Operation
er or upper 16 bits) \ IMM16; 16 bits of rS1 are copied to rD. 2 (normal or complemented).
upper 16 bits) ♦ rS1 (lower or upper MM16. Remaining bits ♦ zero.
er or upper 16 bits) V IMM16; 16 bits of rS1 or copied to rD. 2 (normal or complemented).
er or upper 16 bits) ⊕ IMM16; 16 bits of rS1 are copied to rD. 2 (normal or complemented)

Operation
И16
И16
М16 2
16
16
ИM16 2
И16
И16

er instructions, these instructions are executed

(continued on inside back cover)

Programming
the Motorola® 88000

Michael Tucker & Bruce Coorpender

FIRST EDITION
FIRST PRINTING

Library of Congress Cataloging-In-Publication Data

Tucker, Michael, 1957 –
    Programming the Motorola 88000 / by Michael Tucker, Bruce
Coorpender.
        p.   cm.
    Includes index.
    ISBN 0-8306-3533-5
    1. Motorola 88000 (Microprocessor)—Programming.   I. Coorpender,
Bruce.   II. Title.
QA76.8.M73T83   1990
005.365—dc20   90-44940
                                                        CIP

TAB Books offers software for sale. For information and a catalog, please contact
TAB Software Department, Blue Ridge Summit, PA 17294-0850.

Questions regarding the content of this book should be addressed to:

Reader Inquiry Branch
Windcrest Books
Blue Ridge Summit, PA 17294-0850

Acquisitions Editor: Ron Powers
Technical Editor: Dave Harter
Production: Katherine G. Brown
Book Design: Jaclyn J. Boone
Cover photograph courtesy of Motorola Inc.

Contents

11 Programming examples   **319**

Index   **362**

Acknowledgments

We'd like to express our thanks to the various people and organizations that made this book possible: Motorola Corp., which provided a wealth of information on the 88K and its underlying technology; 88open, which provided equally invaluable data on the BCS; the various users and developers who gave us the benefit of their experience; and, most importantly, our families and friends, who put up with us while we wandered about with the glazed looks and imbecilic expressions common to authors in mid-struggle.

We wish to explicitly thank those individuals who reviewed the book: Dean Herington of Data General; Steve Bunch, Dale Farnsworth, and Matt Holle of Motorola; and Glenn Kasten of Ready Systems.

Introduction

No one actually reads the Introduction. The authors are aware of this fact, and fully expect you to skip ahead to chapter 1, and beyond, where you can get to the stuff that's actually useful.

However, if you are of the select elite who like to know what they are getting into before they start to read: This book is a software developer's guide to the Motorola 88000 processor chip set—or, the "88K" as it's known to its friends. You'll note that this statement of mission neatly divides into two parts: the book's subject, and the software developer.

Let's start with the 88K.

RISC and revolution

As we move through the 1990s, the computing industry finds itself in the midst of a fundamental transformation. Quite literally, it is being remade from the ground up—almost as completely as it was remade in the late 1970s and early 1980s by the commercialization of the microprocessor, when, in less than a decade, computers vaulted the walls of the glass house to drop with a satisfying thud on the desktops of individuals.

This time, though, the agent of change will be RISC—Reduced Instruction Set Computing. The fundamentals of RISC are covered in chapter 1, and even if they were not, it is fairly certain that anyone who's picked up a book on a RISC processor is already rather familiar with the concepts at hand.

However, on the off chance that there might be something to be gained from restating the obvious, RISC is a philosophy of processor design which holds that minimalist poets had it right—less is really more.

As everyone knows, the microprocessors that made the desktop computer a possibility were CISC—Complex Instruction Set Computing—machines. These are, of course, machines that attempt to put as much functionality as possible into themselves, and thus rely very little on slower mechanisms that lie outside the processors. They will, for instance, have large sets of instructions, and those instructions will be complicated and powerful.

In theory, RISC is the antithesis of all that. A RISC processor tries to keep things to a minimum on much the same argument that produced condensed novels and study guides. The complete *War and Peace* might be the better work, but if you're cramming for an exam, and have only 24 hours in which to do so, then the *Cliff Notes* version is quite a bit quicker and for the Philistine business of getting a passing grade instead of a literary education, almost as good.

Thus it is that a RISC processor attempts—among other things—to keep its instruction set to a bare minimum, and to execute the few it does have in a single clock cycle. It tends to be rather like a 50's B-movie cowboy, of few words and those that it does have, sparse and to the point. But, because it is terse and simple, it is —like the cowboy at high noon—fast on the trigger.

This speed, combined with the fact that RISC processors have proven easier than their CISC cousin to design complete computers and embedded systems around, has made for a boom market in RISC processors. System vendor after system vendor has turned, slowly and in many cases most reluctantly, to RISC. And, in turn, software developers are finding that they are writing for RISC machines.

The problem is, of course, that this requires a bit of rethinking on the part of the developer. Programming for RISC is not exactly like programming for CISC. Concepts have to be unlearned, and new ideas embraced.

On the other hand, RISC also presents the software developer with an unmatched opportunity. The vast majority of code in the world is for CISC devices. That code has to be rewritten, or abandoned in favor of something new.

Perhaps never before have software professionals been faced with quite the same possibility and peril. Not only must new software be developed, but also old software must be shifted to entirely different architectures. It is as if they were asked to create a new world—and people it with an unruly mob that must be shepherded there through desert and swamp.

The 88000

There are a number of RISC processors on the market. These sport a variety of designs, and varying degrees and interpretations of RISCness. None can be called "pure" RISC in that some will not execute all their instructions in a single clock cycle, while others are densely populated with transistors (in theory, those ought to be kept to a minimum too). But, what they have in common is that they all demonstrate RISC design techniques somewhere.

The 88000 chip set is Motorola Corp.'s entry into the game. It is actually two chips: the processor (the 88100) and the memory management units (the 88200). The 88200 may be omitted in some specialized systems, or up to 8 88200's may be used in a single design.

Why should the software developer write for the 88K? Two reasons, one technical and the other related to money. The money side of it has to do with the fact that the 88K has been racking up some pretty exciting design wins. While it was a late comer to the game—shipping in volume only in 1989—and faces stiff competition from several strong rivals, it has still managed to be one of the more successful RISC processors.

In the first year it was generally available, the 88K had already been incorporated in machines from such diverse vendors as BBN Advanced Computing, Data General, Everex, Opus Systems, Sanyo/Icon and Tektronix, not to mention Motorola itself, which has its own systems business.

More designs are certain to come, if only because there are already so many Motorola CISC users in the world. Companies that have long relied on Motorola as a supplier, but who now long to move up to RISC, will be strongly tempted to go with the 88K chip-set if only because its origins are familiar.

In short, there are going to be a reasonably large number of 88K machines around. Software for the 88K, therefore, cannot help but have a reasonably large number of customers.

The technical argument for the 88K is even more compelling, though more subtle. The 88K is a very well-defined and complete chip set. Much of the functionality that many other processor vendors leave to support chips is included in the 88K as part of the sticker price. Things like floating-point math, cache control, memory management, and so on, all come standard.

For hardware developers this means that it's remarkably easy (and cheap) to put together a machine based on the 88K. The process is almost a system in itself. With a remarkably modest investment in R&D, companies (or even individuals, and we'll yet see an 88K-hobbyist's market) could design and configure extremely powerful systems in a very short period of time.

As an aside, that very fact accounts for some of the chip-set's popularity. With it, companies that can ill-afford doing their design and development can still get into the RISC game. It's not surprising, then, that its buyers include underfunded start-ups who must begrudge the expense of every additional support chip. For them, the 88K is a happy means of shifting their development costs to someone else—i.e., Motorola.

But the 88K appeals to the other end of the spectrum as well. Among the companies who've gone with the 88K are old and established mainframe and minicomputer vendors saddled with aging product lines. Such companies have suddenly discovered themselves falling behind. Their machines seem to have no place in an age that belongs to RISC processors and generic operating systems, such as UNIX. They have the resources to do their own development work, of course—some could even produce their own RISC chips—but that takes time. And time is what they lack the most. With each passing day, another customer defects.

Where the start-ups want for money, the older firms are desperate for speed *in terms of time to market*. The 88K offers them that. With it, they can get into the RISC game quickly—overnight, if they need to. In effect, they aren't buying the 88K at all, but rather the years of development work that it represents.

Naturally, the vast majority of 88K users fall somewhere between these two extremes. Most of the companies with 88K-based products are healthy, established firms who want a fast processor, but who aren't going to turn down any advantages that processor might happen to offer in the way of being a complete solution to a number of problems. But, where all this completeness business impacts software people is that it removes unpleasant surprises.

That so much comes standard in the 88K means that you can expect much to be consistent. Memory management, cache control, etc., does not vary from 88K-based system to 88K-based system, as they would if those things were left to the vagaries of the various designers.

Thus it is that your software can expect that consistency as well. You can simply take for granted that much of the hardware will remain the same regardless of the vendor. While, of course, there will be differences from device to device, at least you don't have to worry about really fundamental rewrites to reflect the choice of some hardware engineer who decided on brand X cache controller chips because it happened to be on sale that day.

But, that's only the foundation for the really impressive part of the story—the binary compatibility standard (BCS).

BCS

Shortly after the 88K was announced, Motorola and several of its customers formed an organization known as the 88open Consortium. This group promotes the 88K architecture while at the same time developing standards for it.

In 1989, 88open published its magnum opus to date—the BCS. This document specifies a standard interface between applications programs and operating systems running on the 88K. Write to it and, so long as the hardware maker plays by the rules, your application will be at home on any 88K machine. Period.

There will, naturally, be exceptions, problems, glitches, and misalliances. This low-end accounting package is simply lost in the engineer's workstation. That graphically oriented CAD/CAM package will find little love in a multi-user system that links only to dumb character terminals. Such is life in the real world. But, even so, all BCS-compliant 88K machines will look enough like home to all BCS-compliant applications that they will reside happily therein.

That is new among high-end machines. Never before have software developers had such vendor independence, save for the PC and its followers—and even there, differences between this clone and that clone, my XT and your AT, his Mac SE and her PS/2, could make the race neck-and-neck.

The 88K software market

Which brings us back to where we began—money. Software may be an art, but it's one of the rare arts, in that it can and does pay the rent. The 88K lends itself to the rent-paying side of the software aesthetic in that it provides a broad market which is, at the same time, inexpensive to address in its entirety. Do a single port to a single 88K system, and all the others can be had with zero or only minor tweaking.

And, that market will be broad indeed.

The spectrum of 88K machines already extends from embedded systems (up to 40% of 88K sales went into embedded systems in 1989, according to Motorola sources), to the desktop in the form of engineering workstations, to multi-user systems as well.

That last is a rarity, by the way. While, of course, almost every healthy processor can find itself in a multi-user machine, most of the current crop of RISC chips were designed with workstations in mind. The 88K has a place in workstations as well—witness the Data General and Tektronix products—but it appears to have been designed with a multi-user mission as well. It includes a number of on-chip features, such as register scoreboarding, which lend themselves superbly to multi-user applications.

As a result, the 88K is carving out a niche for itself as the multi-user RISC machine of choice. Even before the 88K began to ship in quantity, in June of 1989, it had been adopted for multi-user systems and servers by such companies as Data General, Sanyo/Icon, and Motorola itself. In the summer of that same year, Unisys Corp. announced that it too had adopted the 88K for an upcoming line of machines that would be, in effect, mainframes in everything but name.

Moreover, the 88K may be unique among the popular RISC processors in that it takes parallel and multiprocessing very seriously. Again, the model that guided designers of many of the other commercial RISC chips was that of the workstation—a single processor working for a single user. By contrast, the 88K assumes that it may be part of a set of processors. This might be for the purpose of fault tolerance, or parallel processing, or for who knows what else.

Suffice to say, though, that just as software developers might expect the 88K market to extend from the desktop to the glass house, so too will it range from machines of one bare processor to many hundred. Already, in July of 1989, BBN Advanced Computers introduced a multiprocessor system that included up to 504 88Ks.

In fact, Motorola itself markets what it calls a "Hypermodule," a package of four 88Ks. This means, again, that quite small companies (or even . . . well, why not? . . . our dedicated hobbyist) could produce multiprocessor machines for the cost of some minor board work.

You, the reader

That brings us, at long last, to you the reader. Specifically, this book is meant for *software professionals,* a handy term into which may be catalogued programmers, software engineers, systems analysts, computer scientists, value added resellers, academics, systems integrators, and those who manage all of the above.

In general this large, amorphous mass breaks up into two primary groups. In order of appearance, are those who are writing software which must, in some fashion, directly address the hardware—such as operating systems, real time executives, compilers, and so forth. Such people have an obvious need to understand the processor at hand rather well.

The second group of readers, meanwhile, will be application developers writing new software for, or porting existing applications to, any of the dozens of new 88K-based machines now on the market. Obviously, such folks need less information on the hardware. The whole idea, after all, of things like operating systems was to keep the nasty business of interfacing to the hardware as far removed from software folks as possible.

Yet, there will be times when even the developer operating at the most Olympian levels of detachment will find it necessary to have a little familiarity with the chip at hand. If nothing else, it makes for a bit better morale among the staff when you have to go charging off into places where you're not quite certain that what's wanted is also what's possible.

In addition, we'll be assuming that many, albeit not all, of those readers developing applications for complete computer systems will be working in some form of UNIX. This is not, however, to suggest that there aren't or won't be other operating systems running happily on the 88K—not to mention dozens of assorted real time executives. We're merely reflecting the fact that, at the moment, UNIX is the dominant OS among RISC machines in general, and 88K-based machines in particular.

And, finally, we've tried to have no assumptions at all about what you are writing for. In other words, we have tried to keep in mind just how broad a market the 88K represents, and that you might well be turning out software for anything from a single chip system to some parallel processing brute that's destined to do battle with mainframes.

Naturally, we don't succeed. At least, not consistently. But we plead good intentions—even though we all know which road is paved with those.

1

88K basics

The 88K

As a software developer you will, of course, have only passing interest in what the 88K looks like as a piece of silicon. However, if you were to pry off the top of whatever 88K based machine it is that you wish to write code for, you'd find the processor to be — most likely — a collection of three chips.

In the center would be the 88100, the actual RISC processor. To either side would be two cache memory management units—each an 88200. At least, this would be the most likely configuration. It shows up, for instance, in many of the 88K based workstations, as well as some of the multiuser boxes from Motorola.

However, other designs are entirely possible. There's no reason why the 88100 couldn't operate by itself, for instance, and in some cases (particularly embedded systems, where timing has to be more predictable than can be managed with cache) it does. By like token, there are some applications where there are advantages to having only one 88200. That might be the case, for instance, if the system was meant for online transaction processing, where the data might be so random that there'd be nothing to gain from caching it particularly. At the other end of the spectrum, for very high performance machines you could have more than two 88200s, running in packs at the heels of a lone 88100.

And, of course, you could have multiple 88100s as well. There is a chance that when you pry the lid off the machine, you'll find yourself facing the Motorola Hypermodule, with its four 88Ks in a row, or even some strapping multiprocessing boardset with dozens or hundreds of 88Ks.

If, when you pulled off the top of the machine, you had a particularly educated eye, you would deduce that an 88K is a Harvard architecture machine. In other words, the 88100 is rather like a Byzantine eagle, looking in two directions at the same time. (One direction is for data, the other for instructions.) The typical three-chip version of the 88K dedicates one 88200 to instructions, and the other to data.

But, for the moment, concentrate on the 88100 itself. Motorola describes the 88100 as "the first processor in the 88000 family of reduced instruction set computer (RISC) microprocessors" (which, naturally, leads one to suspect that if it's the first, then others are slated to follow). The company also adds that the 88100, like the 88200, is "implemented with Motorola's high density CMOS . . . technology." This last is one of those places where software people find themselves nodding off over exactly the same piece of information that sends hardware engineers into suborbital ecstasy. Suffice it to say, though, that CMOS—which stands for *C*omplementary *M*etallic *O*xide *S*emiconductor—is a method of chip fabrication that produces circuits which are very fast indeed. Or, at least, fast for current technology. (Today's state of the art is always tomorrow's passing amusement.)

The 88K is a RISC processor—but this is a relative term. RISC is, after all, more a description of a design philosophy rather than of a specific technology. There might be something to be gained from a quick review of the RISC principals, and how the 88K embodies them.

RISC fundamentals

RISC is, unfortunately, one of those terms that's rather difficult to pin down. The market is now crowded with "RISC" processors, but some of these took very *CISC-y* indeed. Some are huge—over a million transistors, in one case—which doesn't quite fit with the model envisioned by RISC's original partisans. Others fail to execute all their instructions in a single clock cycle, or have instruction sets that number in the hundreds, and so on. To make matters worse, some CISC processors are beginning to look a wee bit RISC-y. Both the Motorola 68040 and the Intel 80486 gained significant performance advantages by using RISC techniques in the way they do their math.

In fact, there's been a new term floating around engineering circles lately—CRISP, Complex Reduced Instruction Set Processor. Some people are arguing that the "RISC" processors on the market, and not a few of the "CISC" ones, are really more CRISP than anything else. But, that's a matter we can leave to the judgement of a distant future when RISC and CISC will be alike obsolete, and no one will care but a few academics in search of ever more obscure topics for their Ph.D. dissertations.

In general though, let's rush in where angels fear to tread and define a RISC processor as one which shows the following characteristics:

- Small number of instructions
- One instruction per clock cycle
- Register-to-register operations
- Simple address modes
- Simple instruction formats

That done, let's see how the 88K conforms to each of those.

Reduced instructions

Keeping instructions to a bare minimum is the whole idea of RISC, and the 88K has only 51 instructions. These are listed and detailed in chapter 7.

One instruction per cycle

The 88100 also does the very RISC-y thing of performing most of its instructions in one clock cycle. That happens two ways. First, all integer arithmetic, logical, bit field and certain flow control instructions can execute in a single clock cycle. That's pretty impressive. However, and second, you can actually go further, and make multicycle operations appear to be single cycle.

For instance, most instructions for floating point and memory access are normally multicycle. But, the 88100 contains dedicated subsections of itself—to be precise, three of its five execution units—that handle memory access and floating point operations exclusively, which means that other parts of the processor are free to take care of other tasks. In other words, when it runs across a two cycle operation, for example, it can simultaneously perform another, one cycle operation. Ergo, even though one instruction took two cycles, two operations were still performed in that time.

Thus, while an individual floating point or memory access instruction might actually be multicycle, it performs as though it was single cycle. It's not the last time we'll find the 88K exploiting parallelism.

This might be, by the way, a good place to bring up a touchy issue— that of MIPS, millions of instructions per second. As the saying goes, there are three ways of telling an untruth in this life: lies, damn lies, and MIPS. The unfortunate reality is that if you apply logic alone to rate the 88K in terms of MIPS, you will find yourself in trouble.

The current version of the 88K is a 33MHz machine. That is to say, its internal clock ticks away 33 million times each second. Because it can execute one instruction once each cycle—and there are 33 million of those each second—it is therefore, logically, a 33 MIPS machine.

Logic lies. The industry standard for MIPS ratings is the Digital Equipment Corp. VAX. A VAX 780 is generally accepted as a 1 MIP machine.

A VAX is a CISC machine, and its instructions are extremely complex. Each individual instruction will do a great deal more work than any individual RISC instruction. Therefore, the really important number is not MIPS, but VMIPS—where "V" stands for "VAX." And, in those terms, the 33 megahertz 88K is generally credited with being a 28 VMIPS machine.

Register-to-register operation

One of the underlying themes of RISC is register-to-register operation. A register is a form of very fast memory included in the processor chip itself. In effect, the processor contains its own specialized collection of RAM.

RISC, in theory, assumes that it operates only on data or instructions within those registers. Although it can address system memory, it never ever performs an operation there. Instead, it carefully gets whatever data or instructions it needs from system memory or cache memory, places them in the registers, and—when told to do so—performs an operation within them.

From your point of view, as a programmer, this can be something of a pain. In a CISC system, after all, you can simply tell the machine to, for example, add memory location one to memory location two and be done with it. In a three-chip 88K, however, two locations in system memory are first accessed by an 88200 cache, then transferred to the 88100's registers, and finally summed there. The general theme is that the 88100 does nothing outside itself except for stores and loads.

But, if it's a pain for you as a programmer, it makes for speedier execution for your program. Things just happen faster in a register. And, besides, if you're lucky, and you're an applications developer working with a clever compiler, you'll never have to worry about the issue. Your system software will hide the whole business from you.

But, if you're not so lucky, and you're the one charged with writing the clever compiler in question, then you have to know about all this stuff.

All of the 88100's registers—which are contained within its "register file"—will be covered individually and, in painful detail later. Briefly, the ones that the user or programmer sees most often are the General Purpose registers, of which there are 32 (or, as they're numbered, r0 through r31). Actually, you can modify only 31, because one of them, noted as r0, is always given the value of 0.

In addition to the general purpose registers, there are several given over to the internal workings of the 88100 itself. There are eight registers (noted as fcr1 through fcr8) used in floating point operations, and another two (fcr62 and fcr63) that concern themselves with monitoring the status of floating point. There are 20 more registers (cr0 through cr20) which are for use by system software. And, finally, there are four registers (XIP, NIP, FIP, and SB) meant to be used only by the processor itself for such things as pointers to what it should fetch and execute.

One of these last four, SB, is a particularly interesting little fellow. This is the scoreboard register. Like all the 88K's registers, it can contain 32 bits of information. Each of the SB's bits represents one of the 88100's 32 general registers. The SB keeps track of the status of its sibling registers, keeping a one-bit note as to whether an operation is pending within each. It thus prevents a piece of information that is still needed from getting tramped on by other, incoming data. Likewise, it notes when a register is available for new tasks.

The 88100 manages its registers via a piece of itself known as the *Sequencer*. This is the part (the "functional unit") of the 88100 that controls register reads and writes, exception recognition, and program flow. It performs writeback arbitration and exception arbitration.

Both these have to be defined. *Writeback arbitration* occurs when the 88100—or rather, when some part of the 88100—wants to write the results of some operation to one of its registers. It must request a time for the write to happen. The writeback arbiter part of the sequencer picks the opportune moment, based on whether an exception is pending and if the scoreboard register shows that the register is free for the write.

Exception arbitration is a bit more complex. This happens when there is an exception—i.e., an unusual condition, or an error, which requires special handling. When such a thing crops up, it is the exception arbiter of the sequencer that controls exception processing, and which resolves any conflicts if more than one exception appears at the same time.

Simple address modes

One of the assumptions of RISC is that the designer will make everything as simple as possible, everywhere—right down to the way in which data and instructions are addressed by the system. The 88100 has only three data addressing modes, and four instruction modes. These will be covered fully in chapter 6.

Simple instruction formats

CISC processors can have variable instruction lengths. That's good, because instructions in computing, like those everywhere else, will often vary according to the complexity of the task at hand.

But, it's bad because it slows the processor down. The CPU may need two or three cycles just to decode an instruction, much less do anything productive with it. Therefore, RISC people believe that it is best to not only limit the number of instructions, but also to keep them short. Complex tasks can then be built up of multiple, simple instructions.

The 88K follows this philosophy to the letter. Within it, all instructions are exactly one word long—in the 88K's case, 32 bits. No more, no less.

88100 characteristics

So much for the 88K as a RISC machine. Now take a look at it as a device in its own right.

The execution units

You'll recall that you were pretending that you had popped the lid off your computer to more closely observe the 88K. Now, pretend that you could peel the top off the 88100 itself and stare inside it. (See Fig. 1-1.)

If you could manage that neat trick, you would see the registers and then the sequencer. But, you would see as well four "Execution Units." These are not, as the name would suggest, enforcement agents for the RISC revolution, but rather are subsections of the processor, each handling a different aspect of its operation. They are:

- Integer Unit—which executes all integer, bit field, and control register instructions.

- Floating Point Unit—which executes all floating point arithmetic instructions, plus integer/floating point conversions and integer multiply and divide instructions. (The Floating Point execution unit is fully compatible with both single and double precision IEEE 754 standard for how floating point shall be done.)
- Data Unit—which executes all instructions that access memory and controls the interface to the 88100's own data bus, the data P bus.
- Instruction Unit—which prefetches instructions, begins the process of decoding them, and then ships them off to the appropriate execution unit.

The execution units are exciting to hardware people because they include within one chip much that they would otherwise have to buy elsewhere. For them, it is truly lovely that the 88K has, for example, floating point right out of the package, with no fiddling around with additional floating point chips that might or might not work with the processor, and will certainly take up space on the board one way or the other.

For software people, though, the real kicker is performance. All the execution units may operate at once, on different tasks. It's like having a multiprocessor computer shrunk down to a single chip. The Integer Unit can be doing a sum, while the floating point does a multiply and the Data Unit simultaneously obtains the data specified by the instruction which the Instruction Unit is even then decoding.

88100 internal buses

The 88100 is also a bit of an I/O fanatic in its own right. It contains no less than three internal buses.

The first of these is the "D" bus, which connects the execution units to the registers. It is bidirectional, taking data from the registers to the execution units as well as back again when that data must be stored.

The other two buses—S1 and S2—take data source operands to the integer unit, the data unit, the instruction unit, and the FPU. Source data, in turn, comes from the 88100's 32 general purpose registers, or from 16-bit immediate values in the instruction itself. Either way, though, the S1 and S2 buses are unidirectional.

88100 external buses

And what are internal buses without external ones to match? The 88100 has two external buses, each called a "P" bus. These link the 88100 to its

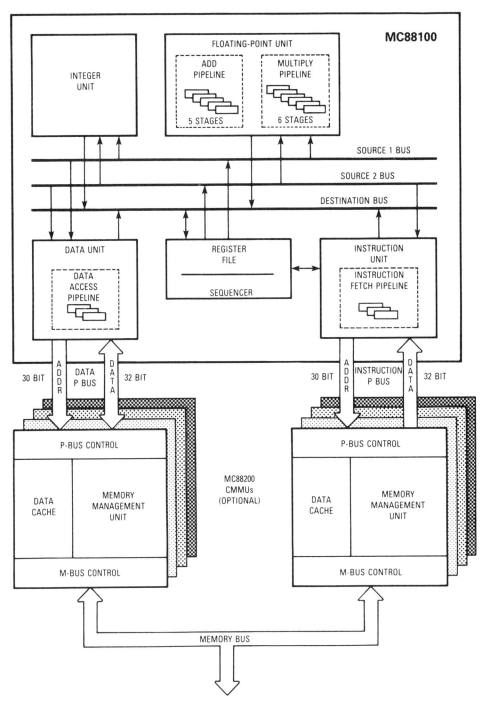

1-1 MC88100/MC88200 block diagram. (Reprinted with permission of Motorola Inc.)

companion 88200 cache memory management units. Each is fully 32 bit.

The P bus which links the 88100 to the *data* 88200 consists of two paths, one for addresses and the other for data. Naturally, the address path is one way—leading into the 88200. The data path, though, is bidirectional, because the processor will be taking data out of the 88200, modifying that data and storing it again in cache.

The P bus which links the 88100 to the *instruction* 88200, meanwhile, is likewise composed of a one-way address path, and a second instruction path. But the instruction P bus's data path is unidirectional, leading into the 88100.

Other features

Even if you really could pry the lid off the 88K, there would be other, more subtle aspects of the 88100 that you could not see—but which would be important all the same. Specifically, the 88100 contains several operational characteristics that will, probably, have a greater impact on us than its actual physical features.

These include:

Pipelining and parallelism

The concepts of pipelining and parallelism are fundamental to the 88K. For example, the four execution units can perform up to five operations at once. One operation occurs at each execution unit, except for the floating point unit which performs floating point, and also integer multiply and divide functions. At some point, then, the 88100 could simultaneously be fetching an instruction from program memory, accessing data memory, executing an integer operation, executing a floating point add instruction, and executing either floating point or an integer multiply instruction.

And, it gets more complex than that. The floating point, data, and instruction execution units are likewise not limited to doing one thing at a time. You can instruct the 88100 to do up to five floating point add, subtract, compare or convert instructions at the same time. By like token, then you can have six floating point or four integer multiply instructions execute at once. You can have three memory accesses in progress at the same time—with two of them happening on the 88100's external bus, and one as an address calculation underway. And, finally, you can have up to two instruction fetches in progress.

While we're on the subject of parallelism and pipelining in register accesses, the 88100 supports concurrent register reads and writes. In effect, you can have three read/write operations going on at the same time—or to be precise, two reads and one write.

Delayed branching

Typically a processor wastes time when it comes to a point in a program at which it must branch—i.e., when it must give up performing one set of instructions and take up another, completely different set. It must put away one set of tools and pick up another, while not working on anything particularly productive in the process.

The 88K remains productive in this otherwise idle moment via delayed branching. In other words, when it comes to a point where it must branch, it has the ability to perform the next instruction in the program with some subsection of itself, while the instruction unit prepares for the new set of instructions. It might, for instance, execute some calculation which its integer unit would perform while the rest of it starts gathering up the data and instructions necessary for the next part of the program.

This is usually done by the compiler, if you are working with a clever compiler. The clever compiler will often just perform minor sleight of hand and place the instruction which would normally occur prior to the branch, just after the branch. This assumes that the instruction doesn't generate results that the branch depends on. Therein lies the clever part. If the compiler is not so clever, and not so optimized, then it will at least have the good grace to hide the delay from you. It may do so by throwing away the use of the delay slot and putting a no-op in it. Simple. It works, but elegant it isn't.

Big Endian and Little Endian

The 88100 is Big Endian by default, but the programmer may set it to Little Endian. Change should be done with care, however. It is easy to get things confused.

Big Endianism and Little Endianism are not normally doctrines about which software people need to concern themselves. However, as with all religious disputes, there are advantages to knowing at least what the issues are so that you can avoid making enemies and irritating people at cocktail parties.

The two terms refer to different means of ordering bytes. The 88K has double word memory—that is, it can store information in two 32-bit words, in case you have something that must be contained in 64 bits rather than the standard 32. In the Big Endian approach, the most significant word is the one on the left. (See Fig. 1-2 and Fig. 1-3.)

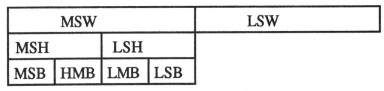

1-2 Big Endian byte ordering.

LSW			MSW
LSH		MSH	
LSB	LMB	HMB	MSB

1-3 Little Endian byte ordering.

It breaks up still further, so that each individual 32-bit word is divided into a most significant half (on the left), and a least significant half (on the right). In each half, then, there is a most significant byte (on the left), and a least significant byte (guess where . . . on the right).

Little Endian, meanwhile, has the very same arrangement—except that it is flipped. The most significant word is on the right . . . as are the most significant halves and bytes.

Happily, from there we get a touch more consistency. In both Big and Little Endian approaches, the bits are ordered in exactly the same way, left to right.

Thus the difference between the two is representational only. It's like, for example, the difference between European Languages that are read left to right and those Asian languages which are the reverse of that.

It seems like a trifling difference, and it is. But, as in Gulliver's Lilliput, where wars were fought over which was the correct end to open an egg, it can be important because Big Endian mode hardware won't run Little Endian software, and vice versa.

And still more

In addition, the 88100 has a host of other little features that are interesting and useful, even if they're not particularly glamorous. These include:

- Levels of privilege—the 88100 has two levels of privilege: user and supervisor. The supervisor mode is the higher of the two, and usually this is reserved for system software. It is here, for instance, that many of the functions of the superuser in UNIX would reside. Basically, in supervisor mode, a program or programmer has access to everything within the 88100. The user mode is a step down in privilege. Typically, it's assigned to application software, where not so many doors need to be open.
- Full 32-bit combinational multiplication—the 88100 can use all 32 bits of one of its words to do a multiply.
- High speed interrupt processing—the 88100 supports only one level of interrupt. This goes back, again, to the RISC design philosophy. If you have only a select number of choices to make, you can usually make up your mind more quickly.

Extensibility

Finally, there is the issue of extensibility.

The 88100 is uniquely *extensible*. It can gain functions and capabilities via additional circuitry that will execute instructions concurrently with the execution units. Known as Special Function Units (SFU), these will go directly onto the 88100, as Motorola develops them.

The idea is that with them the hardware designer can add in extra functionality, without modifying the fundamental architecture. Interested in having a system with capability X? Fine. You just buy the version of the 88100 that contains capability X. Prefer function Y instead? No problem. The 88100 with function Y is another option.

This, of course, means your software has the best of two worlds. Because the 88K will remain pretty much unchanged and unchanging (so long, again, as the hardware vendors play by the rules), you can expect your software to be easily portable across most 88K based machines. However, for additional product functionality, the hardware vendors can pile on SFU's to their heart's delight, and your software can take advantage of them when you decide to write with a specific SFU in mind.

The 88100 has room for up to seven SFUs, with its own Floating Point Unit designed as SFU #1.

The 88200

Now, shift your perspective a bit and look at the 88200, which provides both cache memory and memory management for processor.

Again, if this is a fairly standard, vanilla-flavored 88K system, then there are two of them. One is dedicated to instructions and the other to data. The distinction is based on function alone. Physically, they're identical.

Each, however, would have—among other things—16 Kbytes of high speed cache memory. In this standard, vanilla configuration, the 88K is a cache-oriented machine. It is designed with the assumption that the processor isn't going to address main memory directly. The 88200 will do that instead, and then hold the necessary data and instructions until they're needed by the CPU. This is, in theory, faster because it means the processor can get on with the business of processing rather than wading through the memory.

Cache is much faster than standard memory, and correspondingly more expensive—which is why most hardware designs don't use more of it. The 88K goes with the assumption that most of what an application needs can be done with just two 88200s (though, as before, there's no reason why you couldn't have more if you wanted them).

As an aside, the fact that the 88K does come with its own cache right out of the box is one of the areas where it differs from most (but not all) RISC processors. Most of the commercial RISC processors make few assumptions about the amount or kind of cache hardware designers will choose. That's good, in that the designers can tailor their system exactly. They buy only the amount of cache their applications need.

On the other hand, that's bad, in that it adds yet another level of complexity to the design process. If the developers want to get their product to market in a hurry, or inexpensively, it's a lot easier to go with some system where the cache business has been mostly handled by somebody else.

One way or another, though, most high-performance systems are using cache these days. However, for software people that does lead to one complication. If the processor is not accessing main memory directly, but instead dealing with the cache, then you may have to think about using that cache. You may have to think in terms of what's in there at any one time, and when you'll need it again.

If, for example, an application requires this or that piece of information at such and such a step of the program, and then will require it again a short while later, then you'll want to try to make certain that said information is still in cache when it's needed again. You'll not want to have new information come tramping in on top of it only a few nanoseconds before it's wanted again, causing the system to make yet another time consuming trip into main memory for what had so recently slipped through its fingers.

Again, for applications people working with good compilers, this might not be a big concern. But, for systems people, and for those who are writing (among other things) real time applications, it matters.

88200 registers

Take one of the two 88200s in your vanilla-flavored 88K. As before, you'll pretend to pull the top off it and see what's inside. (See Fig. 1-4).

In there, you would find a number of things. You might be surprised to discover that the 88200, like the 88100, has its own set of registers—virtual registers, entirely software, but no less real for that.

It has them because the 88200 is no passive device. Rather, at the direction of the 88100, it performs diagnostics and the like. There are 13 registers in the 88200. They are covered in detail in chapter 4.

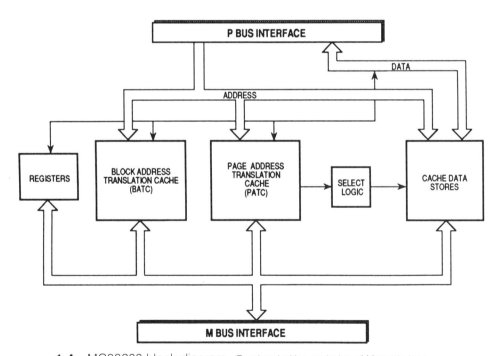

1-4 MC88200 block diagram. (Reprinted with permission of Motorola Inc.)

Cache

Then, you would see the cache devices—all 16 Kbytes of them. What you could not see, but which would be present all the same, would be the underlying design philosophy. Specifically, the 88200 provides a four-way, set associative physical cache. This means that its cache is divided into four subsections which may be searched at the same time—yet another example of the 88K's use of parallelism. The 88200 divides its cache into a quartet of smaller, more easily manipulated pieces. (It is as though you, yourself, were to want to search for a particular piece of paper in a four-drawer filing cabinet. You could go through the drawers one at a time. But, it is much faster if you pull the drawers of the cabinet, lay them side by side on a table, and then assign one each to four assistants.)

Again, there are scales of economics here. The 88K uses a four-way set associative cache because it is a nice compromise between price and performance. There are other ways of organizing cache—such as direct mapped (in which the entire cache is regarded as a single pool of common memory), and fully associative (in which virtually every word is regarded as its own "drawer"), but those range from being relatively poor performers in the first case, to incredibly expensive options, in the second.

Four-way set associative is a nice place right in the middle. You get speed, but you don't go bankrupt in the process.

Virtual memory

The 88200 is designed to support virtual memory—when, that is, it is running an operating system with a virtual memory capability. This is to say that the 88200 allows the 88100 to operate under the benign illusion that the system's mass storage is actually part of the system's main memory.

The 88200 provides for a virtual memory of 16 Gbytes which is divided into two logical address spaces—each called an *area*—of up to 4 Gbytes each for instructions and another 4 Gbytes for data. These are meant for user and supervisor oriented software. Or, to put it another way, the 88200 reserves 8 Gbytes for application software and 8 more for system software.

Depending on your application and your needs, you can adjust that ratio. It might be, for instance, that you're running a very small OS, perhaps a real time executive, and can reduce the supervisor section of the virtual memory down to 1 Gbyte or less. Or, if your operating system is doing most of the work, and is correspondingly large, you could just as easily flip it the other way. In any case, 4 Gbytes for instructions and 4 Gbytes for data is the maximum for either area.

However it is partitioned, the areas are in turn divided into segments of 4 Mbytes, which are then divided into individual pages.

Address translation

However, the 88200 is more than cache memory. It's memory management as well.

When a program on the 88100 processor requires data or instructions, it generates a request for that information and sends it to where the software believes it resides—its "logical address." That request is sent off along one of the P buses that connect the processor to the 88200s.

It then checks two caches within it—its address translation caches (ATCs). These are the page address translation cache (PATC) and the block address translation cache (BATC). Instead of data or instructions, these fully associative caches contain recently used address translations. Every time the system makes a reference to memory, the logical address is passed to both these caches. If the logical-to-physical mapping isn't in either of them, the 88200 supervises a series of table lookups in system memory to find the physical address. It's then held until, in the case of the PATC, something else comes in over it, or in the case of the BATC, you expressly tell the system to write over it. This way, even if the data or instruction is no longer in the regular cache, its physical location may be on hand. The 88200 doesn't have to look it up, and thus can operate more quickly.

The PATC contains 56 recently used address translations on 4 Kbyte page boundaries. The BATC has eight translations for 512 Kbyte blocks (plus two hardwired addresses that refer to control memory, or memory mapped peripheral devices). The difference is that the PATC is used, as a rule, by application software, while BATC is normally used by system software. However, the translation can occur in either regardless of whether the software runs in user or supervisor mode.

It might be that the translation will result in the discovery that the data is in 88200's own caches. After all, that information may have been used recently before, and might be still hanging about. If so, then there's no reason to go back into main memory.

If the 88200 does not score a *cache hit*—i.e., doesn't find the necessary material in its own cache—then it goes to yet another bus, the M bus, which links it to memory. If it knows the address of what it wants (i.e., from the BATC or PATC) then it can go directly where the data or instructions happen to be in system storage.

Either way, it eventually collects what it needs and carts that off to the 88100.

The result of all this business of ATCs and caching is a carefully thought out sting. The 88100, and by extension its user, feels as though it actually has nothing but expensive cache memory, and rather a lot of it, as a supercomputer might. In fact, of course, it's probably got nothing more than inexpensive DRAMs and disk space.

Copyback and writethrough

Naturally, all good confidence men cover all the angles, tie up loose ends and leave themselves an out. The 88200 is no different.

Because it is doing its operation in cache, that means that data in cache might have been modified in the course of events, and be substantially different from that "same" data in main memory. That means, in turn, that main memory has to be updated in a hurry, or future operations could be carried out with old information.

The 88200 has two options for doing the update—copyback and writethrough. You may select between them to suit your purposes.

Under *writethrough*, the 88200 automatically updates the data in main memory each time it modifies the data in cache. That is an advantage, if you need to be absolutely certain that each piece of data in memory is the most recent version of that data. Writethrough is thus tailor made for mission critical and fault tolerant sorts of applications. You could see it showing up, for example, in video display memory.

On the other hand, there is a disadvantage, in that writethrough assures that there will be quite a lot of traffic on the M bus. There will be times when bus performance will be more important than data currency. Ergo, the 88200 offers *copyback* as well. Under this option, the data in main memory is updated only when the cache containing the most recent version of that data is full, or is about to be *flushed*—i.e., emptied, to make room for something else.

The M bus

The 88200 connects to the world two ways: the P bus, which links it to the 88100; and the M bus, which links it to memory. The M bus is 32-bit, and the 88200's relationship with it will vary according to circumstances. Most of the time, it is a bus slave. However, it becomes a bus master when it is accessing main memory.

Bus snooping and cache coherency

The 88200 has *cache inhibit* by area, segment, page, and block granularity—that is, it gives you the power *not* to cache data, if that's useful for you, as it might be in some real time applications.

The 88200 can be *flushed*—emptied—under a number of circumstances. You can direct it to flush itself via software. Or, if you don't care to manage that operation yourself, it will do so automatically when it is full (while, of course, updating main memory as needed). And, the 88200 can be directed to flush by any bus master; that is by any 88100 or other processor which can control the M bus.

Here is where things get really interesting. If more than one bus master may exist in an 88K based system (for example in a multiprocessor box running a number of 88100s), then there could be problems as the various processors directed various 88200s to function without regard to one another. One processor could request for data, only the have another processor modify that data a nanosecond later.

Fortunately, the 88200 has a means of dealing with this sort of conflict: *Bus Snooping*.

The 88200 is, at all times, monitoring the flow of the traffic on the M bus. It is just passively sitting there, listening in—"snooping"—on the bus chatter. But, suppose this is a multiprocessor system, and this particular 88200 contains data that has recently been modified by its 88100. Moreover, the system is in copyback mode. The data in this particular 88200 is now the current version. The stuff in the main memory is out of date.

But, hello! Our snoopy 88200 suddenly hears another 88200 making a request to main memory for that same information for another processor. In addition, the latecomer has raised a flag (more about this later) which indicates that it intends to modify that data.

If that other 88200 goes to main memory, and retrieves that data, it won't have the current version. The program will—shudder—yield incorrect results.

Or, say that the system has been doing writethrough, so that both the data in main memory and our 88200 is current. Once the other 88200 accesses it, and some 88100 modifies it, then our 88200 will no longer have the current version. It could be called upon, later, to use that information, think that it has the right stuff, and—double shudder—once again queer the software.

Either way, there is a problem.

The first 88200, therefore, goes out of snooping mode and puts out a call to hold everything for just a moment. Then, it rushes off to main memory and writes out its version of the data. That way, it knows at least that the data there is current.

Then, it signals the second 88200 to carry on. It also goes to its own cached (and about to be out of date) version of the data and marks it as "invalid."

Via Bus Snooping, the 88K thus maintains *cache coherency*: data and instructions don't become corrupt or obsolete in the rush to conclusions. Snooping isn't something that monoprocessor systems want a whole lot. But, multiprocessor ones need it desperately.

Software standards

Ths chapter has been a brief overview of the 88100—brief, in fact, to the point of being rather breathless. Its purpose has been not so much to provide details (those will come later) but rather to provide a bit of background on the 88K's general architecture.

Yet, as important, if not more so, is the less tangible affair of software standards. Every processor is enmeshed in a network of associations and relationships that are partly technical, but mostly political, that determine how software is written for it. The 88K is no different. It has its place in the world, and its alliances and linkages, just like everyone else. A knowledge of where the 88K falls in the scheme of things can be more useful to the software developer that even the most exacting description of the 88K's size, shape, and silicon.

For that, let's go to chapter 2.

2

UNIX & other standards (but mostly UNIX)

The questionable joy of standards

This chapter is not so much technical as social. It's an attempt to put the 88K more or less into perspective in terms of the great and gory world of standards efforts.

Primarily, though not exclusively, this translates into the UNIX operating system. The standards efforts and organization that forcefully impact 88K software are here, are in UNIX, and are in the various pieces of software (such as the ANSI C programming language) that UNIX programmers tend to use as well.

There are a few lucky souls who might, just barely, escape the world of standards, and thus may avoid reading this chapter entirely—developers working in other operating systems, for example, or in such bare bones embedded systems that they must write directly to the hardware, quite without regard to anything beyond the target system.

But, for the vast majority of programmers, the reality is standards. Either you must work in them directly, or else (if by some miracle our systems are not standards based) they must somehow talk to systems that are.

It used to be, of course, that standards were a rarity in computing. Every vendor had its own operating system. This wasn't entirely a bad thing. You can make good technical arguments against software standards—and many people do. A nonstandard piece of software, which has been optimized for a specific application or processor, will almost always outperform general purpose, standardized software in the same situation.

However, the real advantage of nonstandard software has nothing to do with programming, or indeed, programmers. It has to do with money. The power of proprietary software is that it keeps a company's customers captive. A user isn't likely to throw out a system from vendor X for one from vendor Y—no matter how much superior Y's machine happened to be—when it means also throwing out millions of dollars in training and software development time.

Computer buyers, not being fools as a rule, were perfectly aware of that fact. And, in the 1980s, they revolted. They demanded a common software environment across as many machines as they could.

By the 1990s, it was clear that the users had won. Those vendors who did not adapt themselves to the realities of standards-based computing were dwindling toward bankruptcy or insignificance. The buyers had voted with their feet, and taken their dollars with them.

And UNIX

Where those users were going, most often, was UNIX.

UNIX is, of course, the operating system that was developed at AT&T Bell Labs; and subsequently extended and enhanced at any number of universities, schools, businesses, software companies, and what have you. The University of California at Berkeley was involved. Flavors of UNIX from their work are labeled bsd, for Berkeley Software Distribution. Many innovations in UNIX came from Berkeley. Some are included in various System V implementations, so indicated by "bsd extensions."

In some ways, UNIX's success in the 1980s was largely an accident. It just so happened that UNIX was available—a generic, relatively inexpensive OS, not attached to any one vendor—at precisely the moment that the industry was shopping about for standardized software. Had circumstances been a tiny bit different, it is entirely possible that something else would have taken the same role. (In fact, there were several worthy candidates for the OS crown in the early 1980s. That they are not remembered today is as much a matter of luck as any lack of virtue on their part.)

However, because UNIX was developed in many places and by many different people, it came in many different flavors and versions. Over the last few years, the industry has undertaken a truly heroic effort to pare that population down a bit. Today, as far as the 88K is concerned, there is only one choice for UNIX in the world—AT&T's System V. System V3.2, was the most current production version of the OS as of 1989. In 1990, AT&T

put a new version, System V4 in production. It is V4 which will eventually form the next UNIX standard as far as System V is concerned. Migration to V4 will take a couple of years, while V3 will be around for some years to come.

That said, it is UNIX System V—3.2 and 4—whose various standards efforts will concern us most for the rest of this chapter. But, that is not to suggest that by reduction we're going to limit the chaos dramatically. Rather, we're simply going to pick a particular flavor of bedlam with which to deal.

For the software developers, standards present a host of uniquely diabolic problems. To use them effectively, developers have to understand: first, the relationship between the various standards efforts; second, which of the standards are important to their own particular work.

That can be harder than it seems.

As far as the 88K is concerned—insofar as it is being used in end user computing rather than embedded systems—there are three different levels of standards efforts in operation:

- Source
- Object
- Binary

These levels are here taken one at a time:

Source level standards

Source level standards are those that address source level code. That is, they attempt to regularize the way in which code is written in a human—as opposed to machine—readable form. Source level standards deal with such things as programming languages—but, less obviously, they'll also deal with some aspects of operating systems. Thus, in the sections below, you'll find sections on both ANSI C and POSIX standards for UNIX.

The goal of source level standards is to define the way in which applications are written so that they can be ported from one machine to the other with only a recompilation and relinking. If there is source level compatibility between two systems, then you should be able to take a machine readable source copy of the program for one, and run it through the compiler for the other, and it would execute without problems. Or, at least, without major problems.

There are a number of source level standards that have a role in programming the 88K. They include:

The System V Interface Definition (SVID)

The SVID is a document, issued by AT&T, that defines the way in which an operating system shall interface with the user and with application programs. Note that expression "an operating system." In theory, any operating system, could be made SVID compliant. It might be that we'll see operating systems that are not UNIX, but which are SVID compliant.

However, in practice, SVID defines interfaces for UNIX System V3.2 and System V4 as well as a number of other versions of UNIX. It is of particular interest to developers who need to make their applications easily portable across different versions of System V, and across many different machines which run System V.

As of 1990, there are two versions of SVID. Issue 2 for System V3.2, and Issue 3 for System V4. They are available from:

AT&T Customer Information Center
PO Box 19901
Indianapolis, IN 46219
(800) 432−6600 within the US
(317) 352−8557 outside the US

POSIX

POSIX stands for Portable Operating System Interface for Computer Environments, with "IX" thrown in at the tail to let the reader know that we're inspired by UNIX, if we're not exactly talking about UNIX. ("UNIX" is a trademark of AT&T. As result, there is a booming business in making up names which sound like, but are not quite UNIX.)

Rather like SVID, POSIX defines a standard interface for an operating system—perhaps UNIX, perhaps not. The goal is to support application portability, and the focus has been (to date, anyway) on providing a standardized set of services for a C language interface.

Unlike SVID, POSIX is not the product of any one company. Rather, it is a joint effort of the American National Standards Institute (ANSI) and the Institute of Electrical and Electronics Engineers (IEEE). POSIX's full name, in fact, is ANSI/IEEE Standard 1003.1-1988 Portable Operating System Interface for Computer Environments.

Because POSIX originated with a standards group, it has a broader measure than SVID. If SVID is of most interest to developers who want applications to be source level compatible between different versions of System V, then POSIX is of most interest to those who want source level compatibility across multiple versions of UNIX—including some non-Vish sort of beasts, like Digital Equipment Corporation's ULTRIX or IBM's AIX, Apple's A/UX, and so on.

In fact, there's been a great deal of talk lately about making non-UNIX operating systems POSIX compliant as well.

ANSI/X3.159 C programming language

C is the language that is most closely linked with UNIX. It was in C that UNIX was first written. C was developed, in fact, along with UNIX and in some ways it can be a little difficult to separate the two in terms of their histories.

C itself, meanwhile, is subject to standards. The standards effort which is most likely to immediately impact the 88K is the ANSI C standard. This represents an ANSI attempt to nail down the language as effectively as possible.

The current version of the C standard is:

American National Standard for Information Systems—
Programming Language C
ANSI X3.159-1989

and is available from:

Global Engineering Documents Inc.
2805 McGaw St.
Irvine, CA 92714
(714) 261−1455

The X window system

The X window system is the defacto standard by which windowing and some graphics tasks will be handled on UNIX based machines and within networks of UNIX based machines (see Fig. 2-1). It is a network-transparent window system, which means that applications may be used on any machine of a network as though they were on the user's local machine.

X provides multifont text and two-dimensional graphics in a hierarchy of rectangular windows. Windows can be overlapped, moved, resized, and re-stacked. It is possible to have applications that use several hundred windows.

The application programs are called *clients* and use the network services of X. The program that provides these services is called the X server.

The syntax and semantics of the interprocess communications between clients and the server is the X protocol. The interface library for X, called Xlib, provides the procedures that mask the details of the protocol from the application program. Xlib is currently specified only for the C language—though that will change, and might have already done so by the time you read this.

X Windows was developed at MIT in association with several corporate sponsors. Subsequently, it has become the standard for windowing interfaces under UNIX.

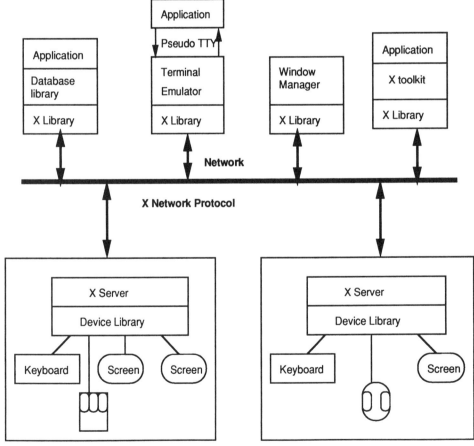

2-1 X window system.

Therefore, the X standard can be thought of as the standard for developers working in basic graphics. The key word here is basic, for while X is powerful, it is very low level, dealing with such things as drawing lines and the barest of windows. It is to computer graphics what the pencil, blank paper, and french curve are to a draftsman.

X is currently in Release II.4, and you'll frequently see it noted as X11.4. Release 3 of X11 is the predominant version in products today.

X materials can be obtained from a number of sources including MIT. However, this is a time for one interesting aside, X is in the public domain. It was made public domain deliberately, in order to encourage its use.

And, increasingly, good public domain X software is being made available by individual programmers who are sharing X concepts and experiments among themselves. It is more than worth the time to take a peek at some of the X freeware that is now flowing over UNIX networks, such as USENET.

The Inter-Client Communication Conventions Manual

The Inter-Client Communication Conventions Manual (ICCCM) is an elaboration and an extension of the X standards. ICCCM defines how X window applications shall play together in the larger world of X. It sets down the rules by which multiple clients may address the X server, without conflicting.

You will recall that X itself is rather low-level. Although that's the secret of X's power, it also can lead to problems. For example, in X11 it is possible for an isolated client application to communicate with the server perfectly, but still be a hazard to other clients. It's like a child in kindergarten who understands clearly that the way to obtain what it wants is through the teacher, but is a bit fuzzy yet on the concept of taking turns. The teacher—the X server—can get a bit overwhelmed by a crowd of clients all demanding immediate attention. Worse, the clients who are really in need of fast action—say, the child who has to go to the bathroom—can get overshadowed by those whose needs are less critical, but whose voices are far louder.

ICCCM came from the X Consortium, and is meant to take care of part of that. It states the conventions that programmers may use to interface client X applications with the server to properly share resources and interact in a predictable manner. ICCCM is distributed along with the X11.4 source materials. It is not currently available from a commercial publisher.

Object level standards

Source level standards are all well and good. They're particularly useful to programmers and to the developers who think in the longer run—that is, in terms of what measures must they take now to ease the application ports to different machines in the future.

But, in the shorter term, source level is of limited commercial value. Except for the rare vendor who actually markets source code, developers sell their products in quite a different form. Their product is normally in binary, machine readable form. And, there is a standard (to be discussed a bare few pages ahead) that is meant to bring binary compatibility to 88K based systems.

But, prior to that, there is an intermediate step. Very often, particularly when the customer is another software vendor and the product is a software development tool or tools (such as a library), a developer will wish to ship a product that is composed of compiled but not yet linked objects. This allows the customer a certain flexibility in how the software's used—not every library routine will be invoked at a time, for instance—while at the same time shielding the source code from competition.

Unfortunately, few if any standards organizations have addressed the problems of standards at this level. As far as the 88K is concerned, there's only one group who has looked at the problem—and that's the 88open Consortium, the ad hoc union of 88K users and developers.

88open has developed the Object Compatibility Standard (OCS). As of press date, it is in Release 1.1, dated April 1990. In general, the OCS is meant to provide standards for any application that is distributed in object form—system libraries, tools such as linkers, and applications that read or manipulate object data. It allows applications to be shipped in a partially linked form, with the final linking to be handled on the target system. Moreover, it allows software modules from different compilers, or even different languages, to be linked together.

Copies of the OCS can be ordered from:

88open Consortium
2099 Gateway Place
Suite 300
San Jose, CA
(408) 436−6600

Binary standards

This is it; the big enchilada; the brass ring on the carousel towards which all fingers must stretch.

Most end users don't care about source compatibility. They don't care about object compatibility. What they care about is binary compatibility. They want to be able to pull a disk out of one system, from one vendor, push it into another system from another vendor, and have that disk read without difficulty. Moreover, they want the application on that disk to run.

It is a tall, tall order. Yet, the customer has spoken. And, at least within processor families, it will be done. It is a pure incarnation of the golden rule—i.e., who has the gold, makes the rules.

By standardizing on UNIX, and by standardizing UNIX, binary compatibility is now within striking distance for the 88K. Two major efforts are currently underway to provide that Grail. The first is the Binary Compatibility Standard (BCS) which was put together by 88open. The second, the Application Binary Interface (ABI), shall come after it, but shall be in the end the more important.

The BCS

When the current push toward binary compatibility began, it was widely understood in the industry that UNIX would be the means by which such compatibility would be achieved. But, it was also widely understood that UNIX System V3.2 was not the UNIX for the job. It lacked functions that users knew and loved from Berkeley UNIX, as well as several other variants.

As a result, AT&T Corporation and (eventually) a number of other UNIX source licensees became involved in an effort to significantly upgrade UNIX. The new version, UNIX V4, is available as a product in 1990.

Unfortunately, when the 88K went into production, V4 was barely a gleam in the collective eye of AT&T and friends. Developers were working with System V3.2. Many of them still are, and will be for years to come. (Changing from one OS variant to another in midoperation is a bit like jumping from one moving train to another. It can be done, but it's best if the trains in question are moving very slowly at the time.)

Some other means of providing binary compatibility had to be devised for System V3.2. 88open came up with one—the BCS. Now in Release 1.1, dated April 1990, the BCS is the standard for interoperability at the executable module level for systems based on the 88K while running System V3.2. It specifies:

- Interfaces between the binary executable file and the operating system.
- Data interchange standards for installing software from removable media.

The BCS provides a commonality of execution to the end user across many 88K based systems. If everyone plays by the rules, then a user can pull that proverbial disk out of the 88K based workstation and have it run without incident on the 88K based multiuser micro. Software developers, meanwhile, know that their software will run on any system that complies with the BCS.

On the other hand, the BCS isn't meant to be a straitjacket. There will be times and places when the developer will want to sacrifice cross vendor compatibility for some extra functionality. To that end, the BCS specifies a facility, sys_local, which provides access to hardware or software which is outside the BCS. In effect, it provides a standard means of incorporating nonstandard capabilities into your application.

A sys_local call includes a vendor identification which designates a specific platform. The call syntax is:

sys_local(*vendor, function, arg1, arg2,..*);

If the implementation does not support the requested vendor function, an error is returned.

In addition, though, the BCS provides a standard "load and go" facility. That is to say, it provides what PC users have had all along—the ability to take a shrink-wrapped application out of its wrapper, stick it in a drive, and have it load and execute in some semiautomatic way.

It specifies standards for installation. The BCS defines the way in which data or program files shall be downloaded from "removable media."

BCS is based on SVID Issue 2 and POSIX 1003.1-1988. The full text of the BCS is available from 88open.

BCS/OCS supplements

In addition to the BCS proper, there are also two networking supplements and one X window supplement. The networking supplements, one for the BCS and one for the OCS, specify how the 88K shall perform networking.

Networking is not required under BCS, but if it is present, then the supplement defines how it shall be done. The X window supplement, meanwhile, describes how X technology shall come to the OCS.

Like the BCS and OCS, the supplements are available from 88open.

The ABI

Beyond the BCS is the Applications Binary Interface. The ABI will define binary compatibility under System V4. If System V4 shall be the shape of UNIX for the foreseeable future, then the ABI will be its texture and its feel.

The ABI comes in two parts: generic, and processor specific. The former was developed by AT&T/US0 under the guidance of UNIX International, and is applicable to all implementations of System V Release 4. The latter was (or is being) developed by the processor vendors: Motorola, Sun Microsystems, Intel, MIPS, etc.

Motorola developed the 88000 ABI, which is available from AT&T. They used the existing BCS and OCS for the foundation of the ABI, and indeed, all BCS software will run on System V4 machines. BCS will be forever linked to System V3.2, which lacks the additional functionality of V4. That's why the ABI has to be required as the successor to the BCS.

Which brings us, curiously, back to where we began, to source level standards.

The developer might or might not have System V4 with which to work. It may be, for instance, that for whatever reason the OS at hand is System V3.2. But, later, the developer might wish to upgrade to V4.

If that's the case, then at some point in the process, the developer will have to invest in the use of a standard Application Programmer Interface, or API, which will make that easier. An API, which is a source level standard, is the sum total of system services, library services, source languages, etc. which the programmer has at hand. SVID Issue 3 and the 88000 ABI, for example, form the 88K's API for System V4.

The BCS and the OCS, meanwhile, provide the API for the 88K in System V3.2. But, BCS applications will run on V4. In other words, by investing now in the BCS/OCS API, the developer will be in a better position to upgrade to V4 tomorrow.

Copies of the 88K ABI are available from Motorola or AT&T.

Standards bodies

Beyond standards themselves are standards setting bodies whose impact on the 88K will vary from small to immense. They range from entire governments to vague associations of like-minded individuals who meet on rare occasions to chat over coffee. It's not quite clear which of the two extremes holds the greatest sway. Maybe, to keep our faith in governments alive, it's best just not to think about it.

Most of the groups below, however, fall somewhere in the middle.

Open Software Foundation

This is a Cambridge, Massachusetts based organization composed of computer system vendors. Its declared aim is to create a common software environment for all its members systems. The basis of its efforts is UNIX, though not System V4. OSF initially worked with AIX, an IBM version of UNIX, but now is developing a micro-kernel independently of AIX.

The OSF grew out of the complex political situation that resulted from AT&T Corp.'s close involvement with workstation vendor Sun Microsystems, in the middle 1980s. At that time, many UNIX source licensees felt they were being cut out of the operating system entirely. Ultimately, their dissatisfaction resulted in the formation of the OSF, whose goal was to create a UNIX that would not be associated with AT&T or Sun.

OSF is somewhat unusual in that it is more than a standards body. It actually produces software, and licenses it to its members or anyone else. Its Motif graphic user interface, for instance, rapidly gained a wide following.

UNIX International, Inc.

When, in the mid 1980s, UNIX source code licensees openly revolted, AT&T quickly took steps to win back popular support. It spun off its UNIX development operation to a separate group within the company, now called the UNIX Software Laboratory (USL). Then, the relationship with Sun was made a bit more arm's length.

At the same time, AT&T and some of the strongest of the revolutionaries formed UNIX International Inc. This group, which effectively functions as OSF's rival, acts to represent the interests of UNIX source code licensees, UNIX systems vendors, and UNIX end users. It provides product direction and advice to the USL.

In effect, if the USL were the executive branch of government, then the UII would be the legislature.

UII has its headquarters in Parsippany, New Jersey.

X/Open

The X/Open Consortium was formed in 1984 by five major European computer systems vendors to develop a common application environment (CAE) based on de facto and international standards. The CAE characteristics, in turn, are described in a document known as the Portability Guide, currently in version 3, and known as XPG3.

While originally limited to those five major European vendors, X/Open successfully colonized first America, and then the Pacific, scooping up both American and Japanese vendors. Today, it has membership of over 20 different companies, organizations, standards bodies, and so on. Among those are UII and OSF, and optimists in the industry hope that X/Open will provide some kind of middle ground between these two groups.

Others aren't so cheery, but only history will tell one way or the other.

In the meantime, X/Open describes itself as having three major objectives: source code portability of applications, connectivity of applications through networking, and consistency of user interface.

X/Open's opus magnum, XPG3, is now a seven volume set (available from Prentice Hall), including:

Volume 1—XSI Commands and Utilities
Volume 2—XSI System Interface and Headers
Volume 3—Supplementary Definitions
Volume 4—Programming Languages
Volume 5—Data Management
Volume 6—Window Management
Volume 7—Networking Services

SIGMA

SIGMA is a bit like X/Open was back in 1984, except that it's from Japan rather than Europe. As such, it is a standards effort that vendors playing in the Pacific Rim markets should get to know rather well.

SIGMA is a five-year project sponsored by Japan's Ministry of International Trade and Industry (MITI). Its goal is to create a common software environment based on System V, Release 2, with certain of the BSD extensions. SIGMA currently leads everybody else in multibyte character support for languages using non-Roman characters (like Kanji).

NIST and FIPS

Finally, consider NIST and all its FIPS.

The United States government is a major standards setter in its own right. In particular, it possesses a specialized body known as the National Institute of Standards (NIST), which was known in less complex days as the National Bureau of Standards.

NIST is putting together something known as the Federal Information Processing Standards (FIPS). This is a set of documents that specify how computers are supposed to operate within the federal government. It's not official yet, and the process by which the FIPS are put together tends to be a bit Byzantine (NIST presents a document to interested groups and gets their opinions), and there are those who've questioned how enforceable the FIPS will be even when they are complete.

Yet, NIST and the assorted FIPS have real power. The government is using the FIPS as a specification for its future computer purchases. If you don't have it on your box, they don't buy it. And, in case anyone missed the fact, the government buys a lot of computers.

Ergo, computer vendors, as a group, tend to be a bit obsessed with the FIPS—which isn't easy, because the FIPS are immense, and positively exhausting in terms of their attention to the sort of details that only a major minutiae freak could really love.

Among the more important of the FIPS, though, is 151-1, which is based on the final POSIX 1003.1 specification. There's also an X FIPS, based on the X Consortium specification for X11 Release 3, though it will be upgraded to Release 4 prior to the FIPS actually becoming official policy.

Other FIPS include such esoterica as the FIPS 33-1 Character Set for Hand Printing, and the hysterically funny FIPS 13, which specifies "Rectangular Holes in Twelve Row Punched Cards."

Actually, there's something sort of comforting about FIPS 13 and its rectangular holes. It rather makes our ruling class seem a little closer, and more human. Because no punched card machine deserves to exist in official Washington outside of the Smithsonian, we could put this one down as evidence that, after all, government does have a sense of humor.

3

MC88100 organization

Overview and features

Actually, when you come right down to it, pin us to the mat, connect us to a lie detector, threaten us with dire consequences, inject us with truth serums, and otherwise treat us in the way that we actually deserve . . . we have to admit this is a sort of unnecessary chapter. We've already been over most of the aspects of the 88100—as hardware—that you, as a software developer, will care much about.

Yet, even so, there is still something to be gained from going a bit deeper into the 88100. (It's a fascinating place, really. A bit like, say, a high-tech version of a Victorian house. You keep finding things in it, not meaning to do so. Here's an unexplored nook and cranny, there's an unopened door, and over to the right is a secret passage.)

First, a bit of review. You'll recall that the 88100 has the following characteristics among others:

- One instruction per clock cycle for integer, logical, bit field, branch and store operations.
- Only 51 instructions
- Fine grain parallelism—via five independent execution units.
- 32 general purpose registers
- Single- and double-precision IEEE 754 Floating Point
- Separate data/instruction memory ports, allowing simultaneous memory access.
- Pipelined load and store operations.
- Big Endian or Little Endian Byte Ordering.

- Extensible (someday quite soon) with Special Function Units (SFUs). (There's already SFU1, the floating point unit, and others are bound to show up, sooner or later, depending on the whims and checkbooks of the systems integrators.)

Execution units

Again, you'll recall from chapter 1 that the 88K boasts five specialized execution units. These divide the processor's work among them. By breaking down the processor's functionality this way, the 88K's design makes it possible for the processor to operate much more quickly. One piece of the processor can work on one part of a problem, while another piece works on another part.

Again, these are:

Integer unit

This execution unit deals with all integer, bit field, and control register instructions—and in one clock cycle to boot. It does not handle integer multiply and divide; those have been farmed out to the floating point unit (see "Floating point unit").

The integer unit contains 11 general control registers, including four supervisor-only storage registers (SR0−SR3), the processor identification register (PID), and the processor status register (PSR). The function of SR0−SR3 is up to the supervisor software programmer to use.

Floating point unit

The FPU is that part of the 88100 which handles floating point arithmetic, integer/floating point conversions, and—on the grounds that it is quicker and easier to do it here than in the integer unit—integer multiply and divide.

The FPU has two pipelines—two pathways, that is, along which things can happen. Addition, subtraction, comparisons, division, and conversion happen in one pipeline. Multiply instructions, meanwhile, happen in another. This means that you could have multiplication going on while, at the same time, something else happens on the other track.

That's good, because FPU operations require more than one clock cycle. But, because the 88K is so very pipelined, it can begin a new instruction every clock cycle, and things average out in the end.

The FPU contains 11 control registers—nine of which are shadow registers for exception recovery. (Shadow registers are copies of other registers that can be used to restore processor context when needed.) The other two are the floating point status register and the floating point control register.

Data unit

The data unit deals with instructions that access data memory, and it also controls the data memory interface portion of the P bus.

In effect, the data unit contains a small, dedicated calculator for computing the address of any particular piece of data in memory that might be specified by an instruction. (With the 88K, data memory access instructions form addresses by adding the contents of one register with that of another, or with a 16-bit immediate value embedded in the instruction. This means that, as hardware at least, the data unit is actually just an adding machine par excellence.)

As with just about everything else about the 88K, memory access is highly pipelined. The memory pipe has, in fact, three stages. It may seem backward, but a request is shown in stage 2 at the start and stage 0 when the data hits the streets. Each time the data unit goes into action, it:

Stage 2—computes the address
Stage 1—drives the external data bus. Or, if this is a store access, it fetches data from registers and drives the external data bus.
Stage 0—monitors the reply. If this is a load operation, then it also reads the data bus and writes the load result to the general purpose register.

This pipelining allows up to two memory accesses to be on the bus at the same time, for two load/store operations.

The data unit has nine data unit general control registers: DMT0−2, DMA0−2, and DMD0−2. All nine are used to reconstruct pending transactions after an exception.

Instruction unit

You'll recall from chapter 1 that the instruction unit is a kind of advance scout for the 88100. It prefetches instructions from memory via the P bus, then starts (but does not complete) the business of decoding those instructions, and finally passes them along to whichever of the other execution units is ultimately supposed to get it.

The instruction unit has, effectively, an instruction pipeline through which instructions are flowing. The unit, therefore, maintains three pointers that indicate the contents of that pipeline at any one time. The eXecute Instruction Pointer (XIP) indicates the instruction that is being executed at the moment at the integer unit, data unit, or FPU. The Next Instruction Pointer (NIP) points at the instruction that is right now being retrieved from memory and decoded. The Fetch Instruction Pointer (FIP) points to the memory location of the instruction that will be accessed next.

The Instruction Unit also has a set of registers of its own so that it can keep track of the contents of the pipeline, just in case that pipeline has to be shut down while the 88100 handles an exception of some sort. That way—even in the event of a really dramatic transfer to exception processing, complete with squealing tires and startled onlookers—the 88K can still recreate the situation as it was before everything got exciting.

When an exception comes along, all the memory accesses in progress are allowed to finish before exception processing begins. Then, while the 88K is off doing exception processing, the processor context is frozen and the FPU is disabled—that way, nothing untoward happens while the processor's attention is elsewhere. When its pipeline is finally empty, the instruction unit can get on with the business of prefetching the exception instruction.

It has an advantage in this. One of its registers is the Vector Base Register (VBR), which points at a memory location containing all the exception vectors. This means exceptions can happen very quickly indeed.

With the use of the VBR, the processor calculates the address of the exception handler. It then writes out that address to the FIP. The exception routine starts up, and everything gets back to normal.

There is one other wrinkle. There are two instructions—bsr and jsr—that cause an 88K program to go to some subroutine, but then allow return to the original position in the program afterwards. To do this, jsr and bsr have to save that original position, the "return address."

It's the instruction unit that does the saving. It identifies and retains the return pointer to the right place, in the register file. The return pointer is either the contents of the NIP at the time the jsr or bsr instructions begin to happen, or else it is the contents of the FIP at the same moment if delayed branching is used. Either way, the return pointer is written to a specific general purpose register. By convention, that is register 1.

The register file/sequencer

There is, however, a fifth execution unit: the register file/sequencer. This subsection of the 88100 is divided into, naturally, the register file and the sequencer.

The register file is where the 88100's general purpose registers make their home—all 32 of them. See chapter 5 for more on them and what you do with them.

The other half of the team is the sequencer. As you'll recall from chapter 1, this sequencer is the traffic cop of the processor. It performs register writeback arbitration and exception arbitration.

In the case of writeback arbitration, this means that when one of the 88100's execution units wants to write a register, it also asks the writeback arbiter for a writeback slot (which is a convenient time to perform the write). The arbiter then checks out the situation. If everything's on the up and up, then it generates a control signal that pops the data over to the D bus and finally to the register in question.

If, however, it picks up an exception about to happen, then the arbiter slams on the brakes. It wouldn't do, after all, to have little lost data wandering around during exception processing. So, it prohibits register writeback except for memory access results.

Moreover, if the arbiter picks up two requests for writeback—one from each of two execution units—then it deals with them according to its idea of their importance. Like most arbiters in life, it's got rather firm ideas about who gets to go first in affairs. One-cycle instructions get the first shot. FPU instructions are number two. And, finally, the data unit is last.

The exception arbiter, meanwhile, controls exception recognition. An exception is, of course, an unusual condition, or an error, which the processor has to handle via some sort of special processing. Upon getting notice of one such situation, the arbiter attempts to figure out what kind of exception is at hand, and to transfer the program to the proper exception handler.

It also deals with multiple exceptions. It's the 88100's flak catcher. If the 88100 finds itself mobbed by a horde of potential exceptions, each demanding action instantly if not sooner, then the exception arbiter will decide which member of the yammering pack the 88100 will recognize. We'll get to the exceptions in chapter 9, but for the moment suffice to say that the arbiter gives preference to precise exceptions (i.e., when the processor knows exactly what happened to bring on the exception). If it can't find one of those, it favors an interrupt (a signal, from outside the processor, which tells the system to take some action). If no interrupt is to be had, it goes to an imprecise exception (one in which the exact cause of the exception isn't known).

The sequencer also generates control signals for the instruction unit and internal buses. But, that's pretty dark, down and dirty in the hardware, and software people usually won't have to worry about it.

Signals

And, speaking of things that are down and dirty in the hardware, turn now to signals—that is, electrical signals sent to and from the 88100 by other board or system level hardware. They are to the buses what a conversation is to a phone.

Fortunately, as a software person, there's a good chance you'll never have to worry about signals. However, there's also a grim possibility that someday, in a remote and terrible future, you'll find that what they do and how they do it will impact your code.

So, to paraphrase Shakespeare, let's screw our courage to the sticking place and face the gruesome little beggars.

And, one last note, here as elsewhere in this book, the authors are using Motorola nomenclature. Motorola, in turn, uses the very hardwarish terms "assert" and "negate" to talk about signals. *Assert* means that a signal is present, or true. *Negate* means that it isn't. Think of them as "1" and "0", or positive and negative, plus and minus.

Data processor signals

These are signals that link the data unit to external memory or 88200s across the P bus. They include:

Data Address Bus (DA31−DA2)—This set of signals provides the 30-bit word address to the data memory space. In other words, it produces the addresses of the data which the 88K needs at any one time. It always addresses an entire data word of 32 bits. But, whether it goes after bytes or half words or a full word is determined by another set of signals: data byte enable (DBE3−DBE0).

Data Bus (D31−D0)—These are a set of 32, two-way data bus signals that interface the 88100 to the data memory space. The data on this bus is the result of addresses produced on the data address bus above.

Data Supervisor/User (DS/$\overline{\text{U}}$)—This is the signal that determines whether the system's into user or supervisor data memory spaces. Asserted means supervisor; negated means user. You choose between the two via the value of the MODE bit in the processor status register (PSR). If MODE is set, i.e., equal to 1, you have asserted. If not, then you have negated.

The exception to this is the ld and st instructions (see chapter 7). These two, which deal with loading a register from memory and storing a register to memory respectively, give you the option of putting them in user space via the .usr (for "user memory") option; but only from supervisor mode.

Data Read/Write (DR/$\overline{\text{W}}$)—This signal indicates whether a memory transaction is a read or a write. If it's asserted, you have a read. If not, you have a write.

Data Bus Lock ($\overline{\text{DLOCK}}$)—This one is rather complex, and it's rather important, because it's one of the things that makes multiprocessing possible with the 88K. Specifically, when the 88K gets an xmem instruction (again, see chapter 7), it takes one of its registers and loads it from some point in system memory, and stores to system memory from that register. The 88K also then puts the $\overline{\text{DLOCK}}$ signal on the memory bus.

So long as the $\overline{\text{DLOCK}}$ signal is asserted—that is, present on the P bus—an 88200 memory management unit won't let any other 88100 (or other bus master) have access to memory. That way, two processors won't try to read or update the same piece of data at the same time.

Once the $\overline{\text{DLOCK}}$ signal is negated (turned off), then the 88200 lets someone else get a crack at system memory.

Data Byte Enable (DBE3 − DBE0)—These signals are presented during the address phase of memory write transaction. Their purpose is to indicate which byte or bytes in memory should be modified. So, for example:

Signal	would access
DBE3	Data Bits D31 − D24
DBE2	Data Bits D23 − D16
DBE1	Data Bits D15 − D8
DBE0	Data Bits D7 − D0

A memory read can be (but doesn't have to be) four bytes wide. When the processor is taking those bytes, it uses the enable signals to do the extracting of the data. This means that, for example, when the 88K gets an ld instruction, it can drive all 32 data signals.

If all the enable signals are negative, however, then the store or load operation being done at the moment is considered a "null transaction." It looks and acts just exactly like any other load or store operation, except that nothing is loaded or stored to memory.

Data Reply (DR1 − DR0)—After the 88K access memory, it must then somehow figure out whether the transaction it has requested has actually been performed. It needs, in short, some sort of response from memory; rather in the way that you get a signed receipt when you send a registered letter. The data reply signals, DR1 and DR0, are the 88K's receipts from memory. These are what the 88K gets back from a transaction, and the combination of the two—if one or the other or both is asserted or negated—reveals the fate of the transaction.

For example, if DR1 were asserted, but DR0 were not, then the 88K could rest assured that the memory transaction had been successful. If, however, both are asserted, then there was "a transaction fault."

The possible combinations of DR1 and DR0 are:

DR1	DR0	Transaction
0	0	Reserved
1	0	Successful Transaction
0	1	Memory Wait
1	1	Transaction Fault

That "0 0" combination is marked "Reserved" because Motorola might or might not do something with it later, and the programmer had best not do anything with it that depends on the current behavior.

Instruction processor bus signals

Instruction Processor Bus Signals link the 88100's Instruction Unit to system memory or the 88200 cache chips. In other words, they look a bit like their cousins, the data processor bus signals, except that they have a different end point (the instruction unit) and different cargo (instructions rather than data).

They include:

Code Address Bus (CA31 − CA2)—These provide the 30-bit word address to the instruction memory space. Instructions are, of course, 32 bits wide. Moreover, they're aligned on 32-bit boundaries. What this means is that the lower two bits of the instruction address aren't needed and don't fit into the 30 bits of CA31 − CA2. So, the system simply assumes they're zero.

Code Bus (C31 − C0)—These are the 32 signals that link the 88100 with its instruction memory space. They're one-way and read-only.

Code Supervisor/User Select (CS/$\overline{\text{U}}$)—This one signals whether we're in supervisor or user instruction memory space. Just as with DS/$\overline{\text{U}}$, if it is asserted, then you're in supervisor space. If it is negated, then you're in user space. And, just as DS/$\overline{\text{U}}$, whether CS/$\overline{\text{U}}$ is asserted or not depends on the MODE bit of the PSR.

Code Fetch (CFETCH)—This one is a sign that the 88100 is fetching instructions for itself. When it is present and asserted at the address phase of a bus transaction, then it means an instruction fetch has just started. If it is present, but it is negated, then a null transaction is at hand.

Code Reply (CR0 − CR1) —These are a bit like DR1 − DR0. The CR0 − CR1 signals are the response that the 88K gets back from instruction memory after a transaction.

If, for example, CR1 is 1 and CR0 is 0, then the transaction was successful. If, however, both are asserted, then there was "a transaction fault."

The possible combinations of CR1 and CR0 are:

CR1	CR0	Transaction
0	0	Reserved
	0	Successful Transaction
0	1	Memory Wait
1	1	Transaction Fault

Interrupt and control signals

These signals are a mixed assortment that the 88K uses to deal with interrupts and to control some of its own internal circuitry. These include some rather dramatic characters—like reset and interrupt—which can be thought of as the processor's version of an air horn to the ear at three in the morning.

But, all told, they are:

Interrupt (INT)—This is the signal that lets everyone know that someone's requested an external interrupt. Everything comes to a halt and the processor proceeds in an orderly manner to exception processing. For more about this, see chapter 9.

Phase Lock Enable (PLLEN)—Here's a jolly little signal that you, as a programmer, will probably never have to worry about. It controls the internal phase lock circuit that synchronizes the internal clocks of the 88100 to another signal, which we'll get to shortly, called the CLK signal. Suffice it to say that this means the PLLEN signal makes certain that the various 88000 chips which make up the 88K system all have their internal clocks set to the same time.

Reset ($\overline{\text{RST}}$)—The $\overline{\text{RST}}$ signal is, of course, a major event in the life of a processor. It brings everything to Ground Zero. All operations under way are aborted. The various pipelines are simply flushed of data and instructions. In one fell swoop, the 88K is returned to a state of primal innocence. In effect, $\overline{\text{RST}}$ takes the processor to what Motorola calls "a known state." No matter how chaotic conditions were before then, and no matter how thoroughly fouled up the program, $\overline{\text{RST}}$ brings everything back to something stable and predictable.

Error (ERR)—To understand this signal, you have to take a quick side trip to the techniques of fault tolerance. Suppose you wanted to build a fault tolerant 88K based system. You want a machine that's so tough that it almost never makes a mistake, or at least catches itself when it does. One way of doing that would be to have every 88100 in the system be shadowed by another, mute 88100. The second, silent 88100 would then do exactly what the first did, performing the very same calculations and operations. Then, it would compare its results with those of the first. If they were the same, then it would assume that nothing was wrong. If, however, there was a difference, then it would know that either its doppleganger or itself had a problem, and it would sound an alarm.

That alarm is ERR. It is the signal which the checker 88100 sends out if it finds there is difference between its answer and that of its mirror image.

P Bus Checker Enable (PCE)—This signal is related to the one above. Obviously, if you're going to have a mirror system like the one above, then you have to have some means of alerting the checker 88100 that its role in life is to be a bank examiner rather than a bank. The PCE is the signal that tells an 88100 to turn itself into a checker.

When it is asserted, the 88100 is in checker mode. When it is negated, an 88100 is active normally.

Power and clock signals

This is hardware country, pure and simple. These signals deal with the clock and with power. The clock signal, CLK, will have some importance to you. But, for software people the power signals can be best described as a fairly effective substitute for Valium.

Clock (CLK)—This signal generates the internal timing signals for the 88100. It is also exported to other parts of the systems—the 88200 chips, for instance—so it is fairly important in that it determines the beat to which the whole system marches.

Power Signals (V_{cc})—These signals are the power lines for the processor. There are 18 of them, and they pump a steady +5 Volts to the various parts of the 88100.

Ground (GND)—These are the ground pins for the 88100. Again, there are 18 of them, matching those of the power signals.

   If you remain awake, the authors applaud you. If you merely cruised through the chapter and looked at the end only to find out if the butler did it, that's all right too. Just recall that you can come back to this part of the book to decode those incoherent mumblings from your hardware counterparts.

4

The 88200

The 88200: A perspective

Now that you've got the 88100 more or less sketched out, move on over to the CMMU—the 88200. The 88200 is a complex bit of goods—in some ways, more complex than the processor it serves. Think of it as being like the Jeeves character in the comic novels of P.G. Wodehouse—in theory, subordinate; in practice, the brains of the outfit and constantly getting the young master out of all sorts of sticky wickets.

But, like Jeeves, it tends to fade into the background when it can. Ergo, this chapter, and this chip, will be of little interest to some programmers. Many applications people, for instance, will be happy to leave the CMMU to systems software, which they themselves never see, and have no desire to meet. For such people, this chapter will be just a casual read, falling in usefulness somewhere between *TV Guide* and John LeCarre.

On the other hand, for the systems or diagnostics programmer, the operation of the 88200 is critical. For them, this chapter will be anything but casual.

If you're of the former group, and you plan to write the next great spreadsheet for the 88K, then you might want to glance through "Features" in this chapter, and then jump on to the next chapter. If, however, you are the person "delegated" with implementing the virtual memory of "*NIX," or whatever it is that the folks up in marketing have decided to call it this week, then read on.

88200 features

Overview

You will recall the 88200's characteristics and features from chapter 1. As a device for memory management, it has:

- Two 4 Gbyte address spaces (one user and one supervisor).
- Address translation capability, via two address translation caches (Block Address Translation Cache—BATC, and Page Address Translation Cache—PATC).
- Write protection for user and supervisor space.
- Address protection for supervisor memory.

In terms of cache, meanwhile, the 88200 boasts:

- 16 Kbytes of four-way, set associative cache
- zero wait state physical cache accesses
- cache addresses that are physical addresses
- copyback and writethrough, both specified by page, area, and segment
- cache flush and invalidate which can be initiated by software
- cache inhibit, by page, area, and segment
- concurrent address translation and cache memory access

And finally, the 88200 supports multiprocessing via:

- bus snooping, to maintain cache coherency
- lockable M bus tenure to synch multiple processors
- data cache and ATCs that can be flushed by any processor of I/O device

See Fig. 4-1 for the MC88200 block diagram.

88200 registers

Perhaps the best place to start describing the CMMU is at its registers, because they form the nucleus of the communications headquarters of the device. The 88200 has registers, just like the 88100. But these are registers that a software person could actually love. Where the 88100's are hardware, the 88200's are virtual. They exist, in short, as software.

In fact, they don't even reside in the chip itself. Instead, they live in system memory; specifically, in the control memory. Control memory

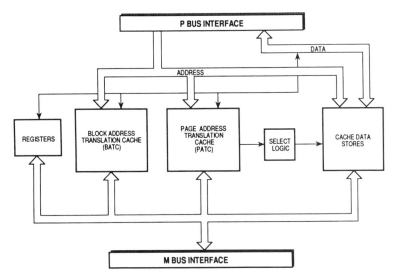

4-1 MC88200 block diagram.

occupies the upper 1 Mbyte of the supervisor address space. (Its address is 0xFFF00000 where, of course, the "0x" means that you're in hexadecimal; more about addresses later.)

Each 88200 has 26 of these virtual registers, which together occupy 4 Kbytes of memory. The registers are listed in Fig. 4-2. Each has a name, each can be accessed in some fashion or another—some can be read from only, some can be written to, some can be both. And, each has a "Base Address Offset."

To explain this offset, we have to talk a bit about IDs. Each 88200 has an ID Register—that is, a register that identifies the 88200 to the rest of the system and declares the location of its registers in system memory. The 88200 needs such a thing because, of course, the actual physical location of those registers will vary with wherever the hardware designers happen to drop the chip in relation to the electronics of system memory. It gets still more complex, in that each 88K-based system will probably have more than one 88200 in it.

Thus, to function, the 88200 must at some point consult a map to the 4 Kbyte page in system memory, which its registers—but not those of any other 88200—call home. The map is contained within each 88200's ID register, which is automatically initialized at powerup. (See Fig. 4-2.)

Now, envision the supervisor address space. Its top 1 Mbyte is control memory. Pretend that it is in fact a little city composed of idividual apartment buildings or, because this is the 1990s, we'll make it condos instead. Each building is of the old type that used to be called a shotgun house—that

Name	Symbol	Access	Base Address
ID Register	IDR	Read/write	0x000
System command	SCR	Write	0x004
System status	SSR	Read	0x008
System Address	SAR	Read/write	0x00C
System Control	SCTR	Read/write	0x104
P Bus fault status	PFSR	Read	0x108
P Bus fault address	PFAR	Read/write	0x10C
Supervisor Area Pointer	SAPR	Read/write	0x200
User Area Pointer	UAPR	Read/write	0x204
BATC Write ports	BWP0-7	Write	0x400 - 0x41C BWP0 = 0x400
Cache data ports	CDP0-3	Read write	0x800 - 0x80C CDP0 = 0x800
Cache Tag ports	CTP0-3	Read/write	0x840 - 0x84C CTP0 = 0x840
Cache set data	CSSP	Read/write	0x880

4-2 88200 registers.

is, a structure with one door opening on the street, a long corridor down its middle, and individual condos opening up off the main hall. And, in each building, there is naturally a resident manager. This person's apartment is the one which is closest to the street. His or her apartment is the one that actually bears the street address of the building as a whole.

Each building is, of course, really a 4 Kbyte page of registers, and each individual condo is actually an individual register. The resident manager is the ID Register, and his or her street number is the Base Address, that place in system memory that marks the beginning of any one set of registers.

As a rule, the Base Address is 0xFFF*ii*000, where FFF stands for the high 1Mbyte of the address space, and *ii* is the value of the ID field in the ID register, while the 000's position the register at the lowest byte of the 4K page it happens to occupy.

Then to deal with multiple 88200s in the system, *ii* specifies which particular 88200 this Base Address belongs to. For most (but not all) implementations, the ID is 0x7F for the first 88200, 0x7E for the second

88200, and so on. Each 88200 is wired so as to contain a different value in the ID field of the ID register.

Consider a system with 4 CMMUs wired to have ID values of 0x7F through 0x7C, leaving the details of how these are wired to the hardware engineers. Suffice it to say that when the system powers up, by magic, they look that way. The result lines up as shown below. The base address is the physical address of the bottom of that 4K page.

Therefore, the base addresses for our CMMUs would be:

CMMU	ID	Base Address
1	0x7F	0xFFF7F000
2	0x7E	0xFFF7E000
3	0x7D	0xFFF7D000
4	0x7C	0xFFF7C000

For CMMU #1, the end of its registers is at 0xFFF7FFFF, which is 4 Kbytes from its base address. In order to speed access to control memory (which contains, among other things, the CMMU registers), BATCs 8 and 9 point to control memory, and are always translation inhibited. BATC 8 points to the lower half megabyte and 9 to the upper half megabyte.

For the few, the proud, and the unfortunate, we can go deeper still. Remember our little city? Give it another glance, and this time go to one of the individual buildings. Go inside one. You'll see that each of the doors opening up off the main hallway has its own address. The one closest to the street is number one. As you move into the building, the numbers go up, so that the last door is marked "26."

Each door is a register. Each register's position is measured by its distance from the street—by the degree to which it is *offset* from the base address. Thus it is, for example, that the P bus Fault Status register isn't far from the door, at 0x108 bytes from the base address. By contrast, the Cache Set Status Port is rather deep, at 0x880.

Any reference to the CMMU registers is taken to be a physical address. So, to load something to the System Command Register for CMMU#1, you would write your data to physical address 0xFFF7F000 plus the offset of 12 bytes, or 0xFFF7F00C.

Commands

And, of course, the 88200's virtual registers may be manipulated just as easily as the 88100's physical registers. They respond to two types of commands—probes and control commands.

Probes are exactly what the name implies: CMMU transactions that you can use to explore—to probe—specific pages or addresses in memory. For example, suppose your system needed to know if a page in cache was "dirty"—that is, if it has been modified. Perhaps this system uses copyback, and at this moment the virtual memory management software needs to determine if a cache line has been written to.

To find out, the operating system could launch a probe. It would parachute in, take stock of the situation, and then perhaps signal that the address of the data in question did indeed indicate a need to update system memory.

In addition, you can use probes to load page descriptors into the PATC. This isn't something that will concern applications people a whole lot, but it can be handy for systems programmers in that it allows them to have the system automatically load predetermined pages of frequently used data the minute it turns on, or when a task is started. This isn't absolutely necessary, but it might improve performance a bit.

Cache control commands, meanwhile, allow ATC and cache flushing. Flushing, in all its awesome grandeur, will be covered in detail in the Cache section of this chapter. In the meantime, the CMMU commands are listed in Fig. 4-3.

Command	Description
1x0gg	Invalidate User PATC descriptors
11x1gg	Invalidate Supervisor PATC descriptors
10x0xx	Probe user address
10x1xx	Probe supervisor address
0100xx	No-op
0101gg	Invalidate data cache
0110gg	Copyback data cache to memory
0111gg	Copyback data cache to memory and invalidate
00xxxx	No-op

gg	granularity
00	line
01	page
10	segment
11	all

4-3 88200 commands.

As for using them, we've been good long enough. Let's now get down and dirty with bit-level details.

To perform a CMMU command, you:

1. Write the address to the System Address Register (SAR) at base +0x00C.
2. Write the selected command to the Systems Command Register (SCR) at base +0x004 (note bits 31−6 are reserved and should be zero).
3. Read the result from the System Status Register (SSR) at base +0x008.

So, for example, say you wished to perform a cache probe. Further, say that the address you want to probe is in register 3, and that register 4 has the base address of the selected CMMU. So, you would write the following assembly language code:

What you write		What it means
st	r3,r4,0x000C	Store the logical address in the SAR
or	r5,r0,0x0020	load r5 with the command "user probe"
st	r5,r4,0x004	Write the command to the SCR
ld	r5,r4,0x008	Read the results from the SSR

And there it is, your probe has done its work.

A probe results in a search of the BATC and the PATC for the logical address written in SAR. If the address isn't in the ATCs, a table search is performed (user or supervisor space, as appropriate). If the table search is successful—i.e., if no invalid descriptor is encountered—a new PATC entry is created. The probe status is then written to the SSR, and the physical address is written to the SAR, overwriting the logical address. If an invalid descriptor is encountered in the table during the search, then the search is aborted and a fault is generated.

If an M bus error is encountered in the probe, the BE (bus error) bit in the SSR will bet set and the V bit—that is, the "valid" bit—will be cleared. The BE bit must be checked periodically by the task that initiated the probe to determine probe success. If it is set, the probe is not successful and the SAR contains the physical address of the fault. Only a bus error or invalid descriptor will halt the probe transaction.

Suppose now that you want to flush all of data cache with copyback to memory. You can manage that fairly easily—Again assume that r4 has the CMMU base address. Just write:

```
or      r5,r0,0x001F   Load r5 with the command to "copyback and
                       invalidate all of cache"
st      r5,r4,0x0004   Write this command to the SCR
```

And the flush is finished. These have been your first fragments of 88000 code. Looks remarkably like every other assembly language you've ever seen, right?

CMMU Reset

The CMMU Reset is a major event in the life of the 88K. When an 88200 gets an $\overline{RST}$, it comes to a complete stop. No queued or in-flight transactions are retained or completed. No half finished business is tidied up. No last few details are swept under the rug. You just slam on the brakes and hope everyone is wearing seat belts.

The process of brake slamming looks a bit like this: first, all address translation and data caching stops. The 88200 registers and signals enter certain predetermined states—all of which are shown in Fig. 4-4. Basically they all enter a sort of suspended animation, with the nature of the suspension varying from register to register and signal to signal. The System Command Register (SCR), for example, is cleared, while the P Bus Address Status Register (PFAR) is left undefined. Meanwhile, the P Address Bus Signals are ignored—the 88200 simply won't respond to them at all.

Register	State after reset
System Command Register	Cleared
System Status Register	Cleared
System Address Register	Undefined
P Bus Fault Status Reg	Cleared
P Bus Address Status Reg	Undefined
Supervisor Area Pointer	CI bit set, all others cleared
User Area Pointer	CI bit set, all others cleared
BATC Write ports	Undefined

4-4 88200 state following $\overline{RST}$.

P Bus Signals	State after reset
Address	Ignored
Supervisor/User	Ignored
Chip Select	Ignored
Data Byte enable	Ignored
Data	Undefined
Read/Write	Ignored
Lock	Ignored
Reply	Undefined

M Bus Signals	State after reset
Bus Request	Cleared
Bus Grant	Ignored
Bus Acknowledge	Cleared
Arbitration Busy	Ignored
Bus Busy	Ignored
Address/Data	Undefined
Address/Data Parity	Undefined
Control	Undefined
Control parity	Undefined
Local Status	Set
System Status (SS3-SS0)	Ignored

Miscellaneous Signals	State after reset
Reset	Set
Clock	Set
Phase Lock Enable	Set

Miscellaneous Signals	State after reset
Tag Monitor	Undefined
Trace	Undefined
Cache Static RAM Mode	Active for input
P Bus Checker enable	Active for input
M Bus Checker enable	Active for input
Error	Cleared
Power	Hopefully it is there
Ground	Hopefully it is there

Software initialization after reset

Now that the CMMU is at a standstill, you're ready to move forward to the next task. But that takes a bit of effort. If sending the 88200 an $\overline{RST}$ is like slamming on the car brakes, then starting it again requires you to ease off the clutch, reengage the engine, and make certain you're in first gear rather than reverse.

So, following $\overline{RST}$, the operating system must initialize the area pointers, data cache and translation tables—and it must initialize access and protection data! You, or rather the operating system, therefore initialize the 88200 data cache status and control information, by doing the following:

1. Write the cache set number $(0-255)$ in bits $11-4$ of the SSR base +0x008. Then write 0x3F0FF000 to the CSSP at base +0x880 (cache set status port). This is done for each of the 256 sets. The operation initializes the LRU bits, denotes all lines as operational, and the VV bits for each line to *invalid*.
2. Set the SCR at base +0x104 to set the parity enable, snoop enable, and priority arbitration. The default is 0x0, no parity, no snoop, fairness arbitration.
3. Set WT, G, and CI (writethrough, global, and cache inhibit, respectively) appropriately in one or both of the area pointers. If address translation is disabled, the TE bit is set to 0, and software initialization ends. If address translation is enabled, set TE=1 and load area pointers with valid segment table base addresses.

4. Initialize the segment table for the mapped space(s). Either mark each descriptor invalid by setting the V bit of the descriptor to 0 or load a pointer to a valid page table. Set WT, S, G, CI, WP.
5. Initialize the page tables. Either mark descriptor invalid by setting the V bit to 0, or load the address of a page frame in memory. Set WT, S, G, CI, WP. (See BATC or PATC for a definition of these bits.)

CMMU ID initialization

We've already noted that to an 88200, ID is a fairly big deal, because it is rarely on its own. There are usually other 88200s around. The thing which establishes the identity of one 88200 is its ID Register (IDR). It determines the base address of the 88200 in control memory space.

Remember the metaphor of the shotgun condos? Think of the IDR—and indeed, of all the 88200's registers—in rather the same way. It, too, is a line (in this case, of bits). Along that line of bits, the different parts of the register (the fields) have their residence. In the case of the IDR, it looks like this:

31	24 23	21 20	16 15	0
ID	Type	Version	Reserved	

In other words, the ID field is like the number on the door of the condo. It occupies bits 31 through 24. The particular component type of this 88200 is further identified by bits 23 through 21. The chip version is bits 20 through 16 (it is here, for instance, that the 88200 would say what generation it is). From 15 to 0, finally, is reserved by Motorola for use some time in the future.

Though the 88200's registers are software, they are manipulated and managed by electrical signals coming into the machine, just as the 88100's are. As a rule, these won't trouble most programmers. They're the stuff of hardware folks. There will be a few, however, that violate that rule with a passion—such as $\overline{RST}$. Programmers will find themselves getting to know $\overline{RST}$ rather better than they'd ever like.

The IDR is particularly important for $\overline{RST}$. For an 88200, recovering from reset rather resembles what it is like for a human being to wake up after a particularly hard night. The alarm clock goes off like an air raid siren, you groggily roll over and hit the snooze button, fumble for the light, somehow find your glasses, and then, try to remember your name.

In other words, the 88200 has to reestablish its identity. It does so with the help of signals from board-level hardware that determine the ID at reset ($\overline{RST}$) time (bit 31 is set to 0 internally). How the signals are connected is a matter of hardware design. The value of these signals to the 88200 will give it its ID value. For example, if each of the signals in the following diagram were *asserted* or on, the ID value would be 0x7F.

bit 31	30	29	28	27	26	25	24
Signal 0	ST0	ST1	ST2	ST3	TM0	TR0	TR1

All 8 bits can be reprogrammed by writing to the IDR at base +0x000—you'll recall that the Base Address is 0xFF*ii*000 where *ii* is the value of ID.

As an aside, all the 8 bits above are hardwired at board level to set a specific ID value for the 88200. If, for some strange reason, you should wish to do so, you could reprogram the base address to switch the CMMU to work off a completely different set of data—rather as if you had a virtual CMMU. Heaven only knows why you would want to do so, but doubtlessly, somewhere, some clever person will find an advantage in it.

Signals

We've spent several pages now talking about signals—even though we've also noted that, with the exception of a few major players, like $\overline{RST}$, the average programmer isn't going to get intimately involved with them. However, they are a regular diet for hardware people, and because hardware and software folks do have to communicate occasionally, it isn't a bad idea to have some concept of what the other signals are. Therefore, think of this section as a handy reference, foreign phrase book, and lightweight Rosetta Stone to assist in translation.

Thus, when one of your hardware counterparts trots up and says something compelling like "Well, we're having problems with the prototype right now, MCE doesn't get asserted, and we think that we have a metastable on PLLEN causing timing skew," you can smile sagely, wait until they're out of view, and then dash for this chapter to figure out what they said.

CMMU signals are grouped into five categories—P bus, M bus, Interrupt and Control, Power and Clock, and Miscellaneous (see Fig. 4-5). Before getting into these, here's a quick note about words.

P Bus Signal	Mnemonic	Count
Address	A31-A2	30
Supervisor/User	S/U	1
Chip Select	PCS	1
Data Byte enable	DBE3-DBE0	4
Data	D31-D0	32
Read/Write	R/W	1
Lock	DLOCK	1
Reply	R1-R0	2

M Bus	Mnemonic	Count
Bus Request	BR	1
Bus Grant	BG	1
Bus Acknowledge	BA	1
Arbitration Busy	$\overline{AB}$	1
Bus Busy	$\overline{BB}$	1
Address/Data	AD31-AD0	32
Address/Data Parity	ADP3-APD0	4
Control	C6-C0	7
Control parity	CP	1
Local Status	ST3-ST0	4
System Status	$\overline{SS3\text{-}SS0}$	4

Miscellaneous	Mnemonic	Count
Reset	$\overline{RST}$	1
Clock	CLK	1

4-5 88200 signals.

Miscellaneous	Mnemonic	Count
Phase Lock Enable	PLLEN	1
Tag Monitor	TM1-TM0	2
Trace	TR10-TR0	2
Cache Static RAM Mode	SRAMMODE	1
P Bus Checker enable	PCE	1
M Bus Checker enable	MCE	1
Error	ERR	1
Power	Vcc	18
Ground	GND	18

Within its documentation, Motorola uses two very hardwareish terms: Assert and Negate. A signal showing the property of *assertion* is one that is active, or true. A signal showing the property of *negation* is one that is inactive, or false. It is probably easiest for software people to mentally translate these expressions into something more familiar, like 1's and 0's. Asserted = 1. Negated = 0.

P Bus Signals These provide the link between 88200 and the 88100. They're a diverse group, including:

Data Bus (D31−D0) These 32 signals are the path for data or instructions between the processor and the 88200.

Address Bus (A31−A2) These provide the 30-bit word address for memory access. Because the 88100's instructions are word aligned, the two least significant bits of the address—0 and 1—are perfectly superfluous. Within the cache, the data byte enable signals DBE3−DBE0 specify intraword granularity.

Bus Reply (R1−R0) These signals relay the status of any specific P bus transaction to the 88100. The following table shows each of the signals, and what each means to the processor.

R0	R1	Transaction
0	0	Reserved
0	1	Success, Transaction complete
1	0	Wait, Transaction delayed
1	1	Fault, Transaction aborted

Supervisor/User Select (S/$\overline{U}$)   As the name would suggest, this signal specifies the supervisor or user space in the memory. An asserted (remember? "1") signal means supervisor, and negated ("0") means user.

Chip Select ($\overline{PCS}$)   This signal informs the 88200 that it has been selected to act as a P bus slave. As an aside, if there are multiple 88200s in the system (as there almost certainly will be), then only one of them should be acting as a slave at any one time. That way there won't be nasty little confusions about who is doing what creeping into the picture. The one exception to this is when you have 88200's in a fault-tolerant situation, and one or more of them is acting as a "checker"—i.e., when it shadows another 88200 (more about this later). In that case, you have the first 88200 selected as a slave, and the second selected as the slave of the slave. The second 88200 is selected via $\overline{PCS}$ when its master, the first 88200, is itself selected.

Selection of the CMMUs must be performed by circuitry external to the CMMUs themselves.

Read/Write (R/$\overline{W}$)   This signal indicates whether a memory transaction is a read or a write. If it is asserted, it's a read. If not, it's a write.

Bus lock ($\overline{DLOCK}$)   When $\overline{DLOCK}$ is asserted, the CMMU maintains M bus ownership and bypasses data cache. The 88200 maintains M bus tenure doing the read and write portions of xmem—which is an atomic read and write (atomic in the original Greek sense of the word, in that it cannot be divided. If modern, rather than ancient science were used for the source of language, it would probably be called a "quantum unit" instead, or perhaps a "quark read/write."). This locks out other M bus masters and ensures data integrity of the access. If data is found at that address in the cache, it is invalidated. When $\overline{DLOCK}$ is asserted, then the C3 signal (M Bus Lock) is also asserted.

Data Byte Enable (DBE3−DBE0)   These signals select intraword bytes to be used during a memory access. Unspecified bytes are not affected by the access. If DBE3−0 are all zero, the transaction is a no-op. Only byte, half word, and word access are permitted.

The signals map to data bits as follows:

Signal	Data bits
DBE3	D31−D24
DBE2	D23−D16
DBE1	D15−D8
DBE0	D7−D0

M Bus Signals M Bus Signals provide the link between the 88200 and system memory. You'll recall that the M bus is a shared, multiplexed bus that accesses memory and memory-mapped peripherals. There is a bus arbitration protocol that grants bus ownership to a single M Bus master (for more on this, see P bus and M bus Operations).

Address/Data Bus (AD31−AD0) These are multiplexed address and data lines. What they do depends on what the M bus control (C6−C0) signals tell them to do.

Address/Data Parity (ADP3−ADP0) These signals indicate the parity of AD31−AD0, that is to say, of the M bus information lines. The 88200 uses even parity, and checks parity on reads (if the PE bit is set in system control register) and always generates it on writes and addresses. The signals relate to address lines in the following fashion:

Signal	Lines
ADP3	AD31−AD24
ADP2	AD23−AD16
ADP1	AD15−AD8
ADP0	AD7−AD0

Control (C6−C0) These signals define transaction control, when the 88200 is the M bus master. They are inputs when the 88200 is a slave and during bus snooping. Either way, their names and functions are listed in Fig. 4-6.

Control Parity (CP) This signal indicates even parity of the Control signals C6−C0 when the 88200 is an M bus master.

C0	AP	Address Phase of transaction (asserted)
C1	IM	Intent to Modify
C2	RD	Asserted for read, negated for write
C3	LK	M Bus lock
C4	CI	Cache Inhibit
C5	G	Global data
C6	-	Reserved

4-6 Address phase and data phase control signals.

C0	DP	Data phase (negated)
C1	LDT	Last data transfer
C2	RD	Asserted for read, negated for write
C3	MBE3	M Bus byte enable 3 Asserted if AD31-24 have data
C4	MBE2	M Bus byte enable 2 Asserted if AD23-16 have data
C5	MBE1	M Bus byte enable 1 Asserted if AD15-8 have data
C6	MBE0	M Bus byte enable 0 Asserted if AD7-0 have data

Local Status (ST3 − ST0)   This signal indicates the local M bus status when the 88200 is a slave, or when it is snooping a global M bus transaction:

ST3	ST2	ST1	ST0	Meaning
0	x	x	x	Error
1	0	x	x	Retry
1	1	0	x	Wait
1	1	1	0	End of data in Data phase
1	1	1	1	Phase Completed

System Status ($\overline{SS3 − SS0}$)   These are signals that slaves send as replies to requests and data phases (i.e., that period of time during M bus access in which data is actually available on the bus). Usually, they are the wired-NOR of the local status signals of all M bus devices. Non-CMMU slaves may drive the lines directly:

$\overline{SS3}$	$\overline{SS2}$	$\overline{SS1}$	$\overline{SS0}$	Meaning
0	x	x	x	Error
1	0	x	x	Retry
1	1	0	x	Wait
1	1	1	0	End of data in Data phase
1	1	1	1	Phase Completed

Request (BR)   This signal requests M bus ownership. This is the signal that an 88200 sends to the world when it wants to have the M bus all to itself. The only time a CMMU can't use BR is when it is already in possession of the M bus.

Grant (BG)   This signal grants ownership of the M bus to an 88200. It's what the 88200 gets back after it makes an M bus request, if it can indeed have the bus to itself. The BG signal is generated by bus arbitration logic. The 88200 recognizes the BG only if the M bus isn't busy.

Acknowledge (BA)   This signal is acknowledgment, by the 88200, that it does indeed have possession of the M bus. BA is maintained during the entire bus tenure.

Busy ($\overline{BB}$)   This signal indicates that the M bus is busy. It is what the 88200 hears if it cannot gain possession of the M bus. This signal is usually generated from the wired-NOR of the BA of all M bus masters.

Arbitration Busy ($\overline{AB}$)   This signal indicates that one or more M bus masters are making a bus request. In other words, it tells the 88200 that bus contention is going on. It may prevent an 88200 from issuing its own bus request until things settle down a bit. This depends on the setting of the priority arbitration bit in the SCR. Typically, the $\overline{AB}$ signal is generated from the wired-NOR of the bus request of all M bus master devices.

Interrupt & control signals   These signals are the tools that the 88200 uses for interrupts and control. They have a peacekeeping and caretaking function.

Checker Mismatch Error (ERR)   This signal indicates a bus comparator error. It is generated either by internal checking circuitry or by a checker CMMU for master/checker implementations. (See Checker Mode CMMU, below.)

P Bus Checker Enable (PCE)   This signal is used in master/checker systems. In effect, it tells the 88200 pair which is the master and which the shadow. It is negated for the master, and asserted for the checker.

M Bus Checker Enable (MCE)   This does precisely the same thing as the PCE, except that it does so for the M bus. It, too, is negated for the master, and asserted for the checker.

Reset ($\overline{RST}$)   We've already covered this one rather well. Let's just note again that it is used to initialize the 88200; that when it hits, all current or pending transactions are ignored, while registers and signals are placed in a known state. The known state of a given register may be that its value is undetermined.

Phase Lock Enable (PLLEN)   This signal controls the circuit that synchronizes the internal 88200 clocks to the clock (CLK) signal. More about the CLK signal follows directly.

Power and clock signals The 88200 also supports a number of signals that deal with things like its own power, and timing. This is hardcore hardware territory, of pretty limited interest to software people. But, on the chance that it might come in handy some day:

Clock (CLK) This signal is used to generate internal timing signals. The internal clock is phase-locked to minimize timing skew between internal and external signals.

Power (V_{CC}) These signals provide the +5 volts that powers the 88200. It comes in via 18 pins. The V_{CC} supply lines are divided into two separate power buses. External line drivers are supplied by one, all other circuitry by the other.

Ground (GND) These are ground pins for the power supply. They too are 18 pins, divided as is the V_{CC} above.

Miscellaneous And, finally, there's a mixed bag of other signals:

Trace (TR1 − TR0) These signals indicate which cache line is being accessed during normal operation. They work with the tag monitor signals (TM1 − TM0, covered below) to indicate the cache line number of the affected cache set when changes are made to the data cache address tags (see Fig. 4-7).

BR	AP	RD	TR1/TR0	TM1	TM0	Operation
1	1	1	<line #>	0	1	M Bus read, tag is or remains loaded
1	1	1	<line #>	0	0	M Bus read, invalidate tag
1	1	1	<line #>	1	1	M Bus read, no effect on tag
1	1	0	<line #>	0	1	M Bus write, tag is or remains loaded
1	1	0	<line #>	0	0	M Bus write, invalidate tag if CI=1; or else indicates control register access
1	1	0	<line #>	1	1	M Bus write, no effect on tag
x	x	x	AH DH	1	0	P Bus result (AH = 1 for ATC hit DH = 1 for data cache hit)

4-7 Trace (TR1 − TR0) and Tag Monitor (TM1 − TM0) signals.

Tag Monitor (TM1 − TM0)   These provide information about cache address tags. They allow the external maintenance of duplicate tags by indicating when changes are made to the tags.

BR is the bus request. AP is address phase of M Bus control (C0 asserted). RD (C2) is asserted for memory read. (See Fig. 4-7.)

< line/#/figure > is encoded as:

TR1	TR0	
0	0	Line 0
0	1	Line 1
1	0	Line 2
1	1	Line 3

Cache static RAM mode (SRAMMODE)   This allows two uses. It puts the 88200 into a mode, such that you can run diagnostics on it, or it can be accessed simply as a 16 Kbyte memory. In the latter, cache is accessed with no wait states through the P bus A11 − A2 (10 bit address), DBE3 − DBE0 (byte address) and TR1 − TR0. They are combined as:

A11 − A4	cache set
TR1 − TR0	cache line
A3 − A2	word number
DBE3 − DBE0	byte enable

While in SRAMMODE, all M bus transactions are ignored, and no memory management is performed. The 88200 may be placed in SRAM-MODE only during the RESET sequence.

Checker mode CMMU

You'll recall that several of the signals above deal with checker mode. This seems like a good time to discuss what that means.

For some applications, redundancy is mandatory. The 88200 allows a checker mode of operation in which two 88200s are wired-ORed together, pin for pin, one acting as the master, the other acting as the checker. The PCE and MCE signals are asserted for the designated checker mode 88200. If the checker detects any difference between the internal results and the results it reads on the pins, it asserts the ERR signal. If the ERR is asserted, the 88100 would have to take action to resolve the problem. For example, it could perform diagnostics on both chips and so determine which is operating correctly. The other could then be removed from service and that fact would be signalled to a real live human being type operator with the suggestion that something constructive be done.

P and M bus operations

First, a cop out. If you really want the details of the Bus Operations, bail out of this book and get a copy of Motorola's own *MC88200 Cache/Memory Management Unit User's Manual*. Open it up to chapter 5 and you too can have it all in mind-numbing minuteness, with lots of pages of timing diagrams to boot.

However, for most software people, that sort of thing is overkill. So, we'll just sort of skim along here, touching a few of the more important features.

Both the M and P buses are fully synchronous. This means that their use is orderly, and they don't get interrupted by untimely disturbances. They can accommodate byte, half word and full word transactions. The 88100 is master of the P bus at all times.

P bus transactions are pipelined, and the 88100 can start another P bus transaction before it finds out how the last one did. In the event of a bus error, the next transaction must be flushed. The pipelining is the reason.

The M bus is the access path to memory and peripherals. An 88200 can act as both a master or a slave on the M bus. It's a master when accessing memory in response to a processor request, and a slave when bus snooping other M bus transactions. Default is the slave state.

To gain access to the M bus, an 88200 arbitrates for ownership. The BR, BG, $\overline{AB}$, and $\overline{BB}$ signals are involved in the process.

M bus arbitration can operate either in fairness mode or priority mode, depending on the setting of the PR (priority arbitration) bit in the SCTR (system control register). In fairness mode, the 88200 only requests the M bus when no other masters are requesting it. In priority mode, it requests the bus regardless of other masters. Both modes require external hardware to prioritize simultaneous requests. Trust that your hardware counterparts have implemented this, and have sympathy when they seem to be pounding their heads against walls. Little items like this almost justify their frequent use of phrases like "That can be done more easily in software," a translation of which is roughly "I'm exhausted. Let those guys solve some problems for a while."

Operations timing

Although the 88200 is a very high performance cache memory implementation, attuned to feeding its 88100 in one cycle, some CMMU operations can be quite lengthy. It is wise for the programmer to be aware of the different effects on the system of different operations.

For example, consider the consequences of different ways to invalidate data cache:

Invalidation	Clock Cycles Required
Line	1
Page	256
Segment	1024
All	256

Note that invalidating by segment takes four times as long as invalidating the entire cache. These numbers don't take into account the overhead of the operation, which can take up to 10 clock cycles. (See "Cache flushing".)

The next timing data is more complicated. It has to do with copyback, and the timing varies with the number of entries that must be copied back. Those are marked with the VV bits indicating exclusive modified (EM) in the cache line. In the table below, n represents the number of lines marked as EM, and $CB = 7 +$ memory waits $+$ arbitration delays.

Copyback	Clock Cycles	Range of n
Line	$1 + n$ (CB)	$0 - 1$
Page	$256 + n(CB)$	$0 - 256$
Segment	$1024 + n(CB)$	$0 - 1024$
All	$1024 + n(CB)$	$0 - 1024$

For example, to do copyback by page with 100 lines marked EM would require:

$$256 + 100(7 + 2 + 0) = 1156 \text{ cycles}$$

for a system with two wait state memory, and no bus arbitration delays. And, lastly, the timing for M bus transactions will vary with the type of transaction. (See Fig. 4-8.)

Type	Clock Cycles required
Write miss	$14 + MW + CB$
Read miss	$10 + MW + CB$
Table search No U/M update	$11 + (2*MW)$
Table search U/M update	$15 + (2*MW)$

4-8 M bus timing.

Table search violation in segment portion	7 + MW
Table search violation in page portion	11 + (2*MW)
CI Read Access	7 + MW
CI Write Access	7
Write once	7
SCR Write	7
IRA Write	7
Probe ATC Hit	PIRA + 3
Probe ATC Miss	PIRA + 2 + Probe table search
Probe table search	
No U/M update	11 + (2*MW)
U/M update	14 + (2*MW)
Invalid Seg Des	6 + MW
Invalid Page Des	10 +(2*MW)

CI - Cache is inhibited

CB - 7 cycles required if it is necessary to perform a copyback for instance if the cache was full and a the least recently used line was marked exclusive modified

MW - 1 cycle for all but fast static RAMS (SRAMS)

IRA - internal control register access

PIRA - 6 for processor IRA

U/M - used or modified bit in page descriptor

Memory management

The 88200 has two great callings in life: caching and memory management. We'll cover caching shortly, but we'll start with memory management.

The 88200 supports demand paged virtual memory management. Actually, memory management takes place in the operating system, but the 88200 provides the facilities to increase the performance of virtual memory (see "Virtual memory"). Specifically, the support it offers is in translation of the logical addresses to physical addresses. In addition, though, the MMU portion of the 88200 provides access control and write protection.

Address translation

You'll recall from chapter 1 that the 88100 deals in logical addresses, most of the time. Whenever it wants data, it requests that information from wherever the 88100 says it is. But, there's a world of difference between that logical location and the actual piece of electronics—the physical location—where the data resides in system memory.

That being the case, something has to translate those logical addresses to physical ones, and the something in question is the 88200. It manages the transformation via a quick table lookup.

But there's more to it than that. Before performing that table lookup, it also checks the BATC and PATC to see if it's performed that translation before, and might still have the address on file. It does so by caching previous translations, and then performing the table search in system memory for "missed" requests. The BATC and the PATC are fast enough to allow reads and writes to and from the cache in one cycle.

As an aside, there are times and places in which you don't want translation to occur—say, in nonvirtual systems for instance. So the 88200 provides a handy means of turning translation off. Translation can be disabled for the user or the supervisor space by a bit in the appropriate area pointer. When translation is disabled, the 88100 presents a physical address. It interfaces with system memory, by itself, just as would any processor that did not implement virtual memory. However, even with the translation mechanism turned off, the protection and control mechanisms of the 88200 still function, and it still works as a cache.

But, getting back to translation, when the 88100 wants data, the 88200 searches its BATC and PATC simultaneously to see if the address happens to be cached. There is some chance that it will be in both of them. If so, then the BATC takes precedence. If neither has the prize, then a new PATC entry is created once we've performed our table search. (And, to make room, one of our old PATC entries gets kicked out on a FIFO basis.)

If an ATC miss occurs, then, the 88200 issues a "wait" on the P bus (this causes the processor to go to sleep. Nothing deep, you understand. Just a quick nap). Then, it makes a request for the M bus.

The M bus could be busy with another 88200's business, in which case the first 88200 will have to wait its turn. But, one way or another, the first 88200 eventually gets its turn at the bus. It performs the usual handshake stuff and then starts the search of segment and page tables to get the page descriptor of the information it needs.

When the page descriptor becomes available, it's loaded into the PATC and the MMU accesses that memory location. If cache inhibit is not on, the four words in the quad aligned area of the reference are loaded into cache.

By "quad aligned area" we refer, of course, to the fact that the 88200 assumes that information in its memory shall be organized into units of four words apiece. When the 88200 needs a word, it grabs up the other three in that unit as well.

The reason? If a program needed one word in that set, then there's a fairly good chance that it'll want one or more of the others, eventually, as well. This way, they're already present in cache.

But there's more. Any translation refers to a 4 Kbyte page of data. There is a very strong likelihood that a program which has already referred once to some location on that page will soon refer to some other location on the same page. When that happens, the translation will be done and available in the PATC. True, the data isn't in cache, and so the 88200 still has to use the M bus to get it out of system memory. However the translation process uses the M bus heavily during table searches. If translation can be neatly avoided, the 88200 reduces the number of trips it takes on the M bus, and things speed up considerably.

If you're really interested in the actions of the 88200, you can look at it in detail here. If not, skip to "The BATC." When it receives an address on the P bus, the 88200 does the following, concurrently:

1. Recognizes when translation is disabled and presents the address from the CPU to cache. If caching is disabled, it puts the address on the M bus. Having the caches disabled gives worse performance than having no caches at all. This is due to data being loaded and stored through the cache rather than going directly to memory.
2. If translation isn't disabled, it compares bits $31-19$ of the logical address and the user/supervisor bit to each entry in the BATC. If there's a hit (i.e., the translation is in the BATC), the physical address becomes the combination of bits $18-2$ of the logical address with the physical block address (bits $31-19$) from the BATC entry.
3. Compares bits $31-12$ to the logical page addresses in the PATC. If there is a hit, the physical address is the combination of bits $11-2$ of the logical address with the page frame address from the PATC.
4. Selects a cache set by using bits $11-4$ of the logical address. This set will be the one checked when, and if, there is a hit on an ATC. Address translation will continue until there is an ATC hit; or until

a fault, error, or violation occurs (in which case the processor is signalled that such a condition has occurred); or until the table search is faulted due to one of the following reasons:

a. An invalid descriptor (and, a word of caution, it may not be in memory)
b. A supervisor privilege violation (i.e., somebody tried to get their sticky little fingers into data they shouldn't have.)
c. An M bus error
d. A parity error (physical memory error of invalid number of bits)
e. At the end of the search due to a write protection error

The BATC

Turn now to the individual ATCs, and start with the BATC.

As you'll recall, the BATC does translations in 512 Kbyte chunks, and it has ten entries. Eight of these—numbers 0 through 7—are available to the system. The other two, 8 and 9, are hardwired to the control memory space used for I/O and other devices (like CMMUs) which need "known" addresses readily. Use of the BATC entries for high use blocks of memory speeds access times.

The eight accessible entries are loaded by system software using the BATC's write ports. There are eight accessible write ports, one for each accessible entry, and each port is one word (4 bytes) in size. They are at the CMMU's base address + 0x400 through 0x41C for ports BWPO through BWP7 respectively. The format for an entry to a BATC write port is identical to that of the BATC entry.

31	19	18	6	5	4	3	2	1	0
LBA		PBA		S	WT	G	CI	WP	V

BATC Entries 0-7

LBA Logical Block Address field consists of the upper 13 bits of the logical address which corresponds to the associated physical address if address translation is enabled.

PBA Physical Block Address field contains upper 13 bits of the physical address.

S Supervisor mode bit. If the LBA matches the logical address on the P bus, but this bit is different than the bit in the PSR MODE, a BATC miss occurs, not a privilege violation.

WT Writethrough mode selection. 0 = copyback, 1 = writeback. If CI is set, this bit has no effect.

G Global bit indicates if the memory is global (=1) or local (=0).

CI Cache Inhibit bit is used to tell the 88200 not to cache in this address block. The CI bit = 1 for inhibit and = 0 for caching allowed.

WP Write Protect bit value of 1 causes write protection of the memory mapped by this BATC entry, 0 says the memory isn't write protected.

V Valid bit is 1 for valid entry and 0 for entries for which address translation will not occur.

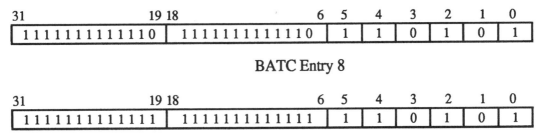

BATC Entry 8

BATC Entry 9

Note that entries 8 and 9 are hardwired as Supervisor, Writethrough, Local, Cache Inhibit, No write protect, and Valid. These two entries are used even if address translation is disabled (TE = 0 in SAPR).

When the 88200 gets a reset signal, BATC entries 0−7 are marked "invalid." In other words, they're history. If you want them in the BATC again, you have to load them again (this isn't true for PATC entries, but more about that later).

Also, no two BATC entries should have the same Logical Block Address value. This is fairly important, because if you have two entries with the same LBA value, you could have unreliable 88100 operations. It's therefore considered a programming error.

Now take a look at how to actually write to a BATC port. (And, by the way, the code you're about to see shows the construction of the BATC entry before writing it.)

Register 4 has the base addresss of CMMU #1, register 6 has a 32-bit logical address, and register 7 has the corresponding 32-bit physical address. For illustration, say that register 6 contains 0x00DAC000 and register 7 contains 0x00EFB000.

You would write:

mask.u	r3,r6,0xFFF8	Clear the lower 19 bits of the logical address, leaving a 13-bit logical block address.
mask.u	r5,r7,0xFFF8	Clear the lower 19 bits of the physical address, leaving a 13-bit physical block address. As a result of these two mask instructions: r3 = 0x00D80000, r5 = 0x00E80000.
rot	r5,r5,0xD	Shift the physical block address down 13 bits, Now r5 = 0x000000740.
and	r3,r3,r5	AND the physical block address into r3. Now r3 = 0x00D80740.
or	r3,r3,0x1	Set control and protection bits. (0x1 means user space, copyback, local, cache not inhibited, entry not write protected, and entry is valid.) Now r3 = 0x00D80741.
st	r3,r4,0x0400	Store the entry in BATC 0.

Normally, BATC entries are not hand made on the fly like this. Usually, they are previously computed in a manner such as above and saved to load to the BATC write ports.

The PATC

The PATC is the other side of the coin. It has no less than 56 entries of addresses of 4 Kbyte pages of data.

45	26	25	6	5	4	3	2	1	0
LPA		PFA		S	WT	G	CI	M	WP

LPA Logical Page Address field consists of the upper 20 bits of the logical address.

PFA Page Frame Address field contains upper 20 bits of the physical address corresponding to the logical address.

S Supervisor mode bit. If the LPA matches the logical address on the P bus, but this bit is different than the mode bit in the PSR MODE, a PATC miss occurs, not a privilege violation.

WT Writethrough mode selection. 0 = copyback, 1 = writeback. If CI is set, this bit has no effect.

G Global bit indicates if the memory is global (=1) or local (=0).

CI Cache Inhibit bit is used to tell the 88200 not to cache in this address block. The CI bit = 1 for inhibit and = 0 for caching allowed.

M Modified bit is set to 1 when a write is performed to any location on this page. It remains until the entry is replaced or invalidated. The initial setting is 0, indicating no modification has occurred.

WP Write Protect bit value of 1 causes write protection of the memory mapped by this PATC entry, 0 says the memory isn't write protected.

Where BATC entries are created via the labor of programmers and their software, PATC entries come into being automatically. Each time there is an ATC miss, and therefore a table search, a new entry is created and placed in the PATC on a first-in/first-out (FIFO) basis.

When a write occurs to cache, the modified (M) bit is set in the PATC entry for that cache line. A translation table search is then begun to set the modified bit in the page descriptor.

PATC replacement occurs when a new entry is required and all existing entries are marked valid. Then, as you'll recall, the oldest entry is shifted out, and all other entries shifted up by one. This maintains PATC as a FIFO queue.

In other words, PATC entries have a lifetime. They are created, enter a queue, and work their way toward the bottom of the heap as new entries are created on top of them. And, eventually, they'll be flushed entirely. Sooner or later, they fall out to make room for still younger entries.

And, in fact, the former can come rather more often than the latter. If the system suddenly finds a need for 56 new entries, then even the youngest of the entries already in the PATC, which has been accessed only nanoseconds ago, is out of the game.

Because we all have birthdays on the near horizon, we'll avoid making deliberate comparisons with the human condition—particularly as things can get even grimmer than that. For instance, there are occasionally situations in which entries cannot be allowed to live out their allotted spans. There are times and places when the memory mapping changes, as it does for a task swap. In said times and places, you can improve performance a bit by giving those entries a nudge toward the door, and leaving their spots open for other, younger entries.

And, happily, the 88200 provides a means of rubbing out entries who aren't wanted any more. You invalidate them by software, by issuing an invalidation command (see "Cache flushing").

Translation table processing

You'll recall that when luck is with you, you don't have to do a table search when the 88100 passes down a logical address to the 88200. When you're very lucky, that information is already in cache. When you're only sort of lucky, the data isn't available, but the physical address of the data is still in one of the ATCs.

But, say that luck is not with you. When both ATCs miss, then you go to a table search.

The virtual address space is divided up into areas (4 Gbyte chunks), segments (4 Mbyte chunks), and pages (4 Kbyte chunks). The area is pointed to by the appropriate area descriptor and is driven by the MODE bit (bit 31) in the PSR, which is set to either user or supervisor. Each of the area descriptors point to the top of their segment table. Each of these segment table entries point in turn to a page table. The page table entry points to a 4 Kpage in physical memory, if it is currently resident. (See Fig. 4-9.)

The MMU follows the tables until it finds a pointer to the requested page, or until it comes across an invalid entry. If it does find an invalid entry, a segment or page fault is signalled. The fault handler would then load a valid descriptor—after bringing in the missing data from secondary memory.

If the table search is successful, the result is a physical address, constructed as shown in Fig. 4-10.

There is, naturally, a table search algorithm, and it's possible to summarize that algorithm without too much detail. When the 88200 performs a table search, this is what is does:

1. First, the supervisor/user bit specifies which area pointer is to be used. There are two parts to this.
   a. If the selected area pointer is marked invalid, then the address is not translated (that is, physical address is assumed), although the WT, G, and CI bits are applied to the address.
   b. If, on the other hand, the area pointer is valid, the WT, G, and CI bits are accumulated.

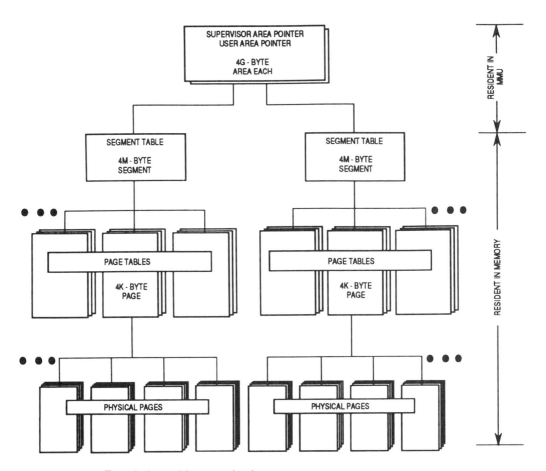

4-9 Translation table organization. (Reprinted with permission of Motorola Inc.)

(Now, a quick aside. In the steps below, if there's an error, a fault, or a violation, the table search comes to a halt. The P Bus Fault Status Register (PFSR) and the P Bus Fault Address Register (PFAR) are updated and the processor receives an exception. It is the responsibility of the exception handler to take the appropriate action, such as loading in a page of segment entries.)

2. Then, the area pointer does what comes natural, and points—specifically, it points to the segment table base address, and bits $31-22$ of the logical address point to the specific segment descriptor in the segment table. Again, you have different possibilities:
   a. If the segment descriptor is invalid, a segment fault occurs.
   b. If a bus error occurs, a bus fault error is signalled.

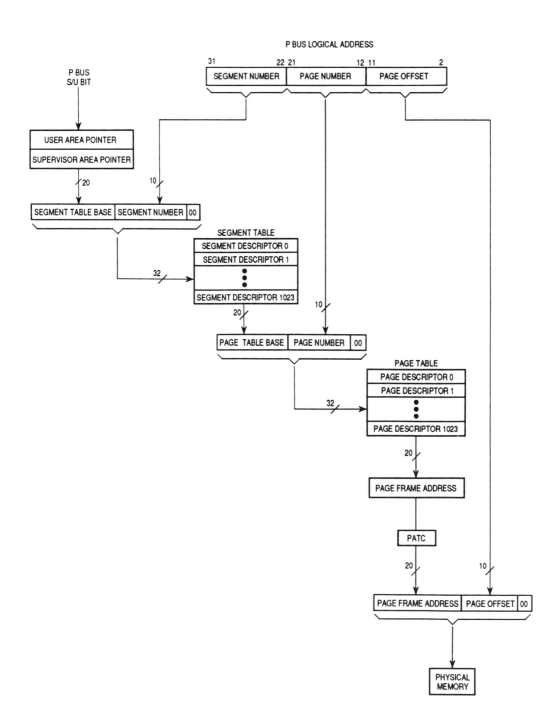

4-10 Physical address generation. (Reprinted with permission of Motorola Inc.)

    c. If the SP bit is set and user access is attempted, an access violation is signalled to the processor.

    d. If the segment descriptor is valid and no error occurred, the protection and control bits (WT, G, and CI) are logically ORed to those values accumulated in 1.b.

3. Next, the segment descriptor entry contains a page table base address, and bits $31-12$ of the logical address specify the entry in that table.

    a. If page table entry is invalid, a page fault occurs.

    b. If a bus error occurs, a bus fault error is signalled.

    c. If the SP bit is set and user access is attempted, a privilege violation is signalled to the processor.

    d. If the page table is valid, the protection and control bits (WT, G, and CI) are logically ORed to those values accumulated in 1.b and 2.d.

4. At this point, the 88200 creates a new PATC entry. If you attempt to get it down in brief, it all sounds a little like DNA reproducing itself.

    a. The S/$\overline{\text{U}}$ bit and bits $31-12$ form the Logical Page Address field.

    b. The PFA from the page descriptor is the Page Frame Address (PFA) field.

    c. The protection and control bits are set from the logical OR and accumulation of 1.b, 2.d, and 3.d.

5. The logical address is then translated through the new PATC entry. The WP bit is tested, and if the page is write-protected and a write is attempted, a write protection violation occurs. If there is no violation, then there is a memory access.

6. And, finally, if cache inhibit is not specified, the four word aligned access containing the referenced word is stored in the data cache, and the accessed data is placed on the P bus from data cache.

Shared and dynamically loaded tables

Now that table searches are out of the way, it's important to know that the behavior of tables themselves can be a bit more complex than you might suspect. They can be shared, paged and dynamically loaded. (See Fig. 4-11.)

    Let's take sharing first. Page frames, page tables and segments can be shared between tasks. To manage it, you simply place a pointer to the table

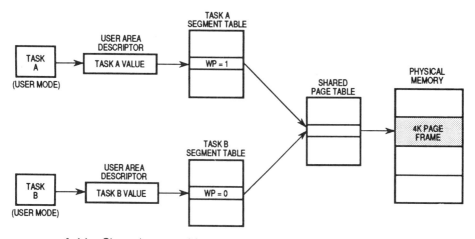

4-11 Shared page tables. (Reprinted with permission of Motorola Inc.)

to be shared in the translation tables of both tasks. You can even set the protection bits so that they are different between the tasks. For example, Task A might access a specific page with write permission, while B has read only access to the same page. The shared area can appear at a different logical address in each set of tables.

Paging, meanwhile, is yet another of the 88K's many little techniques for getting performance gains by making things appear to be in memory when in fact they're someplace else entirely. Not all entries of a table need to be resident in physical memory. If a reference is made to a page frame that requires table entries not in memory, the translation algorithm gives a page or segment fault, and the system software must resolve that the error came from nonresident table entries and effect their acquisition. To the application software, however, it seems like the whole thing was there all along.

Dynamic allocation is an elaboration of the same idea. A complete translation table need not be allocated at task initialization. Rather, the top level entries can be allocated and subsequent ones allocated—dynamically—when needed. At a minimum, one page of segment table and one page of page table information must be allocated in addition to the page frame containing the location referred to be the program counter to start the task. Some tasks might also allocate the same entries for the stack space.

Memory management faults

Now to discuss faults.

When a fault or some other problem is encountered on a P bus transaction, the 88200 does the following:

1. Aborts the transaction which caused the fault in the first place.
2. Updates the PFSR fault code bits $18-16$ (as an aside, that's actually all that's in the PFSR). The possible codes are:

Value	Meaning
000	Success
011	Bus Error
100	Segment Fault
101	Page Fault
110	Supervisor Violation
111	Write Protection Violation

3. The PFAR is updated so that it contains the physical address of the fault.
4. The P bus reply lines, $R0-R1$, report the following to the processor:

Meaning	R0	R1
Reserved	0	0
Success	0	1
Wait	1	0
Fault	1	1

5. The subsequent P bus transaction is ignored by both the 88100 and the 88200 to avoid another fault due to bus pipelining.
6. The 88200 returns to its normal state.

When the 88100 gets a reply $(R1-R0)$ other than "success," an exception is taken, and an exception handler of the operating system is invoked. The exception handler determines the fault type from the PFSR, and may read the PFAR to determine the address which caused the fault. The PFAR contains the physical address. The logical address is still in the 88100 in one of the DMAx registers—where the "x" is $0-2$, depending on the pipeline stage for the particular error.

In the event of a page or segment fault, or an access violation, the 88100 must handle the fault exception. For example, on a page fault, the normal exception response of the operating system will be to fetch the missing page from disk.

If the transaction receives a wait reply, the 88100 exception handler determines if and when to retry the P bus request. Similarly, if the fault is corrected (logical page read in from disk) the exception handler can direct a retry of the P bus request.

You'll recall from the PATC discussion that on a write to cache the PATC modified bit is set, and a table search for the page descriptor is begun. If a bus error happens during that search then the modified bit may not get set in the page descriptor. If so, the exception handler should invalidate the PATC entry to avoid possible inconsistency regarding the settings of the "modified" (M) bits.

Now that you know what the 88200 does once it finds a fault, the time has come to list the kind of faults it's likely to run across. This ghastly crew is:

- Segment Fault—This happens when the 88200 finds a segment marked invalid during a translation table search.
- Page Fault—A page fault occurs when the 88200 encounters a page descriptor with a V bit = 0 (indicating INVALID) during the translation table search.
- Supervisor Violation—This one happens when the 88200 is in the midst of a user mode translation table search for a logical address. Then, quite suddenly, the search runs into a page or segment descriptor with an SP bit = 0, which means supervisor access only.
- Write Protection Violation—This one crops up when a write access to memory finds that the address it wants is write protected. This can occur at the BATC/PATC, or at the segment or page descriptor.
- M bus error—An M bus error can appear to plague any M bus transaction that results from a P bus transaction. (Other kinds of M bus problems exist, by the way. This is just the one unpleasant little beggar that we've chosen to talk about at the moment.) In any case, the 88200 can detect an M bus error either by noting an error in parity, or by getting an error condition report from the system status lines ($\overline{SS3} - \overline{SS0}$). The latter condition could occur in a multiprocessor system when an 88200 detected a write transaction destined for another 88200 to an address which it had cached and modified. (See "Bus Snooping.")

Reset and memory management

And, finally, here's a mention of the effects of the Reset signal on the 88200's efforts at memory management. When the MMU receives an $\overline{RST}$, all partial or pending transactions are flushed. Meanwhile, the memory management registers and ports are initialized as follows:

Register	State After Reset
System Command Register (SCR)	Cleared
System Status Register (SSR)	Cleared
System Address Register (SAR)	Undefined
P Bus Fault Status Register (PFSR)	Cleared
P Bus Address Status Register (PFAR)	Undefined
Supervisor Area Pointer (SAPR)	CI bit set, all others cleared
User Area Pointer (UAPR)	CI bit set, all others cleared
BATC Write Parts	undefined

The operating system must initialize the area pointers, the segment and page tables, and the control and protection data in them.

Data cache

Finally comes the 88200 as a data cache device. It says much about the complexity and power of the 88200 that this section, caching, which would seem to be the definitive function of a "cache" chip actually comes last in the chapter. Caching, while important, is still only one of the 88200's functions.

Cache organization

We've already discussed the fact that the 88200 has 16 Kbytes of 4-way set associative data cache. In combination with the ATCs, the voracious appetite of the 88100 can be fed at a rate of a word almost every clock cycle. That feeding frenzy is the result of a great deal of foresight on the part of the CMMU's designers, and a substantial amount of electronic effort on the part of the 88200 itself.

The four-way set associative cache is a key factor of performance. The 16 Kbytes are arranged as shown below into 256 sets of four lines. Each line contains four data words along with the appropriate control bits and address tags (see below). Although we refer to "data cache" and "data words" you'll recall that these references apply equally well to instructions. You'll also recall that in common configurations there is one CMMU for data and one for instructions.

A single line of cache looks like this:

20 bits	6 bits	1 bit	2 bits	32 bits	32 bits	32 bits	32 bits
Address Tag	LRU	Disable	Status	Word 1	Word 2	Word 3	Word 4

Now to define each of this line's individual sections:

Address tag   is the high 20 bits of the physical address where the data can be found in system memory. This is the address of a 4 Kbyte page.

LRU   which stands for Least Recently Used, is reference data indicating which of the four lines has been used (this is a surprise?) least recently. The LRU is the key factor which determines which otherwise valid line might be thrown out when a new cache entry is needed.

Status   is two bits that denote the status of the data in this particular line. The possible combinations, and their meanings, are:

Bits   Meaning
00   Exclusive Unmodified (this is the only cache line with a copy of the data and it has not been changed from the version which exists in system memory.)
01   Exclusive Modified (this is the only cache line with a copy of the data but it has been modified with respect to memory.)
10   Shared Unmodified (other caches have copies of the data, but none have modified it.)
11   Invalid (this line contains no meaningful data.)

Words 1−4   contain the data actually stored in the cache.
When the 88K makes a reference to data not currently in cache, after the translation, the four-word aligned chunk of memory containing the desired word is written into cache—into words one through four. Its destination in cache is determined by bits 11 through four of the logical address. Those eight bits are used to index into the 256 separate cache sets. One of the lines in the address set will be used to store the four words of data— though which line in particular doesn't matter. It's picked because it happens to be empty, or because it is the oldest.

As an aside, the four-word alignment is consistent. It is used if the line is copied back to memory—four words are written, even if only one byte of one has been changed. However, on a write miss, only the specific word is written to memory.

After the data has been written to cache, it will have a 30-bit address— 30 because the 88K thinks in words. If you want a specific byte, the Data Byte Enable lines let you designate one.

In any case, this new 30-bit address looks something like this:

31   12 11   4 3   2
20 bits from Physical address in address tag	8 bits from Logical address	2 bits from Logical address (denoting word)

The address tag is 20 bits, in which the upper 7 bits of the logical address are appended to the 13-bit physical block address.

Memory update policies

As you'll recall from chapter 1, the 88K lets you pick between a couple of different ways of maintaining coherency between cached data and data in system memory—specifically, copyback and writethrough. You'll also recall that in copyback the first time the cache is written to, the same line is written to system memory as well. But then subsequent writes to the same line just update the cached data. The system memory version grows ever more out of date with each write.

Eventually, the system memory will get the current version of the data, but only when the 88200 is commanded by the software to provide it.

Under writethrough, in contrast, every time data is written to cache, it is also written to memory. Thus, to abandon English and go instead to computerese, with writethrough, system memory and cache are always *coherent*. They always have the same data.

The advantage of that, of course, is that you don't run the risk of something getting lost in the shuffle. You don't have to worry about the possibility of some vital modification not making it from cache to system memory.

Why, then, would you ever want to bother with copyback? Well, in the best of all possible worlds—where software developers dwell in ivory towers and computer users have scandalously large sums of money to spend on computer systems with multiple, super highbandwidth buses and I/O in places where you wouldn't believe it was possible, let alone legal—no one would bother with copyback. Period.

But, unfortunately, this isn't the best of all possible worlds. Instead, we have grim reality to deal with. And, in the grim reality, writethrough is more demanding of computer resources (read "more expensive") than copyback. With writethrough, after all, each time you write to system memory you tax the M bus.

In copyback, though, that happens only the first time and the last time you write the line. As a result, copyback improves system performance by minimizing cache use of the M bus bandwidth. (You will hear hardware folks talking a lot about bandwidth. In situations like this, it is best to tolerate them.)

Actually, there is one fairly good metaphor for bandwidth and the advantages of copyback. In fact, you'll probably live it this evening at five when you hit the most-inaptly-named "expressway" on your way home. As you sit in traffic, horns blaring and exhaust seeping through your window, meditate on this. The cars around you are all trying to use the same road at the same time. However, your expressway was built at least twenty years ago, and it was designed to support roughly half the cars that currently clog its lanes.

Now say the department of transportation launches a particularly successful PR campaign to promote carpooling and 50% of the drivers began to do so. Suddenly, the road seems bigger—it is carrying only its intended load—without any real improvement in the carrying capacity of the route. So it is with copyback. Changes to data are carpooled in the line, and written to memory (getting onto the freeway) only when the trip is mandatory.

So, basically, you have to choose between these two according to your needs. If you want higher performance, and you're willing to gamble a little with the (however remote) chance that you might miss something in transit, go with copyback.

But, if you always want your data to be absolutely current, you'll want to go with writethrough. For one example, you might have a portion of system memory dedicated to the frame buffer or video of a display screen. It's vital that the data in that memory be constantly current. Or the screen might start to show all sorts of nasty little artifacts. For another, you might be dealing with high use global data, in which case you might be far better off with writethrough. The 88200 would avoid loss or error, but at the expense of M bus traffic.

Be warned though, writethrough will always cost in terms of performance. In general, maximum performance for a single processor system is achieved when memory is mapped as local ($G = 0$) and copyback is used. This can be extended to multiple processors by saying that addresses which are normally used by only one processor should be mapped as above; just as if, that is, they were running on a monoprocessor system. If more than one processor uses the data, then snooping must be enabled to maintain coherency between the caches of the processors. The data would be mapped global ($G = 1$). (See "Bus Snooping".)

You select between copyback and writethrough with the WT bit in the ATC entry which maps this cache line, providing that address translation is enabled. If not, then the WT bit in the area pointer (SAPR or UAPR) controls. In either case, the bit setting is:

WT = 1 for writethrough
WT = 0 for copyback

Incidentally, the value of WT has no meaning if the access is cache inhibited. This can come about if the CI bit is set in the ATC, or if the transaction is locked. In the latter case, the signal P bus $\overline{DLOCK}$ would be asserted. (See Cache Avoidance.)

Cache line replacement

Remember those LRU bits, the ones that are present in each cache line? Well, they have a purpose.

When a cache miss occurs, and all the lines in that set are full of perfectly good data, a decision has to be made. Who gets pitched out? The name of the bits gives away the answer. The 88200 will throw out the line that was last used a longer time ago than any other of the lines in the set.

Suppose, for example, that you were incrementing through a giant array and each of the array entries is 4 Kbytes in size.

Now envision what you would see if you were to look at the first word of each entry as it would appear in direct mapped cache, two-way set, and four-way set. Under direct mapped, you would see the line replaced for every entry. In a two-way set, you would see the line replaced at every other entry. In a four-way set, you would have the line replaced at every fourth entry.

However, as with most laws, this one breaks down if applied to infinity. As the array gets bigger and bigger, eventually you reach a spot at which you must pick one of four lines to which you give the old heave-ho. The six LRU bits tell you which of the lines has been used more recently than the others. (The details are about as complex as the Gordian Knot, and not particularly important to boot. However, if for some grim reason you absolutely need to know how the LRU bits are used, see page 3−5 of the *88200 User's Manual*.)

Cache access

Now on to cache access. When the 88100 puts a logical address on the P bus, the 88200 immediately starts working on cache set selection and address translation. It works on translation with the upper bits and picks the cache set with bits 11−4. You'll recall that both ATCs are checked simultaneously—with the BATC using the upper 13 bits of the logical address, and the PATC using the upper 20—and that if a hit is attained on both ATCs, the BATC result is used.

If neither ATC hits, the CMMU performs a translation table search to locate the data and create a PATC entry. When the search is complete, the ATC lookups occur again to get a PATC hit.

Once the physical address is known through translation, the upper 20 bits are compared to the 4 tags in the selected set. (You might want to watch closely after this, because here's where you get the associative part.) The four compares occur simultaneously. Through the use of associative memory, the address tag portions of all four lines are simultaneously compared to the physical address from the ATC.

If one of the address tags matches the physical address, the data is sent from the selected line to the P bus. Bits 3 and 2 of the logical address designate a specific word in the line. If only a byte or a half word is requested, the data byte enable signals tell which ones.

If there is no match to the address tags, then the 88200 selects a cache line to put it in by the rules of LRU, loads it from memory, and then the data access is performed as above.

So, all in all, the cache access process can be summed up as follows:

1. When the 88200 gets a logical address of the P bus, three things happen at the same time:
   a. The CMMU selects the cache set using bits $11-4$ of the logical address.
   b. It also checks the BATC using bits $31-19$ of the logical address.
   c. And, it checks the PATC using bits $31-12$.
2. If 88200 gets an ATC hit, it has a physical address and proceeds accordingly. If not, it does a search and creates a new PATC entry.
3. When the physical address is finally available, the 88200 compares the upper 20 bits against the four cache tags in the set selected in 1a. If there is a match, then it delivers the data—it either reads from or writes to cache with the appropriate information. If there isn't a match, then it goes to memory and gets the selected data.

And that, basically, is all there are to it. But, before moving to details of specific cache accesses, a few more general details ought to be noted. There are some odds and ends that ought to be kept in mind. Specifically:

- If the requested logical is cache inhibited, a memory transation is always done to fetch the data.
- If a cache hit occurs on a cache inhibited address, the line is invalidated.
- The two 2 VV status bits might change during an access.

W

Bits	Meaning
00	Exclusive Unmodified (this is the only cache line with a copy of the data and it has not been changed from the version which exists in system memory.)
01	Exclusive Modified (this is the only cache line with a copy of the data but it has been modified with respect to memory.)
10	Shared Unmodified (other caches have copies of the data, but none have modified it.)
11	Invalid (this line contains no meaningful data.)

- Invalid is used at reset to clear the cache, and bus snooping logic may invalidate a line

That said, move on to individual cache accesses themselves.

Cache reads and writes

Cache access is pretty much a hit or miss operation, quite literally. When either a read or write is requested by the processor, the data either currently exists in cache, or it doesn't. If it is present, you have a hit; if not, a miss.

Now look at the two modes, read and write, in all their gory detail.

Cache read   When the 88100 places a logical address on the P bus (the hardware folks like to say "latches the address"), the address is translated to a physical address, and the CMMU checks its records to see if it has that data on hand. If so, the 88200 achieved a cache hit, and the data, is put back on the P bus within 1 cycle. And the 88200 signals success to the 88100. Sort of a self-awarded "I DONE GOOD!"

If the data is not present, the request "missed" cache; and the 88200 signals the 88100 to wait. Both the success and wait are signalled via the R1−R0 lines on the P bus. Okay, say you missed. Now what? The wait on the P bus is held until the 88200 can acquire the desired data and load it into cache.

So the CMMU requests the M bus (remember the Bus Request signal), and perhaps through arbitration, it gets ownership. If necessary, a line is selected for replacement (by the LRU rules) and if it is marked "modified", it is written to memory. The line is marked invalid, and a read is performed via the M bus to get the data and load it into cache. The M bus is released and the line marked shared unmodified, and the data is put on the

P Bus. R1 − R0 then change to "success" and another happy cache translation is complete.

It is possible that the CMMU receives a "retry" signal when it tries to read the data. As you shall see in the exciting story of "Bus snooping—the private eyes of computers" this could indicate that a snoop hit occurred. If so, the M bus is released and tried again in one clock cycle. The delay allows the snooping device to get mastery of the M bus to update memory with its fresher copy of the data. When it is done, the original requestor will retry, and get the data.

Cache write   Now assume that you have a miss. In that case, the 88200 gets the bus and selects a line in exactly the same way it did with the read. But, it then reads the data with the M bus C1 (Intent to Modify—IM) bit set. This serves notice that the next transaction will write to memory. After the write to memory occurs, the cache entry is updated, and the line is marked "exclusive unmodified." The M bus is released and everyone goes about their business.

On the other hand, if you have a hit, the CMMU checks the status bits to find out if the line is:

exclusive   if so, the cache line is updated and the VV bits set to exclusive modified.

writethrough   the line and memory are updated, VV bits set to shared unmodified.

mapped as global copyback   the line and memory are updated (write once), and VV set to exclusive unmodified. Subsequent writes will only update the line and not memory.

mapped as local copyback   the cache line is updated and VV set to exclusive modified.

If an error occurs, the M bus is released, the PFSR and PFAR have the cause and location of the error. The P bus reply lines (R1 − R0) signal "fault". The processor then runs an exception handler to take corrective action.

Retry is a possibility under the same conditions as above in READ, i.e. caused by a snoop hit, and the CMMU waits one cycle to give the snooper time to grab the M bus.

Xmem   That takes you to xmem. It's covered more fully in chapter 7 on instructions, but you should take a glance here as well. It is a special case because it relates to the 88200 in that it is an atomic instruction which behaves like both a load and a store.

It is a read followed by a write, while maintaining ownership of the M bus the whole time. An xmem transaction is cache-inhibited by the CMMU. If a line is hit, it is invalidated; after writing it to memory if it was marked "modified." This guarantees integrity of data during the bus locked transaction. Errors and retrys are handled as in reads and writes.

The reason for using xmem is to guarantee that the bus is locked. This is quite useful for semaphores or other atomic communications media. It is faster to do the corresponding with discrete load and store instructions than to use xmem but you don't own the bus. By the way, you should avoid use of the I16 form of addressing, because it will not be supported with xmem in future versions of the chip.

Cache coherency Another subject which is covered elsewhere, but which ought to be touched on here is cache coherency. You'll recall that coherency is a term used to refer to the ability of the CMMU to allow multiple processors to have private copies of data in their caches, merrily making changes at will; all without risk that anyone get stale data.

The tool used by the CMMU to perform this minor miracle is bus snooping. It's rather like having someone looking over your shoulder, and as soon as you make a correction to the document (you discovered they spelled your name wrong), that someone immediately tells everyone that has the document that their version is out of date. Note that coherency doesn't say that the various other copies are updated automatically.

Below is an example of cache coherency between two processors via bus snooping. Initially, neither of the 2 CMMUs have any valid data. Then #1 loads a line, followed by #2 loading the same line. #1 then writes the line, causing the line to be written to memory (write once). Each letter represents one word in the cache line (see Fig. 4-12).

Bus snooping

You'll recall that to maintain coherency, the 88200 employs bus snooping. Each and every 88200 watches the M bus to see if any bus master attempts to use data in system memory which it has in its cache, and which might therefore have been modified in some recent operation.

It manages this feat by monitoring the M bus control and information lines. When it spots a Global (G) bit being asserted, the 88200 compares

CPU	Instruction	CMMU1	CMMU2	Memory at 0x0	Action
		?	?	ABCD	Initial State
1	Load 0x0	ABCD	?	ABCD	Cache #1 loaded
2	Load 0x4	ABCD	ABCD	ABCD	Cache #2 loaded
1	Store 0x0	RBCD	ABCD	RBCD	Cache #1 changed, write once Cache #2 is stale
1	Store 0x4	RFCD	ABCD	RBCD	Cache #2 and RAM are stale
2	Load 0x4	RFCD	ABCD	RBCD	#1 gets a snoop hit, tells #2 to retry
2	Retry/Wait	RFCD	RFCD	RFCD	all data current

4-12 Cache coherency example.

the address on the bus with those in its cache. If there is no match, it happily goes back to whatever it was doing in the first place. If, however, it does pick up a match, and if that data is marked "modified," (i.e., if the version of that data in system memory is no longer current) than it preempts the M bus—thus putting the offending transaction on ice for the moment. Then it writes its version of the data to system memory. Then, the transaction attempting to address that data can proceed. If, however, the transaction is itself meant to modify that data (if, that is, it has the intent-to-modify—IM—bit asserted), then the 88200 finding the match in the first place will mark its own copy of the data as invalid.

The IM bit is asserted during any transaction in which the contents of the cache will be modified—this turns out to be any situation other than a normal read. These are: cache line read due to write miss, xmem read, write.

And, by the way, xmem is an interlocked read and write operation that is cache inhibited. Once the issuing CMMU gets the bus, both read and write will be executed without freeing the M bus. Therefore, during an xmem, a snooping 88200 would hit on the read portion, write its data to memory, and invalidate the line, but would not hit on the write portion of xmem.

And naturally, there are all sorts of interesting combinations you can run into with snoops. They include some of the following (and, as an aside, its assumed here that all these actions are taken by the CMMU, unless otherwise noted):

Situation: Read transaction   Data unmodified in snooping cache

In other words, a snooping 88200 spots another 88200 about to do a read of some data in system memory which is also in the snooping 88200's cache. It so happens that this is just a read transaction, and the version of the data in the first 88200's cache has not been modified—i.e., it is the same as the version in system memory. Ergo, the second can pick up that data without picking up stale data in the process.

Therefore, the first 88200's response to the situation is to: mark the line shared, unmodified and get on with its business.

Situation: Read transaction   Data Modified in snooping cache.

This is more difficult. This time, the snooping 88200 picks up another 88200's intent to read data in system memory which also exists—in a modified form—in its own cache. This time, the 88200 has to respond with:

Abort the read (Signal RETRY)
Write the line to system memory
Mark line shared unmodified
Original CMMU does retry

In other words, the 88200 detecting the attempted read of modified data aborts the read by signalling RETRY, copies its version of the data to system memory, and marks the line "shared unmodified." Only then is the original 88200 free to try again.

Situation: Intent to Modify   Data unmodified in the snooping cache.

In other words, the 88200 sees another 88200 about to modify data in system memory which is also in its own cache. But, the snooping 88200 hasn't changed that data. So, the second 88200 is free to go get in. The response is:

Invalidate the line

The snooping 88200 realizes that its own version of that data may shortly be obsolete. So it invalidates the line in question in its own cache.

Situation: Intent to modify   Data modified in snooping cache.

Here, of course, is the same situation as above, except that the snooping 88200's version of the data has been modified. The response is:

Abort the read (Signal RETRY)
Copyback the line
Invalidate the line
Originating CMMU does retry

In short, it prevents the second 88200 from getting to system memory—and from getting unmodified data in the process. Then, it copies back its own version to the system memory, as well as marking its version of the data as invalid. Then the other 88200 is free to try again.

You can also look at this situation from the point of view of the 88200 that is trying to get to system memory. If an 88200 receives a retry signal when it heads for system memory, it responds by releasing the M bus. It then waits one clock cycle. This allows the snooping device (whatever it might be) to gain control of the M bus.

Finally, if the CMMU encounters an error condition, it releases the M bus. Meanwhile, the copyback error control bit (CE) is set in the System Status Register (SSR).

Cache avoidance

Cache is all well and good, but there are times when you just don't want it. Perhaps, you're working with a real time application, where response must be very predictable. If cache were not inhibited, an operation could perform more slowly when data was not in cache, than when it was.

Therefore, memory locations may be marked as cache inhibited to effect cache avoidance. This involves setting the Cache Inhibit (CI) bit at the desired level. Recall that the CI bit is one of the bits accumulated during address translations. This means that if CI is set anywhere in the sequence of area, segment or page descriptor, then cache will be inhibited at that level. Also, the two hardwired BATC entries are always cache inhibited.

Cache is automatically inhibited during table searches. This implies that segment and page descriptors are not cached. This is done without setting the cache inhibit (C4) signal on the M bus, so that off chip secondary caches may be used to cache descriptors. (Some systems might require more cache than you get with even 8 88200 chips. They can use hardware to implement additional cache memory and tie it in using the control signals from the CMMU.)

Finally, cache is inhibited when performing an xmem transaction. Recall that inhibiting cache guarantees data integrity during the bus locked transaction.

Cache flushing

In the course of human events, there ultimately comes a time when you just want to flush everything and be done with it. This applies to cache as well as to other parts of our lives. And, we can deal with that via cache flushing.

At times it will be necessary to flush the cache—that is, to empty it, as could be done when memory management causes a page of physical memory to be paged out. Doing so would leave clean space for new entries, rather than disposing of them one at a time on an LRU basis.

You cause the cache to flush by writing one of three commands in the System Control Register (SCR), in bits 5−0, of the 88200 in question.

These three commands are:

Command	Description
0101gg	Invalidate data cache
0110gg	Copyback data cache to memory
0111gg	Copyback data cache to memory and invalidate

gg	granularity
00	line
01	page
10	segment
11	all

The sequence of a cache flush is as follows:

At times it will be necessary to flush the cache—that is, to empty it, as could be done when memory management causes a page of physical memory to be paged out. Doing so would leave clean space for new entries, rather than disposing of them one at a time on an LRU basis.

3. Finally, you go to each line to be flushed. If the line is exclusive modified, then it is written to memory. But, exclusive or not, the line is marked invalid for commands 0101gg and 0111gg.

If this is a line flush, all 20 bits of the address tag are checked against the SAR, and SAR bits 11−4 specify the cache set. On the other hand, if it is a page flush, then all 20 bits of the address tag are checked in the SAR.

And, finally, if this is a segment flush, then the upper 10 bits of the address tag are checked against the SAR. Any line that was within that segment would be flushed.

And there is one last note about flushing. The cache is not accessible by the processor during flushing. As far as the 88100 is concerned, a 88200 in the act of flushing might as well be on the other side of the moon.

But, and this is an important "but," a flushing 88200 can still perform bus snooping. So, you don't have to worry about its mind being elsewhere when some other 88200 is rushing in where angels fear to tread.

88100 programming model

Processors are like the parable of the blind men and the elephant. They can seem very different according to your point of view. In this chapter, though, we'll attempt to describe how the 88100 appears from the programmer's perspective.

Processor states

We can start by saying that the 88100 has only 3 possible states:

- Reset
- Instruction execution
- Exception

Now, let's take them one by one.

Reset

When the 88K gets an $\overline{RST}$ (reset) signal, it shuts down completely. Everything presently going on within it is abandoned. No calculations are completed, no transactions are finished, and nothing is saved for later. The processor just drops everything, shrugs its shoulders to get the kinks out, and backs into position to start from scratch.

The purpose of the reset state is, of course, to provide a blank slate for new work. So, once the $\overline{RST}$ signal is negated, the processor initializes itself into a known state. Some control registers have defined values, others are undefined, and instruction execution begins at physical address zero.

After $\overline{RST}$ the 88100's registers have the following values:

Register	Value
PSR	Mode bit set, bits 9-0 are set, all other bits are cleared (PSR=0x800003FF) This sets the processor to:
	Supervisor mode
	Big Endian Byte ordering
	Concurrent operation allowed
	Carry not generated by Add or Subtract
	Floating point unit disabled
	No Misaligned data access exceptions
	Interrupts are disabled
	Shadow registers are frozen
EPSR	Undefined
SB	Cleared
SSBR	Undefined
FIP	Physical address 0
NIP	Marked invalid
XIP	Marked invalid
SFIP	Undefined
SNIP	Undefined
SXIP	Undefined
VBR	Cleared
DMT0-2	Bit zero cleared all other undefined
DMA0-2	Undefined
DMD0-2	Undefined
FPECR	Cleared
FPCR	Cleared
FPSR	Cleared
Others	Undefined

This is the starting point for all software execution, which occurs in the state known as *instruction execution*.

Instruction execution

This is the normal operating state of the 88K. It is the plain vanilla mode of the processor. There are two versions of this state. You'll recall that the

88100 operates in either user or supervisor mode, and each has its own address spaces (4GB) allowed by the 88100.

Which mode the 88100 is in at any one time depends on the MODE bit in the PSR. If it is set to 1, the processor is in supervisor mode; if 0, then it is in user mode.

Supervisor mode allows execution of all instructions and access to all control and general purpose registers. If necessary, software can access user space while in supervisor mode through use of the [.usr] option of the memory access instructions.

User mode allows execution of 47 of the 51 instructions, and access to the floating point control and status registers, and the general registers. Instructions not allowed in user mode are:

> ldcr—load from control register
> rte—return from exception
> stcr—store to control register
> xcr—exchange control register

Instructions restricted in user mode are:

> fldcr—load from floating point control register
> fstcr—store to floating point control register
> fxcr—exchange floating point control register

(User mode restricts the above to fcr62 & fcr63, the floating point status and control registers respectively.)

> ld—load register from memory
> st—store register to memory
> xmem—exchange register with memory

(User mode may not execute any of the above three instructions while using the [.usr] option.)

> tb0—trap on bit clear
> tb1—trap on bit set
> tcnd—conditional trap

User mode may not trap to vectors $0-127$, which are hardware vector numbers.

(Note: because of the data in the PSR, some operating system implementations define routines that allow reading and setting certain bits in the PSR—especially SER, C, MXM, BO)

The level of privilege can change automatically. It switches from user to supervisor whenever:

- Exception occurs
- Reset
- User program executes a trap instruction
- Interrupt or memory access fault

When any of these occur, the PSR MODE bit is set to supervisor, and memory access defaults to supervisor space. Access to user space, via ld, st, and xmem requires use of [.usr] option.

It can happen the other way, too. Often, the level of privilege will change from supervisor to user when the processor encounters an rte instruction, and the processor was in user mode previously. The rte instruction restores the processor context as it was prior to a trap or exception.

There is another way that supervisor mode can switch to user mode, though it might be less pleasant. You also go to user mode when the ldcr instruction or the xcr instruction explicitly clears the MODE bit. But, neither ldcr nor xcr changes the FIP and NIP registers. That means you could have something nasty appear in your program's execution.

Exceptions

We've avoided the ugly details of exceptions for too long and must at last delve into them. An *exception* is some condition or event that demands that the CPU be preempted from its current work to recognize and handle the situation. Current execution is halted, although it will usually be resumed.

You may hear the term *exception-time context switch*. This refers to the fact that the processor must change the context from the current task to that of handling the exception. It should do so in a way that is fast and reliable, yet which is also flexible enough to let the processor switch back again to whatever it was doing before the exception came along to spoil an otherwise perfect day.

The 88K provides the latter of these characteristics—the ability to switch back to the original tasks—via its "shadow" registers. These are a set of otherwise silent registers that mirror the activities of the 88100. When an exception occurs, the shadow registers hold information about whatever the processor was doing before. Then, after exception processing is finished, the 88100 can use that information to pick up where it left off.

What sorts of events can cause exceptions? Most often they're the result of interrupts signalled through the interrupt pin on the CPU. These might come from a keystroke on the keyboard, or mouse movement, or a character coming in from a data communications line. In short, they're "normal" exceptional events which the system was designed to accommodate. Most exceptions are of this sort.

Second, and less pleasant, are external errors. These are events outside the control of the processor, but which require action. Common examples of this kind of exception include fault-conditions in virtual memory. Perhaps a page frame was not in physical memory when it was requested. The processor must stop its current tasks (this may be the task that requested the page anyway) and retrieve the page frame from disk.

Third, and least pleasant of all, are internal errors. These are abnormal conditions that occur within the processor itself—usually as the result of some problem in the software. For instance, if you have your program trying to divide by zero or otherwise defying the accepted rules of mathematics, then you'll get an exception. There is a slew of this kind of exception. To get an idea of their numbers, just glance at the exceptions lists in chapter 7 on instructions.

That's *why* they happen. *When* they happen is harder. They're rather like the close relations who never learned to phone ahead. They can turn up any time.

However, when they do show up, the 88100 is a gracious but not excessively attentive host. If the CPU encounters an exception while it is in the middle of an instruction, it first completes that instruction. Only then does it recognize the exception. (With the 88100 averaging 1.1 instructions per clock cycle, the exception won't have long to wait.)

Then, when the 88100 does recognize the exception, the CPU uses the "shadow" and exception time registers to freeze the current context into them so that it can restart later. Note that there is only one set of these guys, so an exception occurring immediately after another one is not allowed. In fact, one of the actions of the processor upon recognizing an exception is to disable interrupts so that no more can occur until it is ready. This means that nothing external can happen. (We presume that the exception handler won't create an internal error.) In addition, the CPU enters supervisor mode. Finally, supervisor software handles the actual exception handling.

All in all, the process looks sort of like this:

- Execution context is frozen in the shadow and exception time registers
- Interrupts are disabled
- The MODE bit is set to supervisor in the PSR
- The FPU is disabled

- The data unit is allowed to complete all pending accesses
- Execution is transferred to the appropriate exception handling routine

Then, to get back from exception handling, use the return-from-exception rte instruction. You need to note that this is a privileged instruction. More detail on exceptions will be forthcoming in chapter 9.

Operand types

The 88100 supports seven types of operands. They are:

Type	Size
byte (signed and unsigned)	8 bits
Half-word (signed and unsigned)	16 bits (2 bytes)
Word	32 bits (4 bytes)
Double word	64 bits (8 bytes)
Single-precision floating point	32 bits (4 bytes)
Double-precision floating point	64 bits (8 bytes)
Bit Field	1 to 32 bits in a 32 bit register

Each instruction has explicit or implicit operand size requirements. The 88100 is very picky about data alignment. It demands that double words be on modulo 8 boundaries. (If it's been a while since that last math class, don't sweat it. Modulo 8 simply means that the address must be evenly divisible by 8 with no remainder, like 0xA8.) Single words must be on modulo 4 boundaries, and half words on a modulo 2 boundary.

The general purpose registers are used for all seven types of operands. The data is organized in, loaded to, and extracted from those registers according to fairly specific rules that are built into the 88100. The rules aren't there because the 88100 happens to be inflexible, but rather the other way around. Because the 88100 supports many different types of operand, it might not always be dealing with nice, neat, well-behaved 32-bit words. It might have half words on its hands, for example. So that it can accommodate some rather eccentric characters, it has to enforce a few regulations about who goes where, and why.

In particular, byte operands are always put into or taken out of a register from the lower eight bits. But when an ld instruction loads a byte into a register, bits 31 through 8 get either sign-extended or zero-extended.

Half words, meanwhile, are loaded or extracted from the lower 16 bits of a register. However, the ld instruction causes bits 31 through 16 to be either sign extended or zero extended.

Word operands load or store their entire 32 bits to and from memory. When there is a double-word operand, though, you have the same thing in duplicate. The double-word operand loads or stores two adjacent registers—known as rn and rn+1. The first of these, rn, always contains the higher order word.

Floating point operations have their own set of rules. For single-precision floating point operations, bit 31 holds the sign bit and bits 30 through 23 contain the exponent, while the remaining bits are the mantissa. Double-precision floating point operands divide the work between two registers—rn and rn+1. The rn register holds the sign bit, an exponent field, and mantissa's upper 20 bits. The lower register, rn+1, holds the rest of the mantissa.

There are some rules about which registers you can use with double-word operands and double-precision floating point operands. Most of the general purpose registers are available to you. In fact, you can use r31 as your rn, in which case r0 becomes rn+1. But here's the rub: You'll recall that r0 cannot be modified. Writes to it are simply ignored. But that might not be a disadvantage if, for some reason, you only need 20 bits of mantissa.

Finally, bit-field operations are specified by an offset and a width. This means that a bit-field's position in a register is defined by its proximity to the register's beginning and ending bits. Thus, the bit-field's most significant bit (MSB) is the one closest to bit 31. Its least signficant bit (LSB) is the one closest to bit 0. The offset, then, is the distance from the LSB to bit 0. The MSB, meanwhile, is automatically equal to the width of the bit-field plus the offset. See Fig. 5-1.

Registers

You've already been through the 88K registers in some detail. But there are advantages to looking at them again—with an eye, this time, toward their impact on software.

You'll recall that there are three types of registers in the 88100:

General purpose: r0−r31
Control: cr0−cr20,fcr0−fcr8, fcr62 and fcr63
Internal: XIP, NIP, FIP, and SB

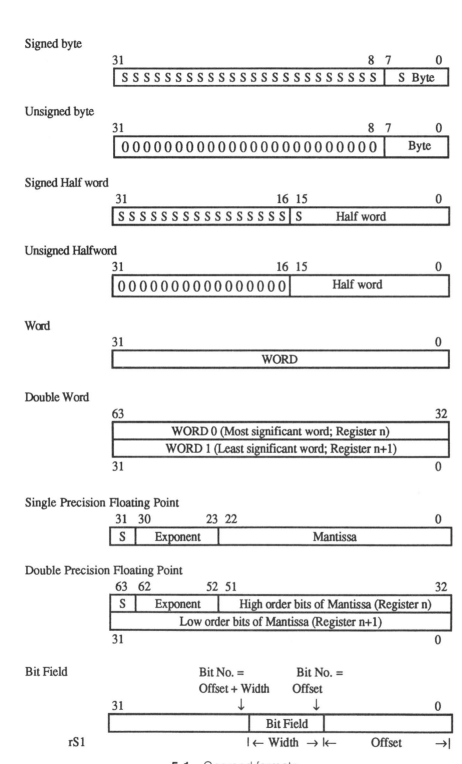

5-1 Operand formats.

The 32 general purpose registers provide data and address information for execution. Control registers cr0−cr20 contain exception recovery and status information for the execution units (integer, data, and instruction). The floating point registers fcr0−fcr8 contain exception recovery and status information for the floating point unit.

Actually there is a fourth type, mentioned in "Exceptions." This fourth is the shadow registers: SXIP, SNIP, SFIP, and SSBR. They shadow the XIP, NIP, FIP, and SB internal registers. Shadowing means that they keep a copy of everything that goes into their "live" counterparts, until they are frozen—which is what happens when an exception comes along. At freeze time, the information in the shadow registers remains constant, and can be used to restart after the exception has been dealt with.

Neither internal nor shadow registers can be accessed in user mode.

General purpose registers

There are specific uses conventionally associated with specific general purpose registers (and these are listed in Fig. 5-2). For instance, r31 is the stack pointer, and r1 is the subroutine return register.

However, convention is meaningless to the processor itself. If you have a good reason for violating convention, by all means do so. But recognize that there's a price for this. If you don't follow convention, your software will be incompatible with any software that does obey the conventions.

Register Number	Name
r0	Zero
r1	Subroutine return pointer
r2−r9	Called procedure parameter registers
r10−r13	Called procedure temporary registers
r14−r25	Called procedure reserved registers
r26	Linker
r27	Linker
r28	Linker
r29	Linker
r30	Preserved register
r31	Stack pointer

5-2 General purpose registers.

We can't think of good reasons to violate some of the conventions listed, because nearly all software will need a stack pointer and a pointer to return from subroutines. However, if you were building a dedicated application that didn't provide software development facilities then the linker registers are certainly fair game.

r0   This register always contains 0. Always. It is there because 0 happens to be one of those happy fixtures that you often find yourself using. You don't have to worry about violating this convention because it is hardwired into the machine. Thus, you're free to write to r0, but you'll still get zero. Your write will have absolutely no effect.

r1   By convention, this register holds a "return pointer." You'll recall that two instructions, bsr and jsr, cause a jump to a subroutine, but they leave behind a pointer to the place in the program to which the application wishes to return, when the subroutine is finished. This register is the place where they'll leave the pointer.

When they do leave that pointer behind, they'll overwrite anything that happens to be in the register before they go there. The pointers aren't immortal either. They too can be overwritten by other software.

r2 through r9   These registers conventionally find employment passing parameters to a called routine. This is a software convention, and the registers can be overwritten by other things.

r10 through r13   These registers are used for temporary storage. They can be overwritten by a called routine, but do not themselves contain the parameters for the called routine.

r14 through r25   By convention, this set of registers is used to store data for the routine that is running at the moment. Again, by convention, these are supposed to have some degree of immunity. A called routine should make certain that the data in r14 through r25 is returned without modifications. These registers can be used within a routine if they are saved first and restored prior to return.

r26 through 29   These are reserved for the linker. Again, this is a software convention.

r30   This register, by a software convention, must be preserved by the called routine.

r31 Finally, this register is reserved for a software stack pointer. Once again, this is a software convention.

Control registers

There are 21 control registers, and 11 FPU control registers. The latter will be discusssed in more detail at the end of this chapter. Normally, control registers are accessible only to the supervisor, although selected registers may be used in user mode. Some system implementation may allow greater access than others. For instance, BCS (see chapter 2) compliant systems have system calls that allow modification of certain bits in the PSR. All of the control registers are listed in Fig. 5-3. Most of these are of only passing interest to most programmers. There are, however, exceptions.

The PID The processor identification register (PID) is the 88100's ID card. It contains information that reveals which version of the chip any particular 88100 might be. This is important for two reasons. First, as the 88K product-line develops, there will be special versions of the chip optimized for particular applications with special function units (SFUs). By checking the PID, a system or application can tell whether this or that 88K is indeed optimized, and if so for what.

Second, the 88K is one of those rare processors that actually assumes that its design isn't carved in stone. It is expected that the 88K will change over time as it is enhanced and upgraded. By checking the PID, software can tell whether the 88K on which it finds itself is one of the older or the newer versions, and react accordingly.

The PID is organized like a name, with different parts of it meaning different things. Bits 31 through 16 are zeros, for the moment. Motorola reserves this space for use later on. Bits 15 through 8 contain the information that reveals which particular 88100 this is—that is, its architecture revision number. The revision number for the current version of the 88100 is 0.

Bits 7 through 1, meanwhile, hold the version number of the chip. This identifies which mask Motorola used when producing this particular 88100. "Mask" refers, of course, to the masking material put down over the raw semiconductor during fabrication. If Motorola decides to change the mask at some time (perhaps for some improvement in performance) there might be changes in the function of the chip, and the version number will alert software to the fact.

Finally, bit 0 is the Master/Checker (MC) bit. This little tag end of the register determines whether the 88K is in checker mode. Checker mode is

Register	Acronym	Name
cr0	PID	Processor Identification Register
cr1	PSR	Processor Status Register
cr2	EPSR	Exception Time PSR
cr3	SSBR	Shadow Scoreboard Register
cr4	SXIP	Shadow Execute Instruction Pointer
cr5	SNIP	Shadow Next Instruction Pointer
cr6	SFIP	Shadow Fetched Instruction Pointer
cr7	VBR	Vector Base Register
cr8	DMT0	Transaction Register 0
cr9	DMD0	Data Register 0
cr10	DMA0	Address Register 0
cr11	DMT1	Transaction Register 1
cr12	DMD1	Data Register 1
cr13	DMA1	Address Register 1
cr14	DMT2	Transaction Register 2
cr15	DMD2	Data Register 2
cr16	DMA2	Address Register 2
cr17	SR0	Supervisor Storage Register 0
cr18	SR1	Supervisor Storage Register 1
cr19	SR2	Supervisor Storage Register 2
cr20	SR3	Supervisor Storage Register 3

5-3 Control registers.

detailed elsewhere, but suffice it to say that checking is done for fault tolerance. When an 88K is a checker it is paired with another, normal 88K. The normal 88K performs the daily tasks of a processor. The checker mirrors the normal 88K. It does exactly the same things as its partner but throws away its output as redundant—unless it finds itself with output that does not match its mirror's. If so, then it knows it has an error on its hands, and sounds an alarm.

An 88K is a normal, "master" processor if the MC bit is set—if, that is, it is "1." If, however, the MC bit isn't set, and has a value of 0, then the 88K is a checker:

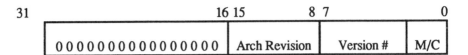

31	16	15	8	7	0
0 0 0 0 0 0 0 0 0 0 0 0 0 0 0 0		Arch Revision		Version #	M/C

For the 88100's in the world to date, here is the correspondence between Version # in the PID, and the "step" level of the parts.

Version #	CPU Level
0x1	A
0x3	B
0x5	C
0x7	D.0
0x9	D.5
0xB	E.0
0xD	E.1
0x11	E.2

The processor status register The processor status register (PSR) is a different beast. It contains information about the current state of affairs within the 88100. The bits within the PSR are set (by hardware or software) to either control those affairs, or simply to report on them. The latter is more important than you might think. It is the PSR which helps the 88K come back from an exception. When the PSR's shadow-freeze bit (SFRZ) is set, then the shadow registers (which you'll recall from elsewhere) are enabled. They take a snapshot of the current situation in the PSR and then provide that information when exception processing is through:

31	30	29	28	27	10	9	4	3	2	1	0
Mode	BO	SER	C	all zeros		all ones		SFD1	MXM	IND	SFRZ

Again, here's a breakdown of the register by function:

Bit 31 is the mode bit. It determines whether you're in user or supervisor mode—when it is 0, you're user, when 1, you're supervisor. Bit 31 is set by hardware, but can be cleared by software. However, it should normally be cleared only by the rte instruction. If you try to clear it with a control register instruction, you might have an incorrect privilege check on the following instruction—or, worse, the following instruction might be taken from the wrong memory space. Default=supervisor.

Bit 30 is the byte order (BO) bit. It determines whether the 88K is going to be Big Endian or Little Endian. If it is set (i.e., equal to 1), then the processor is Little Endian. If it isn't (i.e., equal to 0), then it is Big Endian. You set the bit with the stcr or the xcr instruction. Default=Big Endian.

Bit 29 is the serial mode (SER) bit. If it is set (that is, if it's equal to one), then no concurrent operations are allowed within the 88100. Each instruction completes all operations before the next instruction is begun. The 88100 will still prefetch the next instruction, but that's all. Needless to say, that's a condition you decidedly wish to avoid, because it slows things down to a crawl. But, it's something you want for debugging, when crawling might be the best possible state of affairs. It gives you time and space to see what might be going wrong. When it is cleared (equal to 0), then you're back to the more natural state of concurrent operation. Default=Concurrent.

Bit 28 is the carry (C) bit. In other words, it is what the 88100 uses when it wishes to carry the result of some addition or subtraction. It is used only when some instruction calls for its presence. When, however, it is wanted, it is set (equal to 1) when a carry has been produced, and clear (equal to 0) when one has not. Default=Carry was not generated.

Bits 27 through 10, meanwhile, are reserved by Motorola for future use. Right now, these bits are set to zero, but best not to expect them to be so in the future.

Bits 9 through 4 also deal with things yet to come. They are the SFU Disable bits. When there are more special function units, they will be enabled by these registers. The bits will be zero for enable, and 1 for disable. But, because there aren't any new SFUs around at the moment, these are always set to 1.

Bit 3, the special function disable 1 (SFD1) enables and disables the floating point unit, the one SFU currently in operation. When it is set, the floating point unit is disabled. When cleared, the FPU is enabled. This is done automatically by hardware as the result of an exception of a reset, or it can be done by software via a load or exchange control register instruction. Either way, if you try to start an FPU instruction, or an integer multiply or divide (which also happens on the FPU, you'll recall), when this bit is set, you'll go immediately to a FPU unimplemented precise exception. Default=FPU disabled.

Bit 2 is the misaligned access enable (MXM) bit. Normally, you'll go to exception processing if you try to load, store, or exchange data to and from a memory address that doesn't match the size of the access. An example is a half-word access to an odd byte address.

If this bit is clear, then you will have the normal situation, and such an attempted access will result in an exception. But, there might be times when you want misaligned access. That being the case, you can suppress the 88100's normal rejection of it by setting the MXM bit. When bit 2 is 1, misaligned access doesn't cause an exception. Default=Misaligned accesses do not cause exceptions.

Bit 1 is the interrupt disable (IND) bit. When it is set, interrupts are disabled. When it is clear, interrupts can happen as normal. It is set by hardware and can be cleared and set by the stcr and xcr instructions. One place where interrupts should be disabled is when the shadow registers are frozen. Default=disabled.

Bit 0, finally, is the shadow freeze (SFRZ) bit. If there is an exception, it's automatically set by hardware. When that happens, the shadow registers freeze. Within them is information on the current state of affairs in the processor. Using this information as a reference, the 88K can then find its place in the program after exception processing is complete.

The SFRZ bit can also be set or cleared via software—either directly by the stcr or xcr instructions, or indirectly, as the result of the rte instruction. What stcr and xcr do not do, however, is set the SFRZ bit in the Exception Time Processor Status Register (EPSR). The EPSR, in turn, can be best described as the PSR's doppelganger, or exception time clone. Default=Frozen.

Exception time processor status register   When there's an exception, the contents of the PSR are automatically copied into the EPSR, unless shadowing has already been frozen. In effect, the EPSR becomes the PSR as the PSR was before exception processing began. Then, when the exception is finished, the rte instruction causes the contents of the EPSR to be copied back to the PSR. It can then get on with whatever it was doing before.

31	30	29	28	27		10	9	4	3	2	1	0
*	*	*	*	all zeros			all ones		*	*	*	*

* The value of these bits is determined at exception time.

The shadow registers

That brings you back to those mysterious creatures, the shadow registers. You'll recall that these constantly copy everything that happens within the registers they mirror—until they're frozen. At that time, they go into suspended animation, waiting for the moment when the exception is finished and they can yield up the information contained within them.

They are:

Shadow ScoreBoard Register (SSBR)   You'll recall that the 88100 has a scoreboard register that reflects all 32 of the processor's general registers. Its role is to serve as a reminder about which registers have results pending so they won't be overwritten by another pipeline needing a place to output. Actually, only bits $31-1$ are significant, because register 0 cannot be scoreboarded. The Shadow Scoreboard Register (SSBR) shadows the SB. When there's an exception, and the SFRZ bit is set, the SSBR takes a snapshot of the scoreboard. When the exception is over, the SSBR copies its contents back into the scoreboard via the rte instruction.

31	30	29	28	27	26	25	24	23	22	21	20	19	18	17	16	15	14	13	12	11	10	9	8	7	6	5	4	3	2	1

The SSBR is not a true shadow register in the strictest sense of the word. The whole scoreboard register isn't copied into the SSBR with every clock cycle. Instead, bits in the SSBR are only changed when bits in the scoreboard register are changed. So, there is a chance that the two will be different if the SFRZ bit was set before changes in the scoreboard could be reflected in the SSBR.

The SSBR must be explicitly cleared after a reset. Otherwise, it might not reflect the clean state of the scoreboard after an $\overline{RST}$.

Both read and write access is allowed in the SSBR.

Next Instruction Pointer and its Shadow (NIP/SNIP)   You'll recall that the next instruction pointer (NIP) is always pointing at the location in memory of the instruction which the 88K is accessing right now. The SNIP shadows the NIP. If there is an exception, the SNIP contains a pointer to the address of the instruction that the 88K was about to undertake before the exception came along. With an rte instruction, the 88K uses the SNIP and picks up where it left off.

The SNIP has two unique bits—a V, for valid bit; and an E, for exception bit. E is bit 0 and V is bit 1. They serve as a kind of commentary on the SNIP as a whole.

When the SNIP contains the address of an instruction that was being duly decoded when the exception hit, the V bit is set. The instruction is valid in the sense that the 88K can pick it up and get started again without difficulty. However, if there is a problem with that instruction, then the bit is cleared.

There are three reasons an instruction can be invalid. For instance, it is invalid if it follows a branch or a jump, but the .n option wasn't specified. It's invalid if it has been cleared by software—which you can do, by the way, and this can be useful if you wish to clear the instruction prefetch with a no-op. And, finally, it is invalid if the V bit of the FIP was clear in the first place, so that it was found to be invalid at fetch time.

The E bit, meanwhile, is what the 88K uses to preempt a faulty instruction before it reaches the pipeline. If it is set, and if that instruction is attempted, then there will be an instruction access fault. Sort of an "equipment out of service" tag.

The E bit gets set in the SNIP when it is set in the NIP during shadowing. It can also be set via the stcr and xcr instructions. If both E and V are set when an rte instruction is executed, the NIP instruction generates an instruction access exception.

The E bit is ignored most of the rest of the time. For instance, if V is clear, the result is that the instruction in the NIP is considered invalid and a no-operation happens when the XIP is updated with the NIP information, regardless of whether E is set or clear. Likewise, if V is clear and there's an rte instruction, the instruction in SNIP is not prefetched. SNIP is read/write. See Fig. 5-4.

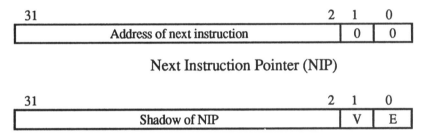

Next Instruction Pointer (NIP)

Shadow Next Instruction Pointer (SNIP) - cr5

5-4 Next Instruction Pointer (NIP).

Fetch Instruction Pointer and the Shadow (FIP/SFIP) The Shadow Fetch Instruction Pointer (SFIP) shadows the fetch instruction pointer (FIP). You'll recall that the FIP always points at the location in memory of the instruction that the 88K will need immediately after it finishes with the instruction which is currently being decoded by the NIP. When there's an exception, the SFIP preserves that pointer. It will hold either the instruction to be next accessed after the 88K finishes, or the target of a jump or branch instruction.

Like SNIP, the SFIP instruction contains a valid (V) and exception (E) bit. The V bit can be cleared by software. When that happens, the instruction that would otherwise be fetched, isn't. We have instead a no-operation, which can nicely clear the decks if you have a need to do so.

If an rte executes when both the V and the E bits are set, then the instruction in question will generate an instruction access exception when it travels on to the NIP address, regardless of whether it actually fails or succeeds.

An rte instruction can be made to go directly to a specified instruction by putting a valid instruction address in the SNIP and the next sequential instruction address in the SFIP with both the V and E bits clear. The rte picks up at the instruction pointed to by the SNIP, and then it proceeds in an orderly fashion to the SFIP. SFIP has both read and write access. See Fig. 5-5.

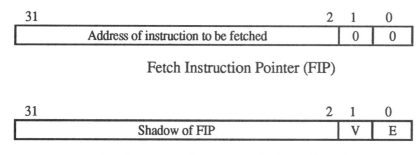

Fetch Instruction Pointer (FIP)

Shadow Fetch Instruction Pointer (SFIP) - cr6

5-5 Fetch Instruction Pointer (FIP).

Execute Instruction Pointer and its Shadow (XIP/SXIP) The Shadow Execute Instruction Pointer (SXIP) shadows the Execution Instruction Pointer (XIP). The XIP, you'll remember, contains the address of the instruction that the 88K is executing right now. The SXIP keeps a record of that instruction in the event of a precise exception. If, on the other hand, there's an imprecise exception, or an interrupt, then the SXIP points to the last instruction executed by the integer unit, or dispatched to the FPU, or data unit.

Moreover, the SXIP too contains a V bit and an E bit. However, in the case of this register, these bits show whether the instruction was successfully executed. If the instruction tried to execute prior to the exception, then the V bit is set. If the instruction couldn't execute for some reason, then the V bit is clear. (The V bit is clear whenever the NIP has a valid bit clear, the NIP is updated to the XIP, and shadowing is enabled.)

The E bit shows whether the instruction was successfully prefetched. If the instruction faulted, then the E bit is set. It is also set if the corresponding E bit on the NIP was set when it traveled up to XIP. As before, if the V bit is clear, the E bit is ignored.

This register is read-only. In addition, the 88K hardware doesn't use

SXIP during a return from exception processing. Instead, an rte takes up with the instruction pointed at by the SNIP. See Fig. 5-6.

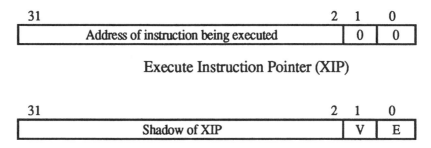

Execute Instruction Pointer (XIP)

Shadow Execute Instruction Pointer (SXIP) - cr4

5-6 Execute Instruction Pointer (XIP).

The Vector Base Register (VBR)

The VBR is loaded by software usually during system start up, and contains a pointer to the top of the vector table.

First, an explanation of the word "vector." When there is an exception, the 88K leaves its regular program to go off and deal with this unexpected or unusual event. It "leaves" and "goes off" in the direction—it is a "vector." In other words, the vectors are simply entry points for the various exception handlers. There are a total of 512 vectors that may be represented by a 9-bit exception number. Each exception or trap has a specific number, and when execution transfers to the handler, it does so by means of combining the VBR and exception number to get an index into the vector list. For a list of vector numbers, see chapter 9.

The VBR can be modified so as to have different pages of exception vectors. However, if this is done, interrupts should be disabled. This means that SFRZ = 1, IND = 1, and SFD1 = 1—thus freezing the shadow registers, and disabling interrupts to the CPU and the FPU. After all, you don't want to have an interrupt while in the middle of changing the vector table. The poor CPU would be lost in space.

There are 20 bits of data in the VBR. When combined with the 9-bit exception number, this adds up to 29 bits. Another three zeros are appended to give a full 32-bit address.

Data unit control registers

There are nine data control registers. These come in three groups of three—each threesome containing a data register, an address register, and a transaction register. The three groups are the pipeline stages of the data unit. Transactions enter at stage 2, and graduate thru to stage 0. In stage 2, addresses are computed, in stage 1 the address (and data if a store) is put onto the address (or data) bus. In stage 0 the data unit waits for the Reply from the P bus.

It is, though, the transaction registers that interest you most. They contain information about the memory access in the data unit when there's an exception. The data and address registers simply hold (you guessed it) the data and address in question. The DMTx registers tell what operation was happening and have enough data to possibly allow software recovery of an exception. The data in DMDx is only valid if the transaction is a valid store. In master/checker mode they should be saved only in that case for exception recovery purposes.

Each of the transaction registers is organized in the same way.

31	16	15	14	13	12	11	7	6	5	4	3	2	1	0
Zeros		BO	DAS	DOUB1	LB	DREG		SD	EN3	EN2	EN1	EN0	Write	Valid

One end of the register—bits 31 through 16—is filled with zeros. To take the rest, though, bit by bit:

BO   Bit 15 is the byte order (BO) bit. When it is 0, we're in Big Endian country. When it is 1, we're Little Endian. As a rule, a system won't change from one to the other during an exception, but there's always a chance that somewhere, somehow, there will be someone who'll see an advantage to doing so. Perhaps for data conversion between the two. However, if there is a difference between the PSR's BO bit and the BO bit here, then the PSR's must be changed before the exception handler can get into memory.

DAS   Bit 14 signifies the data address space. In other words it determines whether you're in user or supervisor mode. If the DAS bit is 0, you're user. If it is 1, then you're supervisor. The DAS bit can be important because the exception handler operates from supervisor space. The .usr option has to be set in instructions that are going to access user memory during the exception.

DOUB1   Bit 13 is the Double Word bit. It's set if the memory access in question is the first access in a double-word transaction, or if it is the load portion of an xmem operation.

Either way, though, if set the bit announces the fact that the next stage in the data unit is the second of a pair of accesses. Exactly what that means depends on the instruction. For example, for an ld.d or an st.d instruction in the second stage of the pipeline, the second access isn't in the pipeline at all. Rather, it is the next word in memory, and the next consecutive general purpose register. The "next word" is another relative term and depends on the byte ordering. The next word address should be generated by inverting the lowest order address bit, bit 2.

In the case of xmem, on the other hand, the second access is a store of the same register to the same address—because after all, the whole purpose of xmem is to exchange contents. (The xmem instruction is, by the way, rather fussy. If you need to retry most of the other instructions, you can do so by generating two load or store instructions instead of one double. But, for an xmem, you have to do it as an xmem.

LOCK Bit 12 is the bus lock bit. It is set if the P bus lock signal ($\overline{\text{DLOCK}}$) is asserted. That only happens when the transaction is part of an xmem instruction. The xmem instruction is a load followed by a store. If the transaction in this register is a load, and the LOCK bit is set, then the next stage contains a store to the same address and destination registers—the data for which is stored in the transaction register's close companion, the data register.

If the load is in stage two of the pipeline, then the store half of the partnership won't be in the pipeline yet. However, the data to be stored is in DMD2. That makes sense, because of the basic nature of xmem. It denotes an atomic load and store. The destination register is set in DREG, and the data to be stored is already known. So the data to be stored is placed in the data register of the load stage. When the store stage comes along, the data will be handy and available.

DREG Bits 11 through 7 are the destination register bits. They indicate the register where the memory access is going. When there's a load or an exchange operation, it is the register indicated here to which the data read from memory should be sent. (In the case of a store or exchange operation, where data isn't going to any register, this field is left empty and the companion data register contains the data to be stored.)

SIGNED Bit 6 is the Sign Extended bit. It's set if the data of a load operation is sign extended. It's cleared if the data is zero extended. The SIGNED bit is only valid when the access is a byte or a half-word.

EN3 – EN0 Bits 5 through 3 are the byte-enable bits. These bits indicate which byte or bytes an instruction is going to access. In brief, if the instruction is going to access a byte of memory (something which is indicated by the .b option), then one of the four is set. If, however, it's after a half-word (indicated by the .h option), then EN3 and EN2 or EN1 and EN0 are set. If what's wanted is a word or a double word, then all four are set.

The value of the enable bits must be encoded to form the least two significant bits of the memory address. (See Fig. 5-7.)

EN3	EN2	EN1	EN0	Meaning
0	0	0	1	Use LSB in data register and .b option
0	0	1	0	Use LMB in data register and .b option
0	0	1	1	Use LSH in data register and .h option
0	1	0	0	Use UMB in data register and .b option
1	0	0	0	Use MSB in data register and .b option
1	1	0	0	Use MSB in data register and .h option
1	1	1	1	Use word in data register and no option

5-7 DMDx byte enable bits.

Write Bit 1 is the Read/Write transaction bit. Under normal conditions, it indicates whether the instruction in question is a read (the bit is equal to zero) or a write (bit = 1).

But to say "normal conditions" is to presuppose that there must be other states of being. If, in fact, the transaction is an xmem, then this bit indicates whether the instruction at hand is the read or write part of xmem.

VALID Bit 0, the Valid Transaction Bit, indicates whether a current transaction should be considered valid. If the Valid bit is clear, then the transaction is considered null and void. If it is set, however, it is considered valid and should be recovered (or put out of its misery) by the exception handler.

That all might be more clear if an example is shown. Here's a sketch of the data unit transaction registers as they process an xmem. So that you can see the data, take this situation:

r1 = 0xC0000   The contents of memory location 0xF0000 are 0xFFFF. CPU is in Big Endian and User mode

r2 = 0xF0000

xmem   r1,r2,0x0   is the instruction to be executed

After the xmem is decoded, and completes stage 2 of the data unit pipeline, things look like this:

Load phase of xmem

DMT2

31 16	15	14	13	12	11 7	6	5	4	3	2	1	0
Zeros	BO	DAS	DOUB1	LB	DREG	SD	EN3	EN2	EN1	EN0	Write	Valid
	0	0	1	1	00001	x	1	1	1	1	0	1

DMD2

Data to be stored - 0xC0000

DMA2

Address of data to be accessed - 0xF0000

In stage 2, the address is computed by adding the immediate value 0x0 to r2, and placing the result in DMA2. The contents of r1 are squirreled away in DMD2. The pipeline advances one stage, and the store phase enters stage 2, and the load phase moves to stage 1.

Store phase of xmem

DMT2

31 16	15	14	13	12	11 7	6	5	4	3	2	1	0
Zeros	BO	DAS	DOUB1	LB	DREG	SD	EN3	EN2	EN1	EN0	Write	Valid
	0	0	0	1	00001	x	1	1	1	1	1	1

continued

DMD2

Data to be stored - 0xC0000

DMA2

Address of data to be accessed - 0xF0000

Note that in the DMT1 register the LOCK bit is still set, and that the Write bit has been set because this is the store phase of the xmem. However, the DOUB1 bit is cleared. The DMA2 and DMD2 values are kept from the previous stage, because this is a locked transaction.

Load phase of xmem

DMT1

31	16	15	14	13	12	11 7	6	5	4	3	2	1	0
Zeros		BO	DAS	DOUB1	LB	DREG	SD	EN3	EN2	EN1	EN0	Write	Valid
		0	0	1	1	00001	0	1	1	1	1	0	1

DMD1

31   0

Data to be stored - 0xC0000

DMA1

31   0

Address of data to be accessed - 0xF0000

In stage 1, the address in DMA1 is put on the address bus. DMD1 still has the data to be stored, but it won't be used in the load phase, and will be overwritten as the load advances to stage 0. So advance the pipeline once more, while nothing new comes into the data unit.

Null transaction in stage 2

DMT2

31	16	15	14	13	12	11 7	6	5	4	3	2	1	0
Zeros		BO	DAS	DOUB1	LB	DREG	SD	EN3	EN2	EN1	EN0	Write	Valid
		0	0	0	1	00001	0	1	1	1	1	1	0

DMD2

Data to be stored - 0xC0000

DMA2

Address of data to be accessed - 0xF0000

Note that the VALID bit was cleared, indicating that nothing is really in stage 2.

Store phase of xmem in stage 1

DMT1

31	16	15	14	13	12	11	7	6	5	4	3	2	1	0
Zeros		BO	DAS	DOUB1	LB	DREG		SD	EN3	EN2	EN1	EN0	Write	Valid
		0	0	0	1	00001		0	1	1	1	1	1	1

DMD1

Data to be stored - 0xC0000

DMA1

Address of data to be accessed - 0xF0000

The data in DMD1, and the address in DMA1, are put on the data and address buses respectively.

Load phase of xmem at stage 0

DMT0

31	16	15	14	13	12	11	7	6	5	4	3	2	1	0
Zeros		BO	DAS	DOUB1	LB	DREG		SD	EN3	EN2	EN1	EN0	Write	Valid
		0	0	1	1	00001		0	1	1	1	1	0	1

DMD0

Contents of memory location addressed in DMA1 - 0xFFFF

DMA0

Address of data to be accessed - 0xF0000

At stage 0, the data unit monitors the Reply lines to find the outcome. When you get a "success" reply, in the load phase, the data will be taken from the data bus and placed in r1. You'll advance the pipeline one more time, to bring the store phase to stage 0. The xmem is now complete. r1=0xFFFF, and memory location 0xF0000 contains 0xC0000.

Supervisor storage registers

Now for the supervisor storage registers—SR0−SR4. Put simply, these are just 32-bit general utility registers that may be used only by the supervisor. No one else need apply. They are read/write accessible.

Floating point operations

The fourth type of registers are the floating point registers. But, before you get into them, take a moment to look at the way the 88K does floating point in the first place.

You'll recall that the 88100 has its own dedicated floating point processor on the chip. The FPU does floating point operating according to the IEEE 754-1985 standard. As such, it follows a number of well established conventions, such as:

Numeric formats

The 88100's FPU, as do all IEEE 754-1985 standard floating point processors, supports single- and double-precision format numbers. Single-precision numbers fit into 32 bits. Double-precision numbers, being exactly twice as long, are 64 bits. Either way, floating point numbers are divided up into three fields of bits.

The first of these is the "sign" bit, which tells you (and the 88K) whether this number is positive or negative. In single precision it resides at bit 31. In a double, it's at 63. In any case, if it is clear (equal to 0) then this is a positive number. If it is set (equal to 1) then the number is negative.

Here is single-precision floating point:

31	30 23	22 0
S	Exponent	Mantissa

Here is double-precision floating point:

63	62		52	51		32

S	Exponent	High order bits of Mantissa (Register n)
Low order bits of Mantissa (Register n+1)		

31   0

In everyday addition and subtraction, the sign bit reflects the sign of the result of the operation, with one exception. If the operation in question is $X + (-X)$, then the result is tagged as negative (sign is 1) if you selected a rounding mode of round-toward-negative infinity (more on rounding later). On the other hand, the result is tagged as positive (sign is 0) if you select any other rounding mode.

In the case of multiplication or division, meanwhile, the sign bit is the exclusive-OR of the sign of the operands.

You'll recall that the FPU also performs a compare operation as the result of the fcmp instruction. If the fcmp encounters a zero in its rounds, it will simply disregard the sign bit. (After all, a negative zero is pretty hard to tell from a positive one, unless you're dealing in experimental mathematics or esoteric physics where all sorts of improbable things really matter.)

The second of the bit fields is the exponent field, which ranges from 8 bits in single-precision numbers to 11 bits in double-precision ones. As the name suggests, it represents the exponent of the floating point number. This exponent is represented in excess 127 notation for single-precision numbers and in excess 1023 notation for double-precision numbers.

Some notes on these are fitting here. Exponents don't need sign bits, or complementary arithmetic for that matter. They're biased, and so can be positive or negative without an additional bit. What bias means is that the 8 bits of the single precision exponent has 127 added to it in interpretation by the FPU. Hence the excess 127 (or 1023) notation. For a number with an actual exponent of 0—such as 1.0×2^0—the biased, excess 127 notation would be 127. An excess 127 notation of 1 is a small number indeed, i.e. $N \times 2^{-126}$.

The third, and last bit field is the mantissa. This is the fractional binary part of a normalized floating point number. It is 23 bits for single-precision numbers and 52 for double.

There are also two exponent values that are reserved for specific cases. The first of these is an exponent value of zero, which indicates a denormalized number where the mantissa is not equal to 0, or 0 when the mantissa is itself equal to zero. The second is an exponent value of all binary ones. This one means infinity where the mantissa is 0, or a not-a-number (NAN), when the mantissa isn't equal to zero. Exponents are always adjusted so the mantissa is constantly normalized. See Fig. 5-8 and Fig. 5-9.

Exponent	Single Precision	Double Precision
Maximum (unbiased)	+127	+1023
Minimum (unbiased)	-126	-1022
Exponent Bias	+127	+1023
Width	8 bits	11 bits

5-8 Floating point exponents.

Sign Bit	Unbiased Exponent value	Mantissa	Representation
0	Maximum	Nonzero	+NAN
0	Maximum	0	+Infinity
0	0 < Exponent < Max	Nonzero	+Real number
0	0	Nonzero	+ denormalized
0	0	0	+0
1	0	0	− 0
1	0	Nonzero	− denormalized
1	0 < Exponent < Max	Nonzero	− Real number
1	Maximum	0	− Infinity
1	Maximum	Nonzero	− NAN

5-9 Floating point domain representation.

As an aside—all normalized, real floating point numbers have a value of one for their integer part. So, the IEEE, being a thrifty bunch, simply leaves that out of the mantissa. We just pretend that it's there.

The more official way of putting it is that the one is "implied" in normalized, real floating point numbers and is therefore called "the hidden bit." In addition to the hidden bit, floating point numbers use the concept of the "binary point." Both can be shown in the following format:

1.<binary fraction>

The 1 is of course the hidden bit. It is followed by the binary world's version of a decimal point, the binary point. What follows is the mantissa, the binary fraction of 1 with which you happen to be dealing. For example, normalizing 1/8 is accomplished by first turning it into .125. From there:

$$.125_{10} = .001_2 = (1.0*2^{-3})$$

Then, in single-precision format:

Sign bit = 0
Biased Exponent = $+124(-3+127)$
Hidden Bit = 1
Mantissa = 0

Here is the single-precision floating point representation of 1/8:

31	30 23	22 0
0	0 1 1 1 1 1 0 0	zeros

Denormalized numbers

If there are normalized numbers, then logic leads you to assume that there are others which aren't. A denormalized number is one which is too big or too little to be represented in the usual format. An example normalized number is $(1.0*2^{-126})$, which is the smallest single number that can be represented as a normalized number.

But, suppose you have a calculation which must divide $(1.0*2^{-126})$ by four:

$$(1.0*2^{-126}) \div (1.0*2^2) = (1.0*2^{-128})$$

The result has a sign bit of zero (positive, an exponent of zero (denormalized number), and a mantissa that has the second bit from the left set. The mantissa is 2^{-2} or $(.01_2)$. That means that the result of the operation is 2^{-128}, which is a bit too tiny for even the 88K's fingers to handle comfortably.

So, when there is a denormalized result like this one, the 88K responds with a floating point exception. In the case of 2^{-128} here, it would be a floating point underflow exception.

Once there's been an exception, the 88K responds by adjusting the result so that the exception handler can go to work. The handler, then, determines the actual value of the denormalized result and does whatever's necessary. It could handle this in software and proceed without mishap.

Not-A-Numbers

The FPU is, of course, a number cruncher. But it can also deal with a couple of things that aren't numbers—referred to generically as a Not-A-Number (NAN). Specifically, it conforms to the IEEE 754-1985 standard in that it can deal with two types of NANs: signalling and non-signalling.

NANs themselves put you into a reserved operand exception. The signalling kind is a NAN with bit 22 clear and it causes you to go to a user exception handler, if there's one to be had.

The non-signalling version of the same has bit 22 set. Such a beast is useful for doing things like representing the results of impossible (or at least invalid) operations like dividing by zero.

Rounding

The FPU can also round numbers. In conformance with the often mentioned IEEE standard for such things, the 88K can do so in four ways—round-toward-nearest, round-to-zero, round-toward-negative-infinity, and round-toward-positive-infinity.

You set which of these you want in the Floating Point Control Register (FPCR). You'll see the FPU's registers, including the FPCR, in a moment. But, for the purposes of rounding, you should really only be interested in two of the FPCR's bits: numbers 14 and 15. It is with them that you select the rounding mode you want (see Fig. 5-10). If, for example, you wish round-to-nearest, then both are cleared to zero.

bit 14	bit 15	Rounding Mode
0	0	Round to nearest
0	1	Round toward zero
1	0	Round toward $-\infty$
1	1	Round toward $+\infty$

5-10   Floating point rounding modes.

Once you've selected the mode, the way that rounding happens has to do with three additional bits:

- The Guard Bit (G)—which represents the bit immediately to the right of the least significant bit (LSB).
- The Round Bit (R)—which represents the bit to the right of the G bit.
- The Sticky Bit (S)—which represents all the bits to the right of the round bit. (You find the value of the S bit by taking the logical OR of all the bits that would be in the result if said result was infinitely precise.)

See Fig. 5-11.

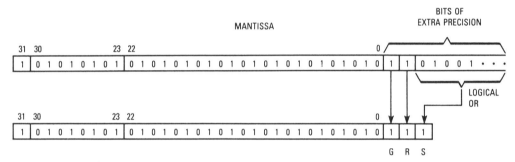

5-11 Guard, Round, and Sticky bits. (Reprinted with permission of Motorola Inc.)

Round-to-nearest   Each of the four methods of rounding has its uses and its place. Round-to-nearest is the default. In it, numbers are routinely rounded up if the G, R, and S bits would make the result closer to the higher number.

There is, however, a special case. If the G bit is one, and the other two are 0, then the 88K rounds up only if the resulting higher number would be even. If it would be odd, the 88K just leaves well enough alone. It checks the oddness or evenness of the situation with the LSB bit. If the LSB is zero, then the result of a round would be even, and so rounding is done. If it is 1, then the result would be odd, and so nothing is done. See Fig. 5-12.

Round-to-zero   When the 88K is set for round-to-zero, then no rounding is done at all. The G, R, and S bits are simply ignored.

Round-toward-positive-infinity   In this mode, a number is rounded to the next highest number when any of the G, S, or R bits is set. When you're

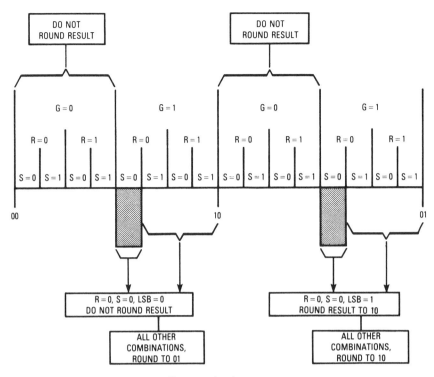

5-12 Round-to-nearest rounding method. (Reprinted with permission of Motorola Inc.)

dealing with positive numbers, this means that an additional one is added to the mantissa, making it even more positive than it was before. When you have negative numbers, though, nothing is done. Under the mode, a negative number stays as negative as it was before, and takes steps toward neither positive nor negative infinity.

Round-toward-negative-infinity   This is the reverse of the case above. In it, a number is rounded down to the next lowest number whenever any of G, S, or R is set. In the case of positive numbers, this means nothing is done at all. But, in the case of negative numbers, a one is added to the mantissa to make it still more negative.

FPU exceptions

The FPU has its own set of exceptions. The FPU's exceptions are covered in greater detail in chapter 9, but they're worth a glance here just the same.

The IEEE standard for floating point mandates only five exceptions:

- Invalid floating point operating exception
- Floating point divide by zero
- Overflow exception
- Underflow exception
- Inexact exception

The FPU is faithful to each of these, but it goes beyond them as well. It incorporates a number of exceptions that aren't part of the standard, but which are very useful, without in any way conflicting with the standard.

Here are the Big 5 that are mandated with the IEEE.

The invalid floating point operation exception   This exception occurs when the 88K decides that an operand is invalid. That doesn't mean that something is an error—merely that it is an operand that can't be handled via normal processing. Trans-infinite numbers and other exotics of higher math have their place in both the real world, and in the programs of software developers. But, they're not something that the 88K is set up to handle as part of its normal routine.

When it does run across such a situation, it must either farm the problem out to software; or, if it discovers a "true" exception, fall back to some pre-defined default. A word about "true" exceptions might be useful here. The IEEE standard says that only a few conditions are considered real, honest-to-goodness exceptions. The others, says the standard, are just problems to be passed to software.

So, when the 88K finds one of these IEEE-approved exceptions, it sets the appropriate bits in its floating point-exception cause register (FPECR). Then, if there's an appropriate exception handler already specified, the FPU calls it up. If not, then the FPU uses the defaults. There are defaults for:

- Operations on NANs—if the 88K discovers a signalling NAN, it sets bit 4 (the accumulated invalid operation flag, or AFINV) in the floating point status register (FPSR) and then writes a non-signalling NAN to the destination. If it finds a non-signalling NAN, on the other hand, the 88K doesn't modify the AFINV, but still writes a non-signalling NAN to the destination.
- Operations on Infinities—if the 88K discovers an operation in which one of the partners is a real number while the other is infinity, then it

writes infinity (properly signed as negative or positive) to the destination. If, however, the operation in question involves the magnitude subtraction of infinities $((+\infty)+(-\infty))$, ∞/∞, or $0*\infty$—then the AFINV bit is set in FPSR and a non-signalling NAN is written to the destination.

- Operations on denormalized numbers—Floating point operations on denormalized numbers are completed. The result might or might not be a denormalized number, but is always written to the intended destination.
- Zero-divide-by-zero—if the 88K is asked to divide zero by zero, the AFINV bit is set and a non-signalling NAN is put in the destination.
- Conversion to Integer Overflow—when this happens, the 88K writes a non-signalling NAN to the destination, and sets AFINV in the FPSR.

Floating-point-divide-by-zero When the 88K finds itself asked to divide something (other than zero) by zero, then it first checks to make certain that this particular case of division by zero is considered invalid in the IEEE standard. If it is invalid, then it calls in the appropriate exception handler. If it isn't invalid, then the result is infinity appropriately signed.

Overflow exception The overflow exception comes along when some operation produces an exponent that's larger than $+127$ for single-precision numbers and $+1023$ for double.

Either way, the 88K responds by calling in the user overflow exception handler, if one's available. When the user overflow exception handler is enabled, the result passed to the handler is the intermediate result (infinitely precise) divided by 2^a, where a (bias adjust) is $+192$ for single-precision numbers and $+1536$ for double-precision ones.

If the user overflow exception handler is not available, then the 88K calls for the user inexact exception handler. If that too is unavailable, then it falls back to a series of a default exception handler, which sets up the result according to a series of rounding modes, which are listed in Fig. 5-13.

Underflow exception As you would expect, the underflow exception is the reverse of the overflow exception—but it is also more than that. The underflow exception occurs when either of two things happens. The first is the obvious one. It happens when some operation has a result with an exponent smaller (more negative) than the 88K can represent in the conventional way. The 88K will round the number, and if it finds that it is too

FPSR		Rounding effect
bit 15	bit 14	
0	0	Signed ∞
0	1	Signed Maximum
1	0	+Maximum for positive value
		− ∞ for negative value
1	1	+ ∞ for positive value
		− Maximum for negative value

5-13 Overflow rounding effect.

small to deal with, the FPU will pass it off to a user exception handler if one is available. If one isn't available, then the default exception handler writes the denormalized result to the destination register.

The second way that an underflow exception can be triggered is loss of precision—that is, if a number begins to become too inexact to use as the result during normalization or rounding.

The 88K can execute a user exception handler only in the first case, when the number is too small. What is passed to the handler is the immediate result (infinitely precise) multiplexed by 2^a, where a is the bias adjust. The bias adjust is $+192$ for single-precision numbers and $+1536$ for double-precision.

If a user exception handler can't be had—either because one isn't specified, or because this is an inaccuracy rather than a size problem—then you get the default handler. It writes the denormalized result to the destination register.

The only way for this exception to occur if a user exception handler isn't specified is for the 88K to detect both loss of accuracy or excessive smallness (i.e., bit 2 or AFUNF set in the FPSR).

Inexact exception   If there's an overflow, but no overflow exception handler is around to deal with it, or if some number is rounded to the point where it isn't accurate at all, then there is an inexact exception.

The FPU responds to these two situations in very different ways. In the case of the overflow problem, the first thing that happens is that bit 0 (the accumulated inexact flag, or AFINX) gets set in the FPSR. That changes the exception from overflow to inexact, and the 88K looks to see if there might be a handy inexact user exception handler available.

If there isn't one, then the result of the operation is written to the destination register, and is either the largest finite number, or infinity, depending on the method of rounding used. (See Fig. 5-13.)

This is the only exception that can be masked by hardware. If the 88K sets bit 0 (Enable Inexact Handler, or EFINX) in the floating point control register (FPCR), then the exception just doesn't happen.

If the exception is caused by a loss of accuracy, then you begin by checking the EFINX bit of the FPCR. If it is set, then it means there is a user handler available, and the exception takes place. Pertinent information—such as the result of the operation, the G, R, and S bits, and whether the result was rounded—are tucked away in the control registers.

However, if the bit is clear, and there is no user handler available, the 88100 writes the rounded result to the destination register.

The FPU exception processing registers

There are 11 FPU exception processing registers with numbers fcr0 through fcr8 and fcr62 and fcr63. The first set, fcr0 − fcr8, contains exception information and can be reached only in supervisor mode. The set is also divided by function. Registers fcr1 − fcr5 are valid only for precise and integer-divide error exceptions. Meanwhile, fcr6 − fcr8 are valid only for imprecise exceptions.

The second set, fcr62 and fcr63, are meant for the user's exception handling software, as well as to report the causes of various exceptions. These can be had either from user or supervisor mode. See Fig. 5-14.

Register	Acronym	Name
fcr0	FPECR	Exception cause Register
fcr1	FPHS1	Source 1 High Register
fcr2	FPLS1	Source 1 Low Register
fcr3	FPHS2	Source 2 High Register
fcr4	FPLS2	Source 2 Low Register
fcr5	FPPT	Precise Operation Type Register

5-14 Floating point control registers.

Register	Acronym	Name
fcr6	FPRH	Result High Register
fcr7	FPRL	Result Low Register
fcr8	FPIT	Imprecise Operation Type Register
fcr62	FPSR	User Status Register
fcr63	FPCR	User Control Register

The Floating Point Exception Cause Register (FPECR)

FPECR, which is register fcr0, is what the 88100 uses to try to indicate the cause of exception. It does so by setting bits within itself to correspond with predefined conditions. For example, it sets a bit within bits $7-3$ to indicate a precise exception, and one of bits $2-0$ for an imprecise one. However, more than one bit can be set after an exception. Here is a picture of the FPECR:

31	8	7	6	5	4	3	2	1	0
all zeros		FIOV	FUNINP	FPRV	FROP	FDVZ	FUNF	FOVF	FINX

Here are the FPECR's individual bit fields:

- Bits 31 through 8 are reserved. Motorola may do something with them in the future. At the moment, they contain zeros, but it is best not to count on that.
- Bit 7 is the Floating Point Integer Overflow (FIOV) bit. When it is certain that a precise exception was caused by a conversion to integer overflow, then this bit is set.
- Bit 6 is the Floating Point Unimplemented (FUNIMP) bit. It is set when a precise exception occurs because the FPU was switched off at the moment a floating point instruction tried to execute. If it's set, then all the other bits are null and void.
- Bit 5 is the Floating Point Privilege Violation (FPRV) bit. This one is set if there's a precise exception caused by a privilege violation of a floating point instruction—something that happens whenever someone tries to get at any of the FPU registers, except fcr62 and fcr63, from user mode.

- Bit 4 is the Floating Point Reserved Operand (FROP) bit. It's set if a precise exception is caused by floating point reserved operand check logic. In other words, bit 4 swings into action if the 88K finds it is supposed to do something it couldn't with infinity, a NAN, or a denormalized number.
- Bit 3 is the Floating Point Divide By Zero (FDVZ) bit. It is set when someone has tried to divide by zero.
- Bit 2 is the Floating Point Underflow (FUNF) bit, which is set when an imprecise exception is caused by a floating point underflow.
- Bit 1 is the Floating Point Overflow (FOVF) bit, which is set when an imprecise exception is caused by a floating point overflow.
- Bit 0 is the Floating Point Inexact (FINX) bit. It is set when an imprecise exception occurs, and the operation which caused it had an inexact result. This bit can be set even though FUNF or FOVF might also be set. FINX is undefined for precise exceptions.

The Floating Point Source 1
Operand High Register (FPHS1)

This register, fcr1, is a read-only beast that holds the sign, exponent, and high-order 20 bits of a single-precision number. Or, it holds the upper word of a double-precision number. It is undefined for integer values. Shown here is the FPHS1:

31	30	20 19	0
Sign	Exponent	High order 20 bits of Mantissa	

To describe its bit fields:

- Bit 31 is the source 1 operand sign bit. It indicates whether the number is positive or negative. In the case of an integer divide error exception, bit 31 is undefined.
- Bits 30−20 hold the source 1 operand exponent. Motorola notes that when dealing with single-precison numbers, the sign is extended. It too is undefined in the case of an integer divide error exception.
- Bits 19−0 hold the high-order 20 bits of the mantissa, except one, which you'll recall is the hidden bit. In the case of an integer divide error exception, these bits will contain all zeros.

Floating Point Source 1
Operand Low Register (FPLS1)

FPLS1 is the flip side of FPHS1. It will hold the three low-order bits of a single-precision source 1 operand, or the low-order word of a double-precision source 1 operand, or the integer operand for integer divide instructions when there's a floating point precise exception. Like FPHS1, the FPLS1 is read-only. Shown here is the FPLS1:

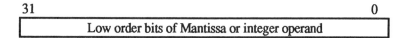

31   0

Low order bits of Mantissa or integer operand

Defining its bits is easy. Bits 31 through 0 contain the lower order bits of the Mantissa or the integer operand in the case of integer operation. For single-precision operands, that means three bits of the source 1 operand only, followed by 29 zeros. For double-precisions operands, however, it means the low-order 32 bits of the source 1 operand. When the FPLS1 is storing integers, finally, it contains the 32-bit source 1 data.

Floating Point Source 2
Operand High Register (FPHS2)

The FPHS2 holds the sign, exponent, and the high-order 20 bits of a single-precision source 2 operand, or else the upper word of a double-precision operand. It too is read-only, and is undefined for integer values. Here is the FPHS2:
Breaking it apart:

31   30   20 19   0

Sign	Exponent	High order 20 bits of Mantissa

- Bit 31 is the Source 2 Operand Sign Bit. Naturally, it holds the sign of the second operand. It is undefined for integer operands.
- Bits 30−20 hold the source 2 operand exponent. When dealing with single-precision numbers, the exponent is sign extended. They are undefined for an integer operand.
- Bits 19−0 hold the high-order 20 bits of the mantissa, except the hidden bit. They are undefined for an integer operand.

Floating Point Source 2
Operand Low Register (FPLS2)

The FPLS2 is just like FPLS1 except that it deals with the Source 2 Operand. It holds the three low-order bits of a single-precision source 2 operand, or the low-order word of a double-precision source 2 operand, or the integer operand for integer divide instructions when there's a floating point precise exception. Like FPLS1, it is read-only.

Bits 31 through 0 contain the lower order bits of the Mantissa or the integer operand. For single-precision operands, that means the lower order three bits only of the source 2 operand, followed by 29 zeros. For doubles, however, it means the low-order 32 bits of the source 2 operand. When the FPLS2 is storing integers, it contains the 32-bit source 2 data.

Floating Point Precise
Operation Type Register (FPPT)

The FPPT register contains two kinds of information about a floating point instruction that has caused an exception: first the opcode, and second the instruction's destination register number. FPPT is read-only and undefined for integer multiply instructions. Here is the FPPT:

31	16 15	5 4	0
Zeros	Operation	Destination	

To take it bit by bit:

- Bits $31-16$ are reserved. At the moment, they contain zeros, but they might not in future versions of the processor
- Bits $15-5$ contain bits $15-5$ of the instruction that caused the exception. This includes a 5-bit opcode and three 2-bit size fields. The upper bit of each size field is cleared. Broken down still further, look at the individual size fields (each will have 00 for single-precision and 01 for double-precision):
- Bits $10-9$ contain the Source 1 operand size.
- Bits $8-7$ contain the source 2 operand size.
- Bits $6-5$ contain the destination size.
- Bits $4-0$ contain the number of the destination register.

The Floating Point Result High Register (FPRH)

FPRH is a read-only register that contains status information and the high-order 21 bits (including the hidden bit) of the partial result that was computed at the time of the exception. In other words, it is like a pathology lab: It holds various odds and ends, some grisly and some otherwise, which the 88K can use to reconstruct the crime, or at least normal processing.

An exception handler can take the information contained in the FPRH (as well as its close relation, the floating point result low register, or FPRL, which is discussed next) to produce a result. Here is the FPRH:

31	30	29	28	27	26	25	24 21	20	0
Sign	RNDMODE		GUARD	ROUND	STICKY	ADDONE	0 0 0 0	High order bits of Mantissa	

Again, to take it bit by bit:

- Bit 31 holds the sign of the result.
- Bits 30−29 show which rounding mode is to be used.
    - 00—round to nearest
    - 01—round toward zero
    - 10—round toward negative infinity
    - 11—round toward positive infinity
- Bit 28 is the Guard bit of the result.
- Bit 27 is the Round bit of the result.
- Bit 26 is the Sticky bit of the result.
- Bit 25 is the add one bit. It is set if the mantissa of the result was rounded by logically adding one.
- Bits 24−21 are reserved.
- Bits 20−0 are the high order 21 bits of the result's mantissa. If the result is an integer, though, bits 20−0 are simply invalid.

Floating Point Result Low Register (FPRL)

FPRL is a read-only register that contains the low-order 32 bits of the partial result that was computed at the time of the exception. In other words, it's a lot like FPRH, but only the lower portion. And, as with FPRH, an exception handler uses the information contained in the FPRL to produce a result. Here is the FPRL:

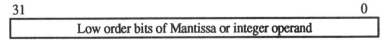

31	0
Low order bits of Mantissa or integer operand	

The bit-by-bit description is a little different here. If the low-order bits in question are double-precision, then bits 31−0 of FPRL contain the low-order 32 bits of the result (except in the event of integers and precise exceptions, in which case they are undefined).

If, however, the result is single-precision, then only the first three bits count. Bits $31-29$ will hold the low-order three bits of the result. The rest of the bits will simply be undefined.

Floating Point Imprecise Operation Type Register (FPIT)

FPIT is a read-only register that holds information on the instruction that caused the exception. It also lets you know which user-supplied exception handler or handlers were enabled to deal with it. Here is the FPIT:

31   20 19   16 15   11 10   9   8   4   3   2   1   0
RESEXP	0 0 0 0	Opcode	DESTSIZ	EFINV	EFDVZ	EFUNF	EFOVR	EFINX	DEST

The describe its internals:

- Bits $31-20$ are the result exponent (RESEXP). That is, they hold the 12-bit exponent of the result. It is formed by taking the 8-bit (in the case of single-precision, 12-bit in the case of double) exponent, and then complementing and extending the most significant bit to 12 bits. As a result, the exponent is equivalent to the unbiased exponent minus one.
- Bits $19-16$ are reserved.
- Bits $15-11$ hold the 5-bit opcode. That is, they hold bits 15 through 11 of the instruction.
- Bit 10 is the destination size (DESTSIZ) bit. It's taken from bit 5 of the instruction.

    0 = single precision
    1 = double precision

The next five bits have to do with enabling, or disabling, a user supplied exception handler. The value of each bit is similar. If it is 1 the user handler is enabled; if 0, it is disabled. Each takes information from the FPCR register at the time the instruction is begun.

- Bit 9 is the enable invalid operation handler (EFINV) bit.
- Bit 8 is the enable divide-by-zero handler (EFDVZ) bit.
- Bit 7 is the enable underflow handler (EFUNF) bit.
- Bit 6 is the enable overflow handler (EFOVF) bit.
- Bit 5 is the enable inexact handler (EFINX).
- Bits $4-0$ contain the number of the destination register.

The Floating Point Status Register (FPSR)

The FPSR is fairly pivotal. The FPSR contains information about the types of IEEE 754 exception that might have occurred in the FPU. It contains five bits that indicate which of the five IEEE standard exceptions has happened.

All of these five are set by software only, except for bit 0, the accumulated inexact flag (AFINX) bit, which can also be set by the hardware. These bits are set by Motorola's default exception handlers.

This register is also unlike the others in that it has read/write access. It can be accessed by user exception handler software. Here is the FPSR:

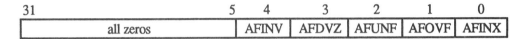

To take it bit-by-bit:

- Bits 31 − 5 are reserved.
- Bit 4 is the accumulated invalid operation flag (AFINV) bit. It is set when there has been an IEEE 754 invalid operation exception. It is cleared by software.
- Bit 3 is the accumulated dividy-by-zero flag (AFDVZ) bit. It is set when there is an IEEE 754 divide by zero exception and the user exception handler is disabled. It too is cleared by software.
- Bit 2 is the accumulated underflow flag (AFUNF). It is set when there has been an IEEE 754 underflow exception. It is also cleared by software.
- Bit 1 is the accumulated overflow flag (AFOVF). It is set when there has been an IEEE 754 underflow exception. It is also cleared by software.
- Bit 0 is the accumulated inexact flag. It is set when there is an IEEE 754 inexact exception and the user exception handler is disabled. It too is cleared by software, though it can also be cleared by the 88100 hardware as well.

The Floating Point Control Register (FPCR)

FPCR indicates which rounding mode you want, and which floating point exceptions you might want your exception handler(s) to process. Like

FPSR, it has read/write access. It is also set by software to enable user exception handler routines. Here is the FPCR:

31		16 15 14 13		5 4		3		2	1		0

```
31              16 15 14 13        5  4       3       2      1      0
┌─────────────────┬────┬───────────┬───────┬───────┬───────┬───────┬───────┐
│      zeros      │ RM │   zeros   │ EFINV │ EFDVZ │ EFUNF │ EFOVR │ EFINX │
└─────────────────┴────┴───────────┴───────┴───────┴───────┴───────┴───────┘
```

In bits, it is:

- Bits $31-16$ are reserved.
- Bits $15-14$ contain the rounding mode, RM.
    - 00—round to nearest
    - 01—round toward zero
    - 10—round toward negative infinity
    - 11—round toward positive infinity

  The RM bits can be set by hardware, or software. All the other bits in this register, except bit 0, are set by software alone.
- Bits $13-5$ are reserved.

For bits $4-0$, their value is:

0—Disable user exception handler
1—Enable user exception handler

- Bit 4 is the enable invalid operation handler (EFINV) bit.
- Bit 3 is the enable divide-by-zero handler (EFDVZ) bit.
- Bit 2 is the enable underflow handler (EFUNF) bit.
- Bit 1 is the enable overflow handler (EFOVF) bit.
- Bit 0 is the enable inexact handler (EFINX) bit. If this bit is clear, the 88K performs the default exception handling without vectoring. EFINX is also unusual in that it can be set by either hardware or software.

This chapter is a combination of read-once material, to catch on to how the 88100 operates and what goes on in its little silicon head, and a good deal of reference material. The latter use will likely cause sections to become dog-eared as you thumb back over the years and ask: "Now what did those guys say about this?"

6

Addressing modes

General features

In chapter 7 we'll get into the nitty gritty of the 88K's instruction set. If you're one of those people who always reads the end of the mystery novel first, and you simply cannot contain yourself, then feel free to jump ahead. We'll forgive you.

This chapter, though, devotes itself to addressing modes—that is, to the ways in which the instructions access information.

Specifically, you'll recall that the 88100 has a bare 51 instructions. All of these—from add to xor—are only one word, or 32-bits, long. Not more. Not less.

And, as if this were a surprise, the instructions contain operands. To be precise, the operands may be contained in that 32-bit long word, or in the general registers. The way it breaks down is that immediate operands and displacements turn up in the instructions, and everything else uses the registers; where data comes and goes from memory via load and store operations.

Meanwhile, there are three types of instructions. They are:

- Flow Control—These instructions alter the sequence of other instructions through the processor. Flow Control instructions include things like bb0, which causes a branch upon the discovery of a clear bit in a specified register.
- Data memory access—These load and store data to memory. An example is st, which stores the contents of a specified register to a specified memory location.

- Register to register—These manipulate data within general purpose registers. For example, the add instruction adds the contents of one specified register to another.

Each of these has unique addressing capabilities. Before getting into them, here are some definitions.

Some of the data has been made as compact as possible, and to be used that data must be transmuted into a 30- or 32-bit address. Although the 88K is a 32-bit device, it is also a word-oriented machine. A 32-bit address references bytes, however, only a 30-bit address is needed for words. In some addressing modes, the 88K clears the low order 2 bits to force addressing to a word boundary. 26-bit branch displacement addressing has a 26-bit field that is transformed into a 30-bit address. 26 bit displacement uses extension of the sign bit. Other modes, like IMM16 fields, require zero extension.

Triadic addressing

Triadic addressing sounds vaguely as though it had something to do with the postal address of secret societies. Indeed, one is tempted to make stupid jokes about Dead Letter Offices and the like, but through a great act of will and no little personal courage, we shall refrain.

Instead, we'll simply admit that triadic addressing is just an esoteric way of saying that an instruction deals with ("addresses") three registers at a time. Specifically, it looks at two source registers and one destination register. These three are usually written as rS1 (register source 1) and rS2 (register source 2) and rD (register destination). For a picture of all this, see Fig. 6-1 and Fig. 6-2.

31 26	25 21	20 16	15 5	4 0
1 1 1 1 0 1	D	S1	Subopcode	S2

D	The D field specifies the destination register for the operations results. Ignored for instructions that do not generate results.
S1	S1 specifies the source 1 register. (For bit scanning and the **rte** instruction, S1 must be zero.)
Subopcode	This field identifies the specific instruction.
S2	S2 field specifies the source 2 register.

6-1 Non-floating point triadic addressing.

31	26	25	21	20	16	15	5	4	0
1 0 0 0 0 1		D		S1		Subopcode		S2	

D — The D field specifies the destination register for the operations results.

S1 — S1 specifies the source 1 register. (For **int**, **nint**, **flt**, and **trnc**, S1 must be zero.)

Subopcode — This field identifies the specific instruction.

S2 — S2 field specifies the source 2 register.

6-2 Floating point triadic addressing.

The registers in question are designated by three 5-bit fields in the instructions. Because $2^5 = 32$, five bits is sufficient to designate one of the 32 general registers. If a specific instruction doesn't need all three, then unused fields should be zero.

Register-to-register instructions use triadic addressing rather a lot. Indeed, they can be considered the classic case for triadic addressing. So, for example, you might have:

    add r1,r2,r3

which would sum the contents of register 2 and register 3 and put the result in r1.

But, flow control instructions use a form of it as well. However, flow control instructions throw in their own little twist. With them, the contents of rD and rS1 are simply ignored. They're just dummy hands as far as the game is concerned. You don't even bother to write them down.

Instead, the instruction pays attention to rS2, which serves as a destination address for a jump (see Fig. 6-3). Thus, for example:

    jmp r2

would transfer program control to the address contained in r2.

Triadic addressing without the use of 3 registers (which is a perfectly lovely contradiction in terms, but we won't go into that) gets used in a couple of other places as well. In particular, when you get to chapter 7, you'll come across a character known as tbnd, or trap generating bounds check instruction. The tbnd instruction compares whatever's in rS1 with whatever is in rS2. It uses triadic addressing, though with only two registers.

31	26 25	21 20	16 15	5 4	0
1 1 1 1 0 1	D	S1	Subopcode	S2	

D	The D field is ignored, but should contain zeros.
S1	S1 field is ignored, but should contain zeros.
Subopcode	This field identifies the specific instruction.
S2	S2 field specifies the source 2 register.

6-3 Jump instructions triadic addressing.

The rD field isn't used. So, for example:

    tbnd r2, r3

would cause a trap if r2 is greater than r3.

Figure 6-4 shows the format for this sort of thing.

31	26 25	21 20	16 15	5 4	0
1 1 1 1 0 1	D	S1	Subopcode	S2	

D	The D field is ignored, but should contain zeros.
S1	S1 field specifies the source 1 register.
Subopcode	This field contains 1 1 1 1 1 0 0 0 0 0.
S2	S2 field specifies the source 2 register.

6-4 tbnd instruction triadic addressing.

Register with 10-bit immediate addressing

This kind of addressing is used with the type of register-to-register instruction that's generally called a "bit-field instruction"—i.e., instructions that manipulate entire fields of bits. For those who cannot wait for chapter 7, that means clr, ext, extu, mak, rot, and set.

Register with 10 Bit Immediate Addressing, then, means that data specified by rS1 is processed as required by the instruction and the result is then placed in rD. The last 10 bits of the instruction word are two 5 bit-long fields. The first is a width, the second an offset. The offset begins at the least significant bit (see Fig. 6-5).

31	26 25	21 20	16 15	10 9	0
1 1 1 1 0 0	D	S1	Subopcode	IMM10(W5,O5)	

D	The D field specifies the destination register for the operation's result.
S1	S1 field specifies the source 1 register.
Subopcode	This field identifies the specific instruction.
IMM10	IMM10 contains two 5-bit fields W5 (width) and O5 (offset).
	Bits 9-5 width
	Bits 4-0 offset

6-5   10-bit immediate addressing.

So, for example:

ext r4,r2,4<5>

would extract a signed bit field from r2, 4 bits wide, starting at bit 5, and place the result in r4. If the contents of r2 were 0x548, then r4 would contain 0xA after the instruction had been executed.

Register with 16-bit displacement/immediate

This form is used by arithmetic and logical register-to-register instructions (see Fig. 6-6). The IMM16 value may be used either as an arithmetic value as in add, or as an address displacement as in bb0. The data in rS1 and the IMM16 field is used according to the instruction, and then dropped into rD.

31	26 25	21 20	16 15	0
Opcode	D	S1	IMM16	

Opcode	This field specifies the particular instruction.
D	The D field will contain the operation's results.
S1	S1 field specifies the source 1 register.
IMM16	This field contains an unsigned 16 bit immediate value.

6-6   16-bit immediate addressing.

For example:

```
add r1,r2,0x1000
```

adds 0x1000 to the contents of r2, and then places the result in r1.

The register-to-register instructions that use this kind of addressing include add, addu, and, cmp, div, divu, maks, mul, or, sub, subu, and xor.

But, a variation of 16-bit immediate is also used by some flow control instructions—specifically, the bit test and branch instructions bb0, bb1, and bcnd (see Fig. 6-7). These instructions test a situation for certain pre-defined conditions, and if those conditions exist, they transfer program control to some specified point.

31	26 25	21 20	16 15	0
Opcode	B5/M5	S1	D16	

Opcode   This field specifies the particular instruction.

B5/M5   For bit tests, B5 specifies the bit to be tested in the register noted in S1.

For conditional tests, M5 specifies the condition to be tested:

Bit 25 - Reserved. must be zero

Bit 24 - Maximum negative number

Bit 23 - Less than zero

Bit 22 - Equal to zero

Bit 21 - Greater than zero

Multiple conditions may be set as follows:

	25	24	23	22	21
eq0	0	0	0	1	0
ne0	0	1	1	0	1
gt0	0	0	0	0	1
lt0	0	1	1	0	0
ge0	0	0	0	1	1
le0	0	1	1	1	0

S1   S1 field specifies the source 1 register.

D16   This field contains a signed 16 bit displacement value.

6-7 Bit-test branch 16-bit displacement addressing.

For bb0 and bb1, the test is administered to the bit specified in the B5 field within the rS1 register. (bb0 checks to see if it's clear, while bb1 checks to see if it's set.) The bcnd instruction, meanwhile, tests the rS1 register for certain conditions present in its M5 field (see chapter 7 for details on that). In the case of bb0 and bb1, if their tests are true, then the 16-bit displacement is shifted left two bits and sign-extended to 32 bits. That result is added to the XIP and placed in FIP. Program execution is transferred to the resulting address.

For example, if the following bb1 instruction is at location 0x30000:

    bb1 20,r5,0x1000

tests bit 20 in r5. If it is set, then it transfers execution to 0x34000.

Yet another variation is used by the tbnd instruction. Here, the data in rS1 is compared to the 16-bit immediate field. Then, a trap is taken if rS1 is greater than IMM16. rD is unused, and should be zero for future compatibility (see Fig. 6-8).

Thus, for example:

    tbnd r5,0x4000

compares r5 to 0x4000 and causes a trap to the bounds check vector if r5 is the larger of the two.

31 26	25 21	20 16	15 0
1 1 1 1 1 0	D	S1	IMM16

D	This field is ignored, but should contain zeros.
S1	S1 field specifies the source 1 register.
IMM16	This field contains a signed 16 bit immediate value.

6-8 tbnd 16-bit immediate addressing.

Control register addressing

This form of address is used by register-to-register instructions to utilize the control and floating point registers of the 88100. This is the form the instructions use to load from, store to, and exchange data between general purpose registers and their more specialized cousins: control and floating point registers (see Fig. 6-9).

```
31         26 25    21 20      16 15  14 13  11 10       5 4      0
┌──────────┬──────┬──────────┬────┬─────┬──────────┬──────────┐
│ 1 0 0 0 0 0 │  D  │   S1    │ OP │ SFU │ CRS/CRD  │   S2    │
└──────────┴──────┴──────────┴────┴─────┴──────────┴──────────┘
```

D   For loads and exchanges, D specifies the destination register.
             For stores, the D field is ignored.

S1   For store and exchange instructions, S1 denotes the source register.
             For load instructions, S1 is ignored.

OP   The OP field identifies the particular instruction.

SFU   SFU specifies the special function unit. 0 specifies the integer unit,
             1 specifies the floating point unit.

CRS/CRD   Specifies the control register. For loads, the control register is the
             source, for stores, it is the destination.

S2   The S2 field must contain the same value as the S1 field.

6-9 Control register addressing.

The exact shape of this depends on what's being done. For instance, the fields used will change according to whether this is a store or a load.

For the first load, the rD field specifies the general register to be loaded with the contents of the designated control register, while rS1 and rS2 are ignored. SFU represents the special function unit selected—and you'll recall that the floating point unit is SFU #1. Others will come in time, but for the moment 1 specifies the FPU, while 0 specifies the integer unit. The CRS field designates the control register whose contents are to be transferred.

For example:

    ldcr r3,cr2

loads the contents of the exception time PSR into r3.

On the store side of the fence, rD is ignored. Meanwhile rS1 and rS2 must contain the same value—that of the general register containing the data to transfer to a selected control register. SFU is 0 for integer unit and 1 for the FPU. CRD indicates the destination control register.

So:

    fstcr r3,fcr62

stores the contents of r3 into the floating point status register.

Register indirect with zero extended immediate index

This form of address is used by data memory access instructions to generate addresses that reference system memory (Fig. 6-10). In it, the contents of the IMM16 field are added to the contents of rS1 to form a memory address. That address is where something is to be taken from, or stored in system memory according to whatever it is the instruction has in mind.

For example:

    ld r3,r2,0x20000

means load the word at the address given by r2 + 0x20000 and then put it into r3.

Or, to go the other direction:

    st r3,r2,0x10000

means store the contents of r3 at the address given by r2+0x10000.

31	26 25	21 20	16 15	0
Opcode	D	S1	I16	

Opcode   This field specifies the particular instruction.

D   D specifies destination for loads, and source for stores/exchanges.

S1   S1 field specifies the source 1 register.

IMM16   This field contains a 16 bit immediate index.

6-10 Register indirect with zero-extended immediate index addressing.

Register indirect with index

Register Indirect with Index is much like the form before it. It's a form of address used by data memory access instructions to generate data addresses. In this case, though, the contents of rS1 are added to rS2 to give an address in system memory (Fig. 6-11). The 88K then either stores to, or loads from, that address—depending on the instruction.

31	26	25	21	20	16	15	5	4	0
1 1 1 1 0 1		D		S1		Subopcode		S2	

D   The D specifies the destination register for a load, and the source register for stores and exchanges.

S1   S1 specifies the source register used in the address calculation.

Subopcode   This field identifies the specific instruction.

S2   S2 field specifies the source 2 register.

6-11   Register indirect with index addressing.

As in:

    ld r3,r2,r4

which means load r3 with the word at the location given by the sum of r2 and r4.

Register indirect with scaled index

Register Indirect with Scaled Index is much like the one before. It too is used by data memory access instructions to generate data addresses. The difference is in the way it's done. Here, the contents of rS2 are scaled by the size of the access and then added to rS2. (Scaling simply means that the scaled register is multiplied by the access size. You'll recall that the 88K can access bytes, half words, words, and double words.)

The result is an address in system memory that's loaded from, or stored to, depending on what the instruction needs to do (Fig. 6-12).

If this is an lda instruction, the resulting address is loaded into rD.

So, for example:

    lda r3,r2,[r4]

means load r3 with the data in the address given by r4*4+r2. This is full word access.

Or, for another look at the same form:

    st.h r3,r2, [r4]

31	26	25	21	20	16	15	5	4	0
1 1 1 1 0 1		D		S1		Subopcode		S2	

D   The D field specifies the destination register for a load instruction. For store or exchange memory instructions, D specifies the source register.

S1   S1 specifies the source 1 register used in address calculation.

Subopcode   This field identifies the specific instruction, including the scaling factor.

S2   S2 field specifies the source 2 register used in address calculation.

6-12   Register indirect with scaled index addressing.

which means store r3 at the address given by $r4*2+r2$. Note that the size is given as the instruction's extension—that is, .h, .d, .b, and so on.

Register with 9-bit vector table index

This sort of addressing (Fig. 6-13) is used in performing tests by the trap flow control instructions—tb0, tb1, and tcnd. For tb0 and tb1, the rS1 register is tested for being set or clear. For tcnd, the rS1 register is tested for conditions specified in the M5 field. In all three cases, if the condition is true, the 20-bit address contained in the Vector Base Register (VBR) is combined with the VEC9 field along with trailing zeros to form an address. Program control is then transferred to that address.
    Thus:

        tb0 30,r2,128

which means test bit 30 in r2. If it is set, then branch to VBR +128 to begin exception processing.

26-bit branch displacement

26-bit Branch Displacement is used by flow control instructions to specify the instruction to which execution control is to be transferred for unconditional branch instructions (Fig. 6-14). Specifically, that means br and bsr.

31	26 25	21 20	16 15	5 4	0
1 1 1 1 0 0	B5/M5	S1	Subopcode	VEC9	

B5/M5   For bit tests, B5 specifies the bit to be tested in S1.

For conditional tests, M5 specifies the condition to be tested:

     Bit 25 - Reserved. must be zero

     Bit 24 - Maximum negative number

     Bit 23 - Less than zero

     Bit 22 - Equal to zero

     Bit 21 - Greater than zero

Multiple conditions may be set as follows:

	25	24	23	22	21
eq0	0	0	0	1	0
ne0	0	1	1	0	1
gt0	0	0	0	0	1
lt0	0	1	1	0	0
ge0	0	0	0	1	1
le0	0	1	1	1	0

S1   S1 field specifies the source 1 register.

Subopcode   This field specifies the particular instruction.

VEC9   This field contains the 9 bit vector number.

6-13   9-bit vector table index addressing.

31	26 25	0
Opcode	D26	

Opcode   This field identifies the specific instruction.

D26   This field contains the displacement to the instruction.

6-14   26-bit displacement addressing.

These instructions use a sign extended 26-bit displacement (marked D26 in Fig. 6-14) to come up with the new target address. The D26 displacement is shifted left two bits and sign extended to 32 bits. (The low 2 bits are cleared to force word alignment.)

For example:

```
br 0x100000
```

means transfer control to the instruction at 0x400000.

Chapter 6 is meant to provide a quick insight into addressing modes of the 88K so that when these terms and modes crop up when describing the 88K's instructions, they will be familiar. You've been very polite. Without further ado, you can plow forward into the details of the instructions: chapter 7.

7

The 88100 instruction set

The 88K is a RISC processor. Its instructions are reduced in number, by definition. We only have to deal with a mere 51 of them. Indeed, it says something about RISC as a technology that a single chapter can list and describe all of the 88K's instructions. To do the same for some CISC processors you would need many chapters.

The following chapter is somewhat different from those that came before it, and those that shall follow. It is mostly just a listing. Each instruction has its own subsection which contains a short description of what the instruction does and what it looks like.

Before getting into the instructions themselves, a bit of discussion of instruction notation might be a wise investment. Each of an 88K's instructions is made up of a number of smaller parts, known as fields. *Fields* specify such things as the register from which data is to come, the register to which it will go, and so on.

Fields have a notational convention. The destination register for an operation is written as "rD", for Destination Register. Each field is defined along with each instruction, but it might be nice to see the collection all in one place. (See Fig. 7-1 and Fig. 7-2.)

And, finally, a quick note on signed and unsigned numbers. Integers can be either signed or unsigned. If the number is to be signed, you have to sacrifice one bit to denote plus or minus. Bit 31 is that bit. If bit 31 is on, the number is negative. If off, positive. Simple! But, you also cut in half the range of positive integers that can be represented. So for signed numbers, you can say $\pm 2,147,483,654$ (2^{31}) while for unsigned, the range is 0 to $4,294,967,304$ (2^{31}).

Without further ado, we present the 88100 instruction set:

Abbrev	Description
eq0	equals zero
ne0	not equal to zero
gt0	greater than zero
lt0	less than zero
ge0	greater than/equals zero
le0	less than/equals zero
x	don't care bit
+	addition operator
−	subtraction operator
÷	division operator
×	multiplication operator
::	comparison operator
∨	logical OR operator
//	concatenation operator
<<	shift left operator
⇐	replacement operator
∧	logical AND operator
⊕	logical Exclusive OR operator
<	comparison operator, true if left operand is less than right operand
>	comparison operator, true if left operand is greater than right operand
{ }	optional
iff	if and only if

7-1 Operation notation.

r1	General register 1
rS1	Register containing the first source operand
rS2	Register containing the second source operand
rD	Register into which the result will be stored
crS	Source control register
crD	Destination control register
crS/D	Source and Destination control register (for **xcr**)
fcrS	Source floating point control register
fcrD	Destination floating point control register
fcrS/D	Source and Destination floating point control register (for **fxcr**)
D16	16 bit signed displacement
D26	26 bit signed displacement
IMM16	Unsigned 16 bit immediate operand
I16	Unsigned 16 bit immediate index
VEC9	Vector offset from VBR
M5	5 bit Match field
B5	Unsigned 5 bit integer indicating bit position within word
<O5>	Unsigned 5 bit integer denoting bit-field offset within word
W5	Unsigned 5 bit integer denoting bit-field width within word
{.n}	Delay branch option
{.c}	Complement option
.ci	Carry In the carry bit
.co	Carry Out the carry bit
.cio	Carry In and Carry Out the carry bit

7-2 Operand notation.

continued

	Memory size options
.b	byte
.bu	unsigned byte
.h	half word
.hu	unsigned half word
.s	single word
.d	double word
	Floating point operand size
.s	single precision
.d	double precision
.usr	user memory option (supervisor only)
[rS2]	Scaled index of source register 2

Integer Add

As the name would suggest, the add instruction adds integers. It adds the contents of the rS1 register with either—your choice—the contents of the rS2 register, or a 16-bit, zero extended operand. The type of addition is unsigned. The result is placed in the destination register—the "rD" register.

You have several options to let you elaborate on this a bit. For instance, there's .ci, which causes the carry bit from the PSR to be added to the result (rD=rS1+rS2+carry). The .co option causes the generated carry bit to be written to the processor status register (PSR). And, finally, there's the .cio option, which allows you to add the carry bit to the result, while also causing the generated carry bit to be written to the PSR.

As an aside, you can also do some interesting tricks with add.ci. You can, for instance, do a "load carry bit" operation by writing:

```
add.ci rD,r0,r0
```

Because r0 contains 0, the result of this little bit of flimflam will be the value of the carry bit—i.e., zero plus whatever the carry bit happens to be—which then shows up in rD. (The carry bit is set when the arithmetic result overflows the container in which you are trying to put it. You would have the carry bit set if you added 100 to 4,294,967,304.)

You can also clear the carry bit by doing this in reverse, via add.co, as in:

```
add.co   r0,r0,r0
```

Because everything here is zero, you can clear the carry bit in one fell swoop. None of the registers are affected by all this.

As with everything in this life, add can get into problems. If you get a result that cannot be represented as a signed 32-bit integer, you'll get an integer overflow exception.

add operation   Destination ⇦ Source 1 + Source 2

Assembler syntax

```
add      rD,rS1,rS2      signed add without carry
add.ci   rD,rS1,rS2      signed add plus carry
add.co   rD,rS1,rS2      signed add propagate carry
```

| add.cio | rD,rS1,rS2 | signed add plus carry & propagate |
| add | rD,rS1,IMM16 | signed add with IMM16 without carry |

Exceptions   Integer Overflow

add instruction encoding

Register with 16 bit Immediate

```
 31            26 25      21 20      16 15                          0
┌──────────────┬──────────┬──────────┬───────────────────────────┐
│  0 1 1 1 0 0 │    D     │    S1    │           IMM16           │
└──────────────┴──────────┴──────────┴───────────────────────────┘
```

Triadic Addressing

```
 31         26 25    21 20      16 15           10 9  8 7    5 4        0
┌────────────┬────────┬──────────┬───────────────┬──┬──┬──────┬────────┐
│  1 1 1 1 0 1│   D    │    S1    │   0 1 1 1 0 0  │I │O │0 0 0 │   S2   │
└────────────┴────────┴──────────┴───────────────┴──┴──┴──────┴────────┘
```

D:	Destination
S1:	Source 1 register
S2:	Source 2 register
IMM16:	16 bit unsigned Immediate value
I:	0 - Disable Carry In
	1 - Add Carry to result
O:	0 - Disable Carry out
	1 - Generate Carry

Unsigned integer add

The addu instruction is like the add instruction—with two differences. First, it can't cause an overflow exception. Second, it uses unsigned integers. In every other respect, though, it looks the same. It adds the contents of the rS1 register with either the contents of rS2 or a 16-bit, zero extended immediate operand, and so on.

addu operation   Destination ⇦ Source 1 + Source 2

Assembler syntax

addu	rD,rS1,rS2	unsigned add (no carry)
addu.ci	rD,rS1,rS2	unsigned add (with carry)
addu.co	rD,rS1,rS2	unsigned add, propagate carry out
addu.cio	rD,rS1,rS2	unsigned add plus carry, propagate carry out
addu	rD,rS1,IMM16	unsigned add with immediate (without carry).

Exceptions   None

addu instruction encoding

Register with 16 bit Immediate

31	26 25	21 20	16 15	0
0 1 1 0 0 0	D	S1	IMM16	

Triadic Addressing

31	26 25	21 20	16 15	10 9	8 7	5 4	0
1 1 1 1 0 1	D	S1	0 1 1 0 0 0	I	O	0 0 0	S2

D:	Destination
S1:	Source 1 register
S2:	Source 2 register

IMM16:   16 bit unsigned Immediate value

I: 0 - Disable Carry In

            1 - Add Carry to result

O: 0 - Disable Carry out

            1 - Generate Carry

Logical and

The and instruction causes the data in register rS1 and the data in register rS2 to be logically ANDed. The result is then stored in the rD register for triadic register addressing.

Tagging .c (for complement) on the end results in the source 2 operand being complemented before being ANDed. With immediate addressing, the lower 16 bits of the rS1 register and the 16-bit unsigned immediate operand encoded in the instruction are logically ANDed. The upper 16 bits of rS1 are copied unchanged into rD. If you use the .u (upper word) option, then the upper 16 bits of the Source 1 operand are ANDed with the immediate operand, and the lower 16 bits of rS1 are copied unchanged into rD, where the result is also stored.

There are no exceptions resulting from and.

and operation   Destination ⇦ Source 1 ∧ Source 2

Assembler syntax

        and   rD,rS1,rS2
        and.c   rD,rS1,rS2
        and   rD,rS1,IMM16
        and.u   rD,rS1,IMM16

Exceptions   None

and instruction encoding

Register with 16 bit Immediate

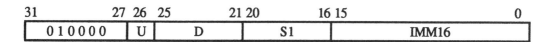

31	27	26 25	21 20	16 15	0
0 1 0 0 0 0	U	D	S1	IMM16	

Triadic Addressing

31	26 25	21 20	16 15	11 10 9	5 4	0
1 1 1 1 0 1	D	S1	0 1 0 0 0	C 0 0 0 0 0	S2	

D: Destination
S1:   Source 1 register

continued

S2:	Source 2 register
IMM16:	16 bit unsigned Immediate value
U:	0 - AND IMM16 to bits 15-0 of S1
	1 - AND IMM16 to bits 31-16 of S1
C:	0 - S2 not complemented before operation
	1 - S2 complemented before operation

Branch on bit clear

This instruction examines a bit of the rS1 register as specified by the B5 field. The B5 field is a 5-bit field in the instruction (bits $25-21$) that designates which bit of the 32 is to be tested. If the bit's clear, then hello!—you have a branch. If not, then you don't.

When you do have a branch, the 16-bit displacement is sign extended and shifted to the left by two bits to form a word displacement. Then, the branch target address is formed by adding that displacement to the address of the bb0 instruction.

With the .n option, you can also make the instruction following bb0 execute before the branch target instruction.

There are no exceptions resulting from bb0, but Motorola says some interesting things about how not to use it. Specifically, "to ensure compatibility" the instruction following bb0.n shouldn't be a trap, a jump, a branch, or anything else that modifies the instruction pointer.

Be wary of this one. If you go to a trap, jump, branch, etc., you could have an error, and the system won't detect it. (This is normally of interest primarily to compiler writers and assembly language hackers.)

bb0 operation   If bit clear: FIP $\hookleftarrow$ XIP + D16 $<<$ 2

Assembler syntax

```
bb0     B5,rS1,D16
bb0.n   B5,rS1,D16
```

Exceptions   None

bb0 instruction encoding

Register with 16 bit Displacement

31	27 26	25	21 20	16 15	0
1 1 0 1 0	N	B5	S1	D16	

N:	0 - Execution suppressed for next instruction in sequence
	1 - Next instruction in sequence executed before branch taken
B5:	5 bit unsigned integer indicating target bit in S1
S1:	Source 1 register
D16:	16 bit sign extended displacement

bb1

Branch on bit set

This instruction is just like bb0, except in reverse. It examines the bit of the rS1 register specified by the B5 field—and, if the bit is set, it causes a branch. In every other respect, it performs exactly like its antithesis, bb0.

The .n option causes the instruction following the bb1 instruction to be executed before the branch target instruction. It also has the same warnings attached. The instruction following a bb1 should not be a trap, jump, branch or anything else that would modify the instruction pointer.

bb1 operation   If bit set: FIP ⇦ XIP + D16<<2

Assembler syntax

        bb1   B5,rS1,D16
        bb1.n   B5,rS1,D16

Exceptions   None

bb1 instruction encoding

Register with 16 bit Displacement

31	27 26	25	21 20	16 15	0
1 1 0 1 1	N	B5	S1	D16	

N: 0 - Execution suppressed for next instruction in sequence

            1 - Next instruction in sequence executed before branch taken

B5:   5 bit unsigned integer indicating target bit in S1

S1:   Source 1 register

D16:   16 bit sign extended displacement

Conditional branch

This one is complex. The bcnd instruction compares the data contained in the rS1 register to zero, and then branches if the value in the register meets some specified condition. For example, you might want to branch if, and only if, the value in rS1 was equal to zero. In that case, you'd write:

```
bcnd eq0,rS1,D16
```

which means branch if what's in rS1 is zero. Note the eq0 part. Remember, that's a mnemonic for exactly what it looks like, "equal to 0." The other comparison mnemonics are allowed.

As with bb0 and bb1, you also have the .n (delayed branch) option. Place it at the end of bcnd, and the instruction following it will be executed before the branch target instruction. And, as with other branches, you have the usual set of warnings attached to the .n option. Don't let the instruction following bcnd.n be a trap, a jump, a branch, or anything else that modifies the instruction pointer.

You can also do something else with bcnd. When it is out there checking the rS1 register, it does so by looking at the value of two of the register's bits—the sign bit (i.e., the most significant bit) and the zero bit (logical NORing of the 31 low-order operand bits). A logical NOR is a Boolean test that says if all of my inputs are zero, then the output is one. If any inputs are 1, the output is zero.

Those two bits are then concatenated to form an index into the M5 field of the instruction. If the indexed bit is set, then the branch is taken. This allows you to have the system do a branch based on comparisons without proceeding the branch instruction with a compare instruction. You can indicate M5 directly, instead of using a comparison code.

As with bb0 and bb1, the 16-bit displacement is sign extended, and shifted left two bits to form a word displacement. Meanwhile, the branch target address is formed by adding that displacement to the address of the bcnd instruction.

There are no exceptions.

bcnd operation   If condition true: FIP ⇦ XIP + D16 $<<$ 2

Assembler syntax   (*cc* represents comparison code)

```
bcnd    cc,rS1,D16
bcnd    M5,rS1,D16
```

```
bcnd.n    cc,rS1,D16
bcnd.n    M5,rS1,D16
```

Exceptions   None

bcnd instruction encoding

Register with 16 bit Displacement

31	27 26 25	21 20	16 15	0
1 1 1 0 1	N	M5	S1	D16

N: 0 - Execution suppressed for next instruction in sequence

          1 - Next instruction in sequence executed before branch taken

M5:   5 bit field for condition to be matched

              Bit 25 - Reserved. must be zero

              Bit 24 - Maximum negative number

              Bit 23 - Less than zero

              Bit 22 - Equal to zero

              Bit 21 - Greater than zero

S1:   Source 1 register

D16:   16 bit sign extended displacement

Unconditional branch

This does just what it says—it produces an unconditional branch. The br instruction causes a transfer of program flow, no questions asked, to the address that's formed by adding the 26-bit, sign extended word displacement (shifted left two bits) to the address of the branch instruction.

The usual warnings apply about not following the .n with a trap, a jump, a branch, or anything else that would change the instruction pointer. There are no exceptions.

br operation   FIP ⇦ XIP + D26 < <2

Assembler syntax

    br   D26
    br.n D26

Exceptions   None

br instruction encoding

26 bit Displacement Addressing

31 27	26 25	0
1 1 0 0 0	N	D26

N: 0 - Execution suppressed for next instruction in sequence

              1 - Next instruction in sequence executed before branch taken

D26:   26 bit sign extended displacement to the instruction.

bsr

Branch to subroutine

The bsr instruction causes an unconditional transfer of the program to a target address—which is formed by adding the 26-bit, sign extended word displacement (shifted left two bits) to the address of the bsr instruction (value of XIP). The return address is saved in register r1.

There's also the usual .n option, with the standard warnings on the pack. According to Motorola, jumps, traps, branches, etc., can be hazardous to your health. But, when you use it, the return address is the address of the second instruction following the bsr.n instruction (value of NIP+4).

Also, one aside—the bsr instruction can be used to do a "load instruction pointer" operation. When you write:

    bsr   *label*
label:

The instruction will then cause a branch to the instruction identified by *label*, which is also the next instruction to come along. A cynic might suggest that this sounds a little like an old-fashioned "goto" statement, but surely there are no cynics here. Instead, we'll just note that the return address—that is, the instruction following the bsr instruction—is then stored in register r1. Ergo, r1 contains the value of the XIP.

bsr operations   FIP ⬅ XIP + D26 < <2
                      r1 ⬅ NIP (+4 if .n option)

Assembler syntax

    bsr   D26
    bsr.n   D26

Exceptions   None

bsr instruction encoding

26 bit Displacement Addressing

31	27	26	25	0
1 1 0 0 1		N	D26	

N: 0 - Execution suppressed for next instruction in sequence
            1 - Next instruction in sequence executed before branch taken

D26:   26 bit sign extended displacement to the instruction.

Clear bit field

It's said that nature abhors a vacuum. However, the clr instruction isn't a big fan of nature, and it loves zeros instead. It copies the contents of the rS1 register into the rD register and inserts a field of zeros, of width W5, into the data. W5 is a 5-bit field in the clr instruction (bits 9−5) that specifies the width of the bit field to be cleared.

The field is offset from bit zero of the rS1 register by the number of bits specified in the O5 field. So, for example, if W5 contains 4, and O5 holds 18, then four zeros are dropped in bits 18 through 21 of the rS1 operand.

With triadic register addressing, bits 9−5 and bits 4−0 of the rS2 register are used as the W5 and O5 fields. The rest of the rS2 register, meanwhile, is simply ignored. And, speaking of ignoring things, if the specified field extends beyond bit 31, those bits numbered 31+n are forgotten about as well.

There are no exceptions to clr.

clr operation   Destination ⇦ Source 1 ∧ (bit-field of 0s)

Assembler syntax

      clr   rD,rS1,W5<O5>
      clr   rD,rS1,rS2
      clr   rD,rS1,{<}O5{>}

Exceptions   None

clr instruction encoding

Register with 10 bit Immediate

31	26 25	21 20	16 15	10 9	5 4	0
1 1 1 1 0 0	D	S1	1 0 0 0 0 0	W5	O5	

Triadic

31	26 25	21 20	16 15	5 4	0
1 1 1 1 0 1	D	S1	1 0 0 0 0 0 0 0 0 0	S2	

D:	Destination
S1:	Source 1 register
W5:	5 bit unsigned integer indicating bit field width (0 = 32 bits)
O5:	5 bit unsigned integer indicating bit field offset
S2:	Source 2 register

Integer compare

Here's one that you'll be using a lot. The cmp instruction compares the data in rS1 with either the data in rS2, or with a zero extended, 16-bit operand. The instruction then returns the evaluated conditions as a bit string in the destination register.

Where this gets complex is in what you get back—in, that is, the bit stream that comes as a response to cmp. It looks something like:

31	12	11	10	9	8	7	6	5	4	3	2	1	0
0 0 0 0 0 0 0 0 0 0 0 0 0 0 0 0 0 0 0 0		hs	lo	ls	hi	ge	lt	le	gt	ne	eq	0	0

You'll note that bits 11 through 2 are the important ones as far as we're concerned at the moment. The rest are zero (although Motorola drops the pregnant warning that they might not be in the future).

Somewhere in 11 through 2 there will be at least one 1, meaning that the condition represented by that bit is, in this case, reality. Each of the different bits stands for a different potential reality. So, for example, if there is a 1 in bit 11, the *hs* bit, S1 is unsigned and greater than or equal to S2.

All told, the different conditions that can be represented are:

Bit	Meaning
hs:	$S1 \geq S2$ (unsigned)
lo:	$S1 < S2$ (unsigned)
ls:	$S1 \leq S2$ (unsigned)
hi:	$S1 > S2$ (unsigned)
ge:	$S1 \geq S2$ (signed)
lt:	$S1 < S2$ (signed)
le:	$S1 \leq S2$ (signed)
gt:	$S1 > S1$ (signed)
ne:	$S1 \neq S2$
eq:	$S1 = S2$

This is a particularly handy instruction. You can, for instance, use it for things like "compare and branch on condition" operations with bb0 and bb1. And, while there are conditions where it's not the most efficient means of doing so (as in out-of-bounds array access checking), you can also use it to trap the results of "trap on bit instructions" (specifically, tb0 and tb1, which will be discussed shortly).

cmp operation   Destination ⇐ Source 1 :: Source 2

Assembler syntax

    cmp   rD,rS1,rS2
    cmp   rD,rS1,IMM16

Exceptions   None

cmp instruction encoding

Register with 16 bit Immediate

31		26	25		21	20		16	15			0
	0 1 1 1 1 1			D			S1				IMM16	

Triadic Addressing

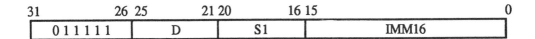

31   26 25   21 20   16 15   11 10 9   5 4   0

| 1 1 1 1 0 1 | D | S1 | 0 1 1 1 1 1 | 0 0* | 0 0 0 | S2 |

* These bits must be zero to ensure future compatibility.

D:	Destination
S1:	Source 1 register
S2:	Source 2 register
IMM16:	16 bit unsigned Immediate value

Signed integer divide

The div instruction is good old fashioned division, without a whole lot of surprises. The data in S1 is divided by either the data in S2, or by the zero extended 16-bit immediate operand specified in the instruction. We're talking here about 32-bit two's complement binary division, with the quotient stored in the rD register.

This one has exceptions, though. If the divisor is zero, or if either operand is negative, you'll get an integer divide exception, and program control shifts over to the integer divide exception handler (more on this in chapter 9 on exceptions). You'll also get a floating point exception if the div instruction attempts to execute when the FPU is disabled.

div operation   Destination ⇦ Source 1 ÷ Source 2

Assembler syntax

> div   rD,rS1,rS2
> div   rD,rS1,IMM16

Exceptions   Integer Divide
Floating Point Unimplemented (if FPU disabled)

div instruction encoding

Register with 16 bit Immediate

31	26 25	21 20	16 15	0
0 1 1 1 1 0	D	S1	IMM16	

Triadic Addressing

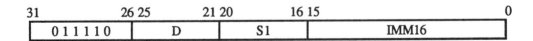

31	26 25	21 20	16 15	11 10 9 8	5 4	0
1 1 1 1 0 1	D	S1	0 1 1 1 1 0	0 0* 0 0 0	S2	

* These bits must be zero to ensure future compatibility.

D:	Destination
S1:	Source 1 register
S2:	Source 2 register
IMM16:	16 bit unsigned Immediate value

divu

Unsigned integer divide

The divu instruction is exactly like div, except that the integers involved are unsigned. Otherwise, everything is the same, right down to the exceptions; except that a negative operand isn't possible.

divu operation Destination ⇦ Source 1 ÷ Source 2

Assembler syntax

    divu   rD,rS1,rS2
    divu   rD,rS1,IMM16

Exceptions Integer Divide
Floating Point Unimplemented

divu instruction encoding

Register with 16 bit Immediate

31	26	25	21	20	16	15	0
011010		D		S1		IMM16	

Triadic Addressing

31	26	25	21	20	16	15	11	10 9	8	5	4	0
111101		D		S1		011010		0 0*	000		S2	

* These bits must be zero to ensure future compatibility.

D:	Destination
S1:	Source 1 register
S2:	Source 2 register
IMM16:	16 bit unsigned Immediate value

Extract signed bit field

The ext instruction does just exactly what its name suggests. It extracts a signed bit field from the rS1 register. The width of that extracted field is specified by the W5 field, and the offset from the least significant bit is specified by the O5 field. Then, the extracted bit field is sign extended to 32 bits and deposited in the rD register.

For triadic register addressing, bits $9-5$ and $4-0$ of the rS2 register are used for the W5 and O5 fields, while the rest of the rS2 register is just ignored. If the bit field extends beyond bit 31, then bit 31 is used as the sign bit and it is then extended in the destination register. The operation of ext is shown here:

Signed bit field

31			0
X X X X X X X X X X	S Y Y Y Y	X X X X X X X X X X X X X X X X X	

rS1 |← Width →|← Offset →|

31		0
S S S S S S S S S S S S S S S S S S S S S S S S S S S	S Y Y Y Y	

rD |← Width →|

When the W5 field contains only zeros (meaning a width of 32 bits), ext operates as an arithmetic shift right operation. The offset specifies the number of positions to shift. The high-order bits are sign-filled in the destination registers.

ext operation   Destination ⇦ (sign extended bit field) of Source 1

Assember syntax

```
ext   rD,rS1,W5<O5>
ext   rD,rS1,rS2
ext   rD,rS1,{<}O5{>}
```

Exceptions   None

ext instruction encoding

Register with 10 bit Immediate

31	26 25	21 20	16 15	10 9	5 4	0
111100	D	S1	100100	W5	O5	

Triadic

```
31          26 25      21 20        16 15                    5 4        0
┌─────────────┬─────────┬───────────┬─────────────────────┬───────────┐
│  1 1 1 1 0 1│    D    │    S1     │  1 0 0 1 0 0 0 0 0 0 │    S2     │
└─────────────┴─────────┴───────────┴─────────────────────┴───────────┘
```

D: Destination
S1:   Source 1 register
W5:   5 bit unsigned integer indicating bit field width (0 = 32 bits)
O5:   5 bit unsigned integer indicating bit field offset
S2:   Source 2 register

Extract unsigned bit field

This is exactly like ext, but unsigned. Just like its sibling, the extu instruction extracts a bit field from the rS1 register. The width of that field is specified by the W5 field, and the offset from the least significant bit is specified by the O5 field. For triadic register addressing, bits 9−5 and 4−0 of the register specified by the rS2 field are used for the W5 and O5 fields respectively, and the rest of the rS2 is ignored. If the field extends beyond bit 31, then the result is zero extended in the destination register. The operation of extu is shown here:

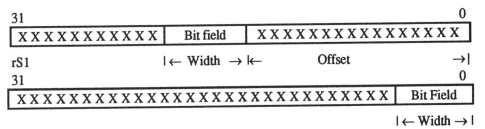

When the W5 field contains only zeros (meaning a width of 32 bits), ext operates as an arithmetic shift right operation. The offset specifies the number of positions to shift. The high-order bits are zero-filled in the destination registers.

extu operation   Destination ⇦ (zero extended bit field) of Source 1

Assembler syntax

        extu   rD,rS1,W5<O5>
        extu   rD,rS1,rS2
        extu   rD,rS1,{<}O5{>}

Exceptions   None

extu instruction encoding

Register with 10 bit Immediate

31	26	25	21	20	16	15	10	9	5	4	0
111100		D		S1		100110		W5		O5	

Triadic

```
 31        26 25      21 20      16 15              5 4        0
┌─────────┬─────────┬─────────┬─────────────────┬──────────┐
│ 111101  │    D    │   S1    │  10011000000    │    S2    │
└─────────┴─────────┴─────────┴─────────────────┴──────────┘
```

D:	Destination
S1:	Source 1 register
W5:	5 bit unsigned integer indicating bit field width (0 = 32 bits)
O5:	5 bit unsigned integer indicating bit field offset
S2:	Source 2 register

Floating point add

This instruction is a little more complex than it might seem at first glance. As the name suggests, it takes the operands of the rS1 and rS2 registers, adds them according to the IEEE 754 standard for floating point addition, and places the result in rD—but, before it does that add, it first checks the rS1 and rS2 operands to make certain that they are not reserved IEEE floating point numbers, specifically:

$\pm$ NAN - not a number
$\pm$ Zero
$\pm$ Infinity
$\pm$ Denormalized numbers

If the instruction finds a reserved operand, then it causes a floating point exception.

The "s" and "d" in the assembler code stand for single- and double-precision, respectively. You can, in fact, use any combination of single- and double-precision that you'd like.

There are also many exceptions. One has already been mentioned: the floating point reserved operand. But there are others. For instance, you'll get an exception if you have an overflow, underflow, or inexact result. If you specified r0 as the destination register, or if fadd attempts to execute when the floating point unit is disabled, you'll get a "floating point unimplemented exception."

Underflow means that the resulting number was too small to represent as a normalized floating point number. Inexact marks a loss of result accuracy. You can "mask" off the inexact interrupt so that it doesn't occur.

fadd operation   Destination $\Leftarrow$ Source 1 + Source 2

Assembler syntax

```
fadd.sss    rD,rS1,rS2
fadd.ssd    rD,rS1,rS2
fadd.sds    rD,rS1,rS2
fadd.sdd    rD,rS1,rS2
fadd.dss    rD,rS1,rS2
fadd.dsd    rD,rS1,rS2
fadd.dds    rD,rS1,rS2
fadd.ddd    rD,rS1,rS2
```

Exceptions   Floating Point Reserved Operand
Floating Point Overflow
Floating Point Underflow
Floating Point Inexact (if not masked)
Floating Point Unimplemented

fadd instruction encoding

Triadic

31	26	25	21	20	16	15	11	10 9	8 7	6 5 4	0
1 0 0 0 0 1		D		S1		0 0 1 0 1		T1	T2	TD	S2

D:	Destination
S1:	Source 1 register
T1:	Source 1 operand size
T2:	Source 2 operand size
TD:	Destination operand size
	Note: for T1, T2, & TD fields,
	00 - Single precision
	01 - Double precision
S2:	Source 2 register

Floating point compare

The fcmp is yet another clever way of using the floating point unit. Like its cousin fadd, this instruction takes rS1 and rS2 and, before anything else, checks both to make certain they don't contain any reserved operands. If they do, it slams out a floating point reserved operand exception.

But, if they don't, it subtracts the rS2 operand from the rS1 operand. Then, like cmp, it evaluates the result for a number of different conditions—i.e., is rS2 greater than rS1? Or equal to? Or less than? And so on. All the choices will be discussed down the page a bit, but suffice it to say that the comparison is done according to the IEEE 754 standard.

The fcmp instruction also does a quick compare with zero, and does a comparison for bounds. That is to say, it asks if subtraction produces something which is in (in range), ob (out of range or just on the boundary), ib (in range or just on the boundary), or ou (out of range).

The result is returned as a bit string in the rD register, while the actual subtraction result is just discarded. Here's a picture:

31		12	11	10	9	8	7	6	5	4	3	2	1	0
0 0 0 0 0 0 0 0 0 0 0 0 0 0 0 0 0 0 0 0			ob	in	ib	ou	ge	lt	le	gt	ne	eq	cp	nc

You'll notice that bits 31 through 12 are zero and have little to do with anything at the moment. Motorola, however, does not guarantee that they will be zero in the future, so it might be that additional functionality will show up there later on. At the moment, though, the important stuff occurs in bits 11 through 0. In fact, these can be divided into two smaller groups: bits 11 through 8 and 7 through 0.

The second group, bits 7−0, contains the results of the comparison of rS2 to rS1. Bit 7, for instance, has the mnemonic "ge" and will contain a 1 (will be true) if and only if rS1 ≥ rS2. All in all, you have the following possibilities:

Bit	Mnemonic	Meaning
7	ge	true iff (rS1) $\geq$ (rS2) (signed greater than or equal)
6	lt	true iff (rS1) $<$ (rS2) (signed less than)
5	le	true iff (rS1) $\leq$ (rS2) (signed less than or equal)
4	gt	true iff (rS1) $>$ (rS2) (signed greater than)
3	ne	true iff (rS1) $\neq$ (rS2) (not equal)
2	eq	true iff (rS1) $=$ (rS2) (equal)

You also have two other possibilities: bits 1 and 0. These deal with whether the comparison is legal under the rules established by IEEE 754-1985.

| 1 | cp | true if and only if the two operands are comparable per IEEE 754 |
| 0 | nc | true if and only if the two operands are comparable per IEEE 754 |

Bits 11 through 8, meanwhile, deal with the comparison of rS2 to bound.

11	ob	true iff out of range, or on boundary
10	in	true iff in range
9	ib	true iff in range, or on boundary
8	ou	true iff out of range

You can use the returned result of the fcmp in a number of ways. For instance, it could be used by branch-on-bit instructions (bb0 and bb1) in "conditional branch on comparison" operations—for example, if you wanted the software to branch if and only if rS1 = rS2 and therefore eq was 1.

There are two exceptions—floating point reserved operand and floating point unimplemented. When one of these happens, the reserved operand exception handler can complete some operations in software. For instance, if you wanted to compare a string of denormalized numbers, which you simply could not do directly with this instruction, then you could handle the problem in software. The exception handler could then generate a return string, exactly as though the comparison had been handled by fcmp all along.

fcmp operation   Destination ⇦ Source 1 :: Source 2

Assembler Syntax

```
fcmp.sss   rD,rS1,rS2
fcmp.ssd   rD,rS1,rS2
fcmp.sds   rD,rS1,rS2
fcmp.sdd   rD,rS1,rS2
```

Exceptions   Floating Point Reserved Operand
Floating Point Unimplemented

fcmp instruction encoding

Triadic

31	26 25	21 20	16 15	11 10	9 8	7 6	5 4	0
100001	D	S1	00111	T1	T2	00	S2	

D:	Destination
S1:	Source 1 register
T1:	Source 1 operand size
T2:	Source 2 operand size
	Note: for T1, & T2 fields,
	00 - Single precision
	01 - Double precision
S2:	Source 2 register

fdiv

Floating point divide

The fdiv instruction causes the rS1 operand to be divided by the rS2 operand according to the IEEE 754 standard for that sort of thing—after it first checks both to make certain that neither is reserved. Then, it puts the result in rD. You can select any combination of single- and double-precision operands that you like.

There are a number of exceptions to fdiv—many of them having to do with the basic nature of division itself. For instance, you can't divide by zero with this instruction anymore than you can anywhere else, and you'll go into exception processing if you try to do so. Likewise, you'll get an exception if you try to use a reserved operand. You'll have them when the 88K detects an overflow, underflow, or inexact result. Moreover, exception conditons will show up if r0 is specified as the destination register, and if fdiv tries to happen when the FPU is disabled.

The sting is in divide-by-zero. There was a bug in some versions of the 88100 that some readers will see. The errata to Motorola's documentation notes that "When executing div or divu which contains a zero in the divisor, the CPU, depending on several conditions, may not take the divide-by-zero exception, but instead would execute the divide resulting in an all ones pattern being written into the destination register."

What this means is that programmers must test the divisor to see if it is zero. Fortunately there is a relatively free way to do so. Execute the div or divu instruction. It then goes off into the FPU pipeline to work away for many cycles. As the next instruction, place a bcnd to the divide-by-zero exception handler. If the divisor is not zero, the program will continue normally. If it is zero, the FPU pipeline can be flushed.

fdiv operation   Destination ⇦ Source 1 ÷ Source 2

Assembler syntax

```
fdiv.sss    rD,rS1,rS2
fdiv.ssd    rD.rS1,rS2
fdiv.sds    rD,rS1,rS2
fdiv.sdd    rD,rS1,rS2
fdiv.dss    rD,rS1,rS2
fdiv.dsd    rD,rS1,rS2
fdiv.dds    rD,rS1,rS2
fdiv.ddd    rD,rS1,rS2
```

Exceptions   Floating Point Reserved Operand
Floating Point Overflow
Floating Point Underflow
Floating Point Inexact (if not masked)
Floating Point Unimplemented
Floating Point Divide-by-Zero

fdiv instruction encoding

Triadic

31	26	25	21	20	16	15	11	10 9	8 7	6 5	4	0
100001		D		S1		01110		T1	T2	TD	S2	

D:	Destination
S1:	Source 1 register
T1:	Source 1 operand size
T2:	Source 2 operand size
TD:	Destination operand size

Note: for T1, T2, & TD fields,

00 - Single precision

01 - Double precision

S2:   Source 2 register

Find first bit clear

The ff0 instruction scans the rS2 register from the most significant bit to the least looking for a clear bit. If it finds a clear bit, then the bit number of that bit is loaded in the destination register—with zero for the least significant bit and up to 31 for the most significant. If none of the bits are clear, then the destination register is loaded with the integer value 32.

ff0 operation   Destination ⇦ (bit number) of Source 2 Scanned for
first clear bit

Assembler syntax

    ff0   rD,rS2

Exceptions None

ff0 instruction encoding

Triadic

31	26	25	21	20	16	15	5	4	0
1 1 1 1 0 1		D		0 0 0 0 0*		1 1 1 0 1 1 0 0 0 0 0		S2	

*These bits are not decoded, but should be zero to ensure future compatibility

D: Destination
S2:   Source 2 register

Find first bit set

The ff1 instruction is ff0's close cousin. It behaves in the same way, except that ff1 looks for the first set bit instead of the first clear one. It scans the rS2 register from the most significant bit to the least. It takes the bit number of the first set bit it finds, and loads that number in the destination register—with zero for the least significant bit and 31 for the most. If no bits are found set, then the destination register is given an integer value 32.

ff1 operation Destination ⇦ (bit number) of Source 2 Scanned for first set bit

Assembler syntax

> ff1   rD,rS2

Exceptions None

ff1 instruction encoding

Triadic

31	26	25	21	20	16	15	5	4	0
111101		D		00000*		11101000000		S2	

* These bits are not decoded, but should be zero to ensure future compatibility

D: Destination
S2:   Source 2 register

fldcr

Load from floating point control register

The fldcr instruction causes the contents of the floating point unit control register specified by the FCRS field to be loaded into the general purpose register specified by the D field. That looks fairly simple, but there are complications. All registers may be equal, but some are more equal than others. Floating point control registers fcr8 − fcr0 are privileged registers and can only be accessed in the supervisor mode. By way of contrast, registers fcr63 and fcr62 are the floating point control and status registers. They can be accessed in either supervisor or user mode.

Registers fcr61 − fcr9 are unimplemented, but when they do get around to happening, they'll be privileged. A load from fcr61 − fcr9, when executed in supervisor mode, results in a string of zeros getting dropped into rD. But, try the same trick in user mode and you'll get a floating point privilege violation exception.

fldcr operation   Destination ⇦ Floating Point Control Register

Assembler syntax

   fldcr   rD,fcrS

Exceptions   Floating Point Privilege Violation

fldcr instruction encoding

Triadic

31	26	25	21	20	16	15	11	10	5	4	0
100000		D		00000*		01001		FCRS		S2	

* These bits are not decoded, but should be zero to ensure future compatibility

D: Destination
FCRS: Floating point control register source

Convert integer to floating point

This instruction causes the signed integer number in the rS2 register to be converted into floating point representation. The result goes to the rD register. Because rS2 holds an integer, it can only be specified as single-precision, but the destination register can be single- or double-precision.

But, the destination registers cannot—repeat, cannot—be r0. Try that, and you'll get a floating point unimplemented exception, just as you would if flt attempts to execute while the FPU is disabled.

flt operation   Destination ⇦ Float (Source 2)

Assembler syntax

    flt.ss   rD,rS2
    flt.ds   rD,rS2

Exceptions   Floating Point Inexact (if not masked)
Floating Point Unimplemented

flt instruction encoding

Triadic

31	26	25	21	20		7	6	5	4	0
100001		D		00000001000000			TD		S2	

D: Destination (r0 not allowed)

TD: Destination operand size
            Note: for T1, T2, & TD fields,
                00 - Single precision
                01 - Double precision

S2:   Source 2 register

fmul

Floating point multiply

The fmul instruction causes the operands in rS1 and rS2 to be multiplied according to IEEE standard 754—after it first checks to make certain that neither is reserved. The result is placed in rD. You can specify any combination of single and double point precision that you like.

If, when it checks its operands, fmul stumbles across the fact that one or both are reserved, then the result is a floating point reserved operand exception. There are also a number of other, familiar exceptions—overflow, underflow, and inexact. And if the r0 is the destination register, or if fmul tries to execute when the FPU is disabled, you'll get a floating point unimplemented exception.

fmul operation   Destination ⇦ Source 1 × Source 2

Assembler syntax

        fmul.sss   rD,rS1,rS2
        fmul.ssd   rD,rS1,rS2
        fmul.sds   rD,rS1,rS2
        fmul.sdd   rD,rS1,rS2
        fmul.dss   rD,rS1,rS2
        fmul.dsd   rD,rS1,rS2
        fmul.dds   rD,rS1,rS2
        fmul.ddd   rD,rS1,rS2

Exceptions   Floating Point Reserved Operand
             Floating Point Overflow
             Floating Point Underflow
             Floating Point Inexact (if not masked)
             Floating Point Unimplemented

fmul instruction encoding

Triadic

31 26	25 21	20 16	15 11	10 9	8 7	6 5	4 0
100001	D	S1	00000	T1	T2	TD	S2

D: Destination (r0 not allowed)
S1:   Source 1 register

T1:	Source 1 operand size
T2:	Source 2 operand size
TD:	Destination operand size
	Note: for T1, T2, & TD fields,
	00 - Single precision
	01 - Double precision
S2:	Source 2 register

fstcr

Store to floating point control register

The fstcr instruction takes the contents of the general purpose register specified by the S1 field and stores it to the FPU control register specified by the FCRD field. If this sounds a bit like fldcr, it should. The two instructions are, of course, each other's mirror image. They share many traits, including the complexities that result from problems of privilege.

Floating point control registers fcr8 − fcr0 are privileged registers, and you can only reach them from supervisor mode. Try to get at them while in user mode, and you'll get back a floating point privilege violation. Registers fcr61 − fcr9 aren't yet implemented, but when they are, they will be privileged too, and will have the same inaccessibility from user mode. A fstcr instruction to these registers performs a null operation and causes a floating point privilege violation exception in user mode.

As with fldcr, fcr63 (the floating point control register) and fcr62 (the status register) can be accessed in either supervisor or user mode. Again, if this sounds like fldcr, it is. However, with fstcr, there is a new wrinkle. Registers fcr8 − fcr1 are read-only, and an fstcr instruction addressing them performs a null operation.

fstcr operation   Floating Point Control Register ⇦ Destination

Assembler syntax

    ftscr   rS1,fcrD

Exceptions   Floating Point Privilege Violation

fstcr instruction encoding

Triadic

31	26 25	21 20	16 15	11 10	5 4	0
1 0 0 0 0 0	0 0 0 0 0*	S1	1 0 0 0 1	FCRD	S2	

* These bits are not decoded, but should be zero to ensure future compatibility

S1:   Source 1 register
FCRD: Floating point control register destination
S2:   Source 2 register
                    Note: S1 and S2 must contain the same value

Floating point subtract

As you would expect, the fsub instruction causes the rS2 operand to be subtracted from the rS1 operand according to the IEEE 754 standard—after both the Source 1 and Source 2 operands are checked to make certain that neither is reserved. The result is placed in the destination register. You can specify any combination of single- or double-precision operands.

If, before there's a subtraction, one of the operands turns out to be reserved, you'll get a floating point reserved operand exception. And, as before, the other exceptions you might discover with fsub can result from an overflow, an underflow, or an inexact result. Moreover, if r0 is somehow specified as the destination register, or fsub tries to execute when the FPU is disabled, then you'll have a floating point unimplemented exception.

fsub operation   Destination ⇦ Source 1 − Source 2

Assembler syntax

fsub.sss	rD,rS1,rS2
fsub.ssd	rD,rS1,rS2
fsub.sds	rD,rS1,rS2
fsub.sdd	rD,rS1,rS2
fsub.dss	rD,rS1,rS2
fsub.dsd	rD,rS1,rS2
fsub.dds	rD,rS1,rS2
fsub.ddd	rD,rS1,rS2

Exceptions   Floating Point Reserved Operand
Floating Point Overflow
Floating Point Underflow
Floating Point Inexact (not masked)
Floating Point Unimplemented

fsub instruction encoding

Triadic

31	26	25	21	20	16	15	11	10 9	8 7	6 5	4	0
100001		D		S1		00110		T1	T2	TD	S2	

D:	Destination (r0 not allowed)
S1:	Source 1 register
T1:	Source 1 operand size
T2:	Source 2 operand size
TD:	Destination operand size
	Note: for T1, T2, & TD fields,
	00 - Single precision
	01 - Double precision
S2:	Source 2 register

Exchange floating point control register

The fxcr instruction is fairly complex. It causes the contents of whatever general purpose register is specified by the S1 field to be transferred to the FPU control register, and also causes the contents of the FCRS/D register to be transferred to the rD register.

There can be lots of complications. For instance, floating point registers fcr8 – fcr0 are privileged registers and can only be accessed in the supervisor mode. By contrast, fcr63 and fcr62, the floating point control and status registers respectively, can be accessed in either supervisor or user mode. Registers fcr8 – fcr1, meanwhile, are read-only, and an fxcr that addresses them performs a load into the general purpose destination registers only.

You'll recall that registers fcr61 – fcr9 aren't yet implemented—but when they are, they'll be privileged. An fxcr instruction to any of them performs a load of all zeros into rD, when executed from supervisor mode. When it tries the same thing from user mode, it will get a floating point privilege violation exception.

fxcr operation   Destination ⇦ Floating Point Control Register
Floating Point Control Register ⇦ Source 1

Assembler syntax

   fxcr   rD,rS1,fcrS/D

Exceptions   Floating Point Privilege Violation

fxcr instruction encoding

Triadic

31	26 25	21 20	16 15	11 10	5 4	0
1 0 0 0 0 0	D	S1	1 1 0 0 1	FCRS/D	S2	

D: Destination register

S1:   Source 1 register

FCRS/D: Floating point control register source/destination

S2:   Source 2 register

Note: S1 and S2 must contain the same value

Round floating point to integer

This instruction causes the single- or double-precision floating point number in the rS2 register to be converted into a 32-bit integer using the rounding mode specified in the floating point register (FPCR). The result is then placed in rD.

There are three exceptions to this one. If the rS2 operand exponent is greater than or equal to 30, then you'll get a floating point integer conversion overflow exception. Also, if any of the operands turns out to be invalid, there will be a floating point reserved operand exception. And, finally, if r0 is specified as the destination register, or if int occurs when the FPU is disabled, the result will be a floating point unimplemented exception.

int operation   Destination ⇦ Round (Source 2)

Assembler syntax

    int.ss   rD,rS2
    int.sd   rD,rS2

Exceptions   Floating Point Reserved Operand
                 Floating Point Integer Conversion Overflow
                 Floating Point Unimplemented

int instruction encoding

Triadic

31	26 25	21 20	9 8 7	6 5 4	0
1 0 0 0 0 1	D	0 0 0 0 0 0 1 0 0 1 0 0	T2	0 0	S2

D: Destination register (r0 not allowed)

T2:   Source 2 operand size
              Note: for T2 field,
                    00 - Single precision
                    01 - Double precision

S2:   Source 2 register

Unconditional Jump

The jmp instruction causes an unconditional transfer of program flow from wherever it is to the absolute address contained in the rS2 register. The two least significant bits of that register are masked to force the FIP to an instruction boundary.

There is, however, a familiar variation on this theme. By tagging .n (delayed branch option) to the end of jmp, you can cause the instruction following the jmp.n instruction to execute before the target instruction. There are no exceptions, but there is a warning that you've also seen before. Motorola cautions that to ensure future compatibility, the instruction following the jmp.n instruction should not be a trap, jump, branch, or any other instruction that modifies the instruction pointers. If it were, then you would have a programming error that would go undetected.

The jmp instruction can also be used to return from subroutines. For example:

```
jmp r1
```

You'll recall that the bsr instruction places the return address in register r1 as a hardware convention. (So, for that matter, does the jsr instruction, which is discussed later.) With jmp, you can get back to that return address once the subroutine is complete.

jmp operation   Fetch Instruction Pointer ⇦ Source 2

Assembler syntax

```
jmp     rS2
jmp.n   rS2
```

Exceptions   None

jmp instruction encoding

Triadic

31 26	25 16	15 11	10 9	9 5	4 0
111101	0000000000*	11000	N	00000	S2

* These bits are not decoded, but should be zero to ensure future compatibility

N: 0 - Next sequential instruction not executed

1 - Next sequential instruction executed prior to branching

S2:   Source 2 register

Jump to subroutine

And speaking of subroutines, the jsr instruction helps handle them. It causes an unconditional transfer of program control to the target address contained in the rS2 register. It also saves the return address in register r1. The two least significant bits of the rS2 register are masked, forcing the FIP to an instruction (word) boundary. The return address is the address of the jsr instruction (value of NIP).

Also, there is the familiar .n (delayed branch option), which causes the instruction following the jsr.n instruction to execute before the jump target instruction. When the .n is specified, the return address is the address of the second instruction following the jsr.n instruction. There are no exceptions, but here is the warning seen before. Motorola cautions that, to ensure future compatibility, the instruction following the jmp.n instruction should not be a trap, jump, branch, or any other instruction that modifies the instruction pointers. If it were to be, then you would have a programming error that wouldn't be detected.

jsr operation   FIP ⇦ Source 2
r1 ⇦ NIP (+4 if .n specified)

Assembler syntax

    jsr   rS2
    jsr.n   rS2

Exceptions   None

jsr instruction encoding

Triadic

31	26	25	16	15	11	10	9	5	4	0
111101		0000000000*		11001		N	00000		S2	

*These bits are not decoded, but should be zero to ensure future compatibility

N: 0 - Next sequential instruction not executed
            1 - Next sequential instruction executed prior to branching

S2:   Source 2 register

ld

Load register from memory

Here's a fairly major instruction. The ld instruction reads data from a specified memory location and loads it into a specified destination register. The memory address is contained in the rS1 register. Added to this base is either a zero extended 16-bit immediate index or an unsigned 32-bit word index contained in the rS2 register. The index in the rS2 register can be scaled or unscaled. The destination register is marked "in use" (in the scoreboard register) until the memory fetch completes.

Just by itself, the ld instruction specifies a 32-bit operation. But, you're not confined to that. The .b option specifies signed byte (8 bits) .bu specified unsigned byte, .h specifies signed half word (16 bits), .hu specifies unsigned half word (16 bits), and .d specifies double word (64 bits). For the scaled index modes, the scale factor is determined by the size option of the instruction. Operations that are byte, half word, word, and double word in size define scale factors of 1, 2, 4, and 8, respectively, when the rS2 field is coded within square brackets.

When the MODE bit of the PSR is set, the memory address refers to supervisor memory space. But, when MODE is clear, the memory address refers to the user memory space. The value of the MODE bit is reflected via the DS/$\overline{U}$ P bus signal. The .usr option specifies that the memory access must be to the user address space regardless of the mode bit in the PSR. The .usr option is privileged and you can get at it only in supervisor mode.

Exceptions are recognized between any two memory transactions on the P bus. Therefore, the double word load (ld.d) can encounter a data access exception between word access. Because this requires two separate words to be loaded, there are two memory transactions. It is important to recognize that ld.d is not *atomic*. Although you make it happen thru a single instruction, ld.d can be interrupted. Also, if the destination register is r31 for the ld.d instruction, the most significant word of the data is placed in r31. The least significant word is read from memory, but is not written in r0. You'll recall that r0 always contains zero.

The two bus transactions required for a double word do not lock the P bus. As a result, if your system interfaces the data P bus to multiple CMMUs, the double word load to memory may be interrupted by an alternate memory bus master.

ld operation   Destination Register ⇦ Source Data

Assembler syntax

Unscaled Immediate		**Unscaled**		**Scaled**	
ld.b	rD,rS1,IMM16	ld.b	rD,rS1,rS2	ld.b	rD,rS1[rS2]
ld.bu	rD.rS1,IMM16	ld.bu	rD,rS1,rS2	ld.bu	rD,rS1[rS2]
ld.h	rD,rS1,IMM16	ld.h	rD,rS1,rS2	ld.h	rD,rS1[rS2]
ld.hu	rD,rS1,IMM16	id.hu	rD,rS1,rS2	ld.hu	rD,rS1[rS2]
ld	rD,rS1,IMM16	ld	rD,rS1,rS2	ld	rD,rS1[rS2]
ld.d	rD,rS1,IMM16	ld.d	rD,rS1,rS2	ld.d	rD,rS1[rS2]
		ld.b.usr	rD,rS1,rS2	ld.b.usr	rD,rS1[rS2]
		ld.bu.usr	rD,rS1,rS2	ld.bu.usr	rD,rS1[rS2]
		ld.h.usr	rD,rS1,rS2	ld.h.usr	rD,rS1[rS2]
		ld.hu.usr	rD,rS1,rS2	ld.hu.usr	rD,rS1[rS2]
		ld.usr	rD,rS1,rS2	ld.usr	rD,rS1[rS2]
		ld.d.usr	rD,rS1,rS2	ld.d.usr	rD,rS1[rS2]

Exceptions   Data Access Exception
Misaligned Access Exception (if not masked)
Privilege Violation (.usr option only)

ld instruction encoding

Register Indirect with Zero extended Immediate Index

31	30 29	28 27	26 25 21	20 16	15 0
0 0	P	TY	D	S1	I16

Register Indirect with Index

31 26	25 21	20 16	15 14 13 12	11 10 9	8	7 5	4 0
1 1 1 1 0 1	D	S1	0 0	P	TY	0 U 0 0 0	S2

Register Indirect with Scaled Index

31 26	25 21	20 16	15 14 13 12	11 10 9	8	7 5	4 0
1 1 1 1 0 1	D	S1	0 0	P	TY	1 U 0 0 0	S2

P:	00 - Load unsigned (for half word and byte operations only)
	01 - Load signed
TY:	00 - Double word
	01 - Word
	10 - Half word
	11 - Byte
D:	Destination Register
S1:	Source 1 Register
I16:	16 bit immediate index
U:	0 - Access determined by MODE bit in PSR
	1 - Access user space
S2:	Source 2 register

Load address

The lda instruction creates a memory address from the specified operands. The memory base address is contained in the rS1 register. Added to that is either a zero extended 16-bit immediate index or an unsigned 32-bit word index contained in the rS2 register. The index in the rS2 register can be scaled or unscaled. Either way, the resulting address is placed in rD. However, a word of warning: the address calculated by this instruction isn't checked for alignment relative to the operation type.

The lda instruction by itself, fresh out of the box and with no options to speak of, specifies a 32-bit operation. But, once again, there are lots of options from which to pick. The .b option specifies byte (8 bits), while the .h specifies half word (16 bits), and .d specifies double word (64 bits). For the scaled index modes, the scale factor is determined by the size option of the instruction. Operations that are byte, half word, word, and double word in size define scale factors of 1, 2, 4, and 8 respectively when the rS2 field is specified within square brackets[ ].

lda operation Destination $\hookleftarrow$ Source 1 + Source 2

Assembler syntax

lda.b	rD,rS1,rS2	lda.b	rD,rS1,[rS2]
lda.h	rD,rS1,rS2	lda.h	rD,rS1,[rS2]
lda	rD,rS1,rS2	lda	rD,rS1,[rS2]
lda.d	rD,rS1,rS2	lda.d	rD,rS1,[rS2]

Exceptions None

lda instruction encoding

Register Indirect with Zero extended Immediate Index

31	28 27 26 25	21 20	16 15	0
0 0 1 1	TY	D	S1	I16

Register Indirect with Index

31	26 25	21 20	16 15	12 11 10 9	8	7 5 4	0
1 1 1 1 0 1	D	S1	0 0 1 1	TY	0	0*	0 0 0	S2

* If this bit is set and the instruction is in user mode, a privilege violation occurs.

Register Indirect with Scaled Index

31	26	25	21	20	16	15	12	11 10	9	8	7	5	4	0
1 1 1 1 0 1		D		S1		0 0 1 1		TY	1	0*	0 0 0		S2	

* If this bit is set and the instruction is in user mode, a privilege violation occurs.

TY: 00 - Double word
                 01 - Word
                 10 - Half word
                 11 - Byte

D: Destination Register

S1:   Source 1 Register

I16:   16 bit immediate index

S2:   Source 2 register

Load from control register (privileged instruction)

The ldcr instruction takes the data contained within whatever integer unit control register that happens to be specified by the CRS field of the instruction, and loads it to the general purpose register specified by the destination field.

There is an exception to this one. The integer control registers may only be accessed in the supervisor mode. Try to get to them from user mode, and you'll have a privilege violation.

ldcr operation   Destination Register $\hookleftarrow$ Control Register

Assembler syntax

    ldcr   rD,crS

Exceptions   Privilege Violation

ldcr instruction encoding

Control Register

31	26	25	21	20	16	15	11	10	5	4	0
100000		D		00000*		01000		CRS		00000*	

* These bits are not decoded, but should be assembled as specified for future compatibility.

D: Destination Register
CRS: Control register source

Make bit field

This one, too, will look a bit familiar to you. The mak instruction extracts a bit field from the rS1 register. The width of that field is specified by the W5 field, with its beginning at the least significant bit of the rS1 register. The extracted field is then deposited in the rD register, offset from the least significant bit by an amount specified by the O5 field. mak differs from ext in that any bits outside the field are cleared to zero.

For triadic register addressing, bits $9-5$ and bits $4-0$ of the rS2 register contain the W5 and O5 fields respectively—but the rest of rS2 is simply ignored. Likewise, if the W5 field specifies bits that are actually outside the destination register, then those bits are ignored. The operation of mak is shown here:

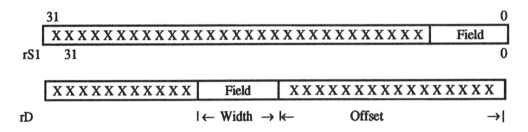

There aren't any exceptions to this one. However, there is an alternative use. If the W5 field contains nothing but zeros—and thus specifies a width of 32 bits—the mak instruction acts as a shift left. The width field selects the entire register, while the offset specifies the number of positions to shift. The low order bits of rD—which, of course, would otherwise be vacant, since everything from rS1 has been shifted to the left—are filled with zeros. The high bits of rS1, meanwhile—which of course have been shifted right out of any available spots in rD—are ignored.

mask operation   Destination $\wedge$ Source 1 $\vee$ IMM16

Assembler syntax

```
mak   rD,rS1,W5<O5>
mak   rD,rS1,rS2
mak   rD,rS1,{<}O5{>}
```

Exceptions   None

mak instruction encoding

Register with 10 bit Immediate

31	26	25	21	20	16	15	10	9	5	4	0
1 1 1 1 0 0		D		S1		1 0 1 0 0 0		W5		O5	

Triadic

31	26	25	21	20	16	15	5	4	0
1 1 1 1 0 1		D		S1		1 0 1 0 0 0 0 0 0 0 0		S2	

D:	Destination
S1:	Source 1 register
W5:	5 bit unsigned integer indicating bit field width (0 = 32 bits)
O5:	5 bit unsigned integer indicating bit field offset
S2:	Source 2 register

mask

Logical mask immediate

The mask instruction takes the lower 16 bits of the rS1 register and logically ANDs them with the unsigned 16-bit immediate value. In addition, it clears the upper 16 bits of the destination register. The result is then deposited in the destination register, rD. mask differs from and in that the non-addressed 16 bits are cleared rather than being copied unchanged.

You have an option. If you tag .u (for "upper word") on the end of the mask, the upper 16 bits of the rS1 register will be ANDed, while the lower 16 bits of the destination register will be cleared. Again, the result is stored in the rD register.

There are no exceptions.

mask operation   Destination ⇦ Source 1 ∧ IMM16

Assembler syntax

    mask   rD,rS1,IMM16
    mask.u rD,rS1,IMM16

Exceptions   None

mask instruction encoding

Register with 16 bit Immediate

31	27	26	25	21	20	16	15	0
0 1 0 0 1		U	D		S1		IMM16	

U:	0 - Apply IMM16 to bits 15-0 of S1
	1 - Apply IMM16 to bits 31-16 of S1
D:	Destination
S1:	Source 1 register
IMM16:	16 bit unsigned immediate operand

Integer multiply

The mul instruction takes the data in the rS1 register and multiplies it by either the data in rS2, or by the unsigned, zero extended 16-bit immediate value. The least significant 32 bits of the product are then stored in the rD register.

There is also an exception. If mul attempts to execute when the FPU isn't on, the result will be a floating point unimplemented exception.

mul operation   Destination ⇦ Source 1 × Source 2

Assembler syntax

        mul   rD,rS1,rS2
        mul   rD,rS1,IMM16

Exceptions   Floating Point Unimplemented

mul instruction encoding

Register with 16 bit Immediate

31	26 25	21 20	16 15	0
0 1 1 0 1 1	D	S1	IMM16	

Triadic Addressing

31	26 25	21 20	16 15	10 9	8 7	5 4	0
1 1 1 1 0 1	D	S1	0 1 1 0 1 1	0 0*	0 0 0	S2	

* These bits are not decoded, but should be assembled as specified for future compatibility.

D:	Destination
S1:	Source 1 register
S2:	Source 2 register
IMM16:	16 bit unsigned Immediate value

nint

Floating point round to nearest integer

The nint instruction is nothing if not straightforward. It takes the floating point number contained in rS2 and converts it into an integer using the IEEE 754 round-to-nearest rounding method, and then drops the result into whatever destination register that you'd care to specify, so long as it isn't r0. You can also have the rS2 operand be either single- or double-precision.

There are three exceptions you're likely to meet with nint. First, if you were to specify r0 as the destination register, or if nint attempts to execute when the FPU is out of commission, there would be a floating point unimplemented exception. Further, if the rS2 operand exponent is greater than or equal to 30, there would be a floating point overflow exception. And, finally, if nint discovers a reserved operand in rS2, there would be a floating point reserved operand exception.

nint operation   Destination ⇦ Round-to-Nearest (Source 2)

Assembler syntax

    nint.ss   rD,rS2
    nint.sd   rD,rS2

Exceptions   Floating Point Reserved Operand
                  Floating Point Integer Conversion Overflow
                  Floating Point Unimplemented

nint instruction encoding

Triadic

31	26 25	21 20	9 8 7	6 5 4	0
100001	D	000000101000	T2	0 0	S2

D: Destination register (r0 not allowed)
T2:   Source 2 operand size
                 Note: for T2 field,
                      00 - Single precision
                      01 - Double precision
S2:   Source 2 register

Logical OR

When it is used via triadic register addressing, the or instruction causes the contents of the rS1 register to logically OR with the contents of rS2. The result is then stored in the destination register. If, however, the .c (for complement) option is tagged onto the end of or, then the source 2 operand is complemented before being ORed.

On the other hand, when the or instruction is used with immediate addressing, the contents of the rS1 register are ORed with the unsigned 16-bit immediate operand, and the upper 16 bits of the rS1 are copied unchanged to rD. If the .u (upper word) option is specified, then the upper 16 bits of the source 1 operand are ORed with the immediate operand, and the lower 16 bits of rS1 are copied unchanged to rD. Again, the result is stored in rD.

or operation   Destination ⇦Source 1 ∨ Source 2

Assembler syntax

  or rD,rS1,rS2
  or.c rD,rS1,rS2
  or rD,rS1,IMM16
  or.u rD,rS1,IMM16

Exceptions   None

or instruction encoding

Register with 16 bit Immediate

31	27 26 25	21 20	16 15	0
0 1 0 1 1	U	D	S1	IMM16

Triadic Addressing

31	26 25	21 20	16 15	11 10 9	5 4	0
1 1 1 1 0 1	D	S1	0 1 0 1 1	C 0 0 0 0 0	S2

U: 0 - OR IMM16 to bits 15-0 of S1

     1 - OR IMM16 to bits 31-16 of S1

D: Destination

S1:   Source 1 register

S2:   Source 2 register

IMM16:   16 bit unsigned Immediate value

C: 0 - Second operand not complemented prior to operation

            1 - Second operand complemented prior to operation

Rotate register

The rot instruction rotates the bits in the rS1 register to the right by the number of bits specified in the O5 field. Simply put, this means that bit 31 is moved to bit 0's old position. Bit 0 is moved to bit 1's old position, . . . etc. The result is placed in the rD register.

For triadic register addressing, the five low-order bits of the data contained in the rS2 register are used as the O5 field—which brings up a matter of some concern. Bits 5 through 9 of the rS2 should be zero to guarantee future compatibility. In any case, the other bits are ignored.

rot operation   Destination ⟵ Source 1 rotated by O5

Assembler syntax

    rot   rD,rS1,<O5>
    rot   rD,rS1,rS2

Exceptions   None

rot instruction encoding

Register with 10 bit Immediate

31	26	25	21	20	16	15	10	9	5	4	0
111100		D		S1		101010		00000*		O5	

* These bits are not decoded, but should be as shown to ensure future compatibility.

Triadic

31	26	25	21	20	16	15	5	4	0
111101		D		S1		10101000000		S2	

D: Destination
S1:   Source 1 register
O5:   5 bit unsigned integer indicating bit field offset
S2:   Source 2 register

rte

Return from exception (privileged instruction)

Once there is an exception, and you have gone off and dealt with it via exception processing, there has to be some mechanism to get you back into regular processing mode. The rte instruction is that mechanism. It provides an orderly termination of exception processing—exception time and shadow registers are restored into their appropriate execution units and pipelines, while instruction execution resumes in the context defined by the SNIP, SFIP, EPSR, and SSBR registers.

The rte instruction "synchronizes" the 88100—meaning that it allows all the previous operations to complete whatever it is they're doing (thus neatly clearing the scoreboard register and data unit pipe) before it executes.

There is one thing to keep in mind about rte. It is a "privileged" instruction. It should be executed only from supervisor mode. If it occurs in the user mode, then there will be a privilege violation exception.

rte operations   PSR ⇦ EPSR
                     NIP ⇦ SNIP
                     FIP ⇦ SFIP
                     SB ⇦ SSBR

Assembler syntax

   rte

Exceptions   Privilege Violation

rte instruction encoding

Triadic

31	26	25	16	15	5	4	0
111101		0000000000*		11111100000		00000*	

* These bits are not decoded, but should be as shown to ensure future compatibility.

Set bit field

The set instruction reads the rS1 register and inserts a field of ones, of width W5, into the data. The offset from bit zero is specified by the O5 field. The result of all this is placed in the rD register.

Say that W5 contains 5 and O5 contains 16. The destination register will contain the rS1 operand with a field of five ones in bit 16 through bit 20. For triadic register addressing, meanwhile, bits 9−5 and bits 4−0 of rS2 are used for the W5 and O5 fields. If the W5 field specifies bits outside the destination register, those bits are ignored.

set operation   Destination ⭠ (Source 1 ∨ (Bit Field of all 1's))

Assembler syntax

        set   rD,rS1,W5 < 5 >
        set   rD,rS1,rS2
        set   rD,rS1,{ < }O5{ > }

Exceptions   None

set instruction encoding

Register with 10 bit Immediate

31	26	25	21	20	16	15	10	9	5	4	0
1 1 1 1 0 0		D		S1		1 0 0 0 1 0		W5		O5	

Triadic

31	26	25	21	20	16	15	5	4	0
1 1 1 1 0 1		D		S1		1 0 0 0 1 0 0 0 0 0		S2	

D:	Destination
S1:	Source 1 register
W5:	5 bit unsigned integer indicating bit field width (0 = 32 bits)
O5:	5 bit unsigned integer indicating bit field offset
S2:	Source 2 register

Store register to memory

The st instruction takes the contents of rD, and writes it to whatever memory location you'd care to specify. rS1 contains the memory base address. To that base address, st adds either a zero extended 16-bit immediate index or the signed 32-bit word index contained in the rS2 register. The index in the rS2 register can be scaled or unscaled.

There are several options with this one. Normally, the st instruction specifies a 32-bit operation. But, tagging the .b option on the end specifies byte (8 bits). Meanwhile, .h specifies half word (16 bits) and .d specifies double word (64 bits, registers rD and rD+1). For the scaled index modes, the scale factor is determined by the size option of the instructions. Operations that are byte, half word, word, and double word in size define scale factors of 1, 2, 4, and 8 when rS2 is specified within square brackets.

Because st is an instruction having to do with memory, it of course has two ranges. It addresses either the supervisor memory space, or the user memory space. When the MODE bit of the PSR is set, the memory address refers to supervisor memory space. When the MODE bit is clear, then the memory address is to the user memory space. Either way, the MODE bit is reflected via the DS/$\overline{U}$ P bus signal. However, there is a way of specifying that the system be in user memory space regardless of MODE. Tagging .usr on to the end of the st instruction, will specify user address space. .usr option is privileged and is only available in supervisor mode.

And st has its share of exceptions—three, to be precise. And by the way, exceptions are recognized between any two memory transactions on the P bus. As a consequence, the double word instruction—that is, st.d—can run into a data access exception between word accesses. Moreover, if the source register for st.d is r31, the data is taken from r31 and r0, because r31+1 maps to r0—which is OK if you wanted zero there. The two bus transactions required for a double word store do not lock the P bus. Therefore, in a system that interfaces the data P bus to CMMUs, the double word store to memory might be interrupted by an alternate memory bus master. Finally, use of the .usr option, in user mode, will cause a privilege violation.

st operation   Memory Location ⟻ Source Register (specified as rD)

Assembler syntax

Unscaled Immediate	Unscaled		Scaled	
st.b rD,rS1,IMM16	st.b	rD,rS1,rS2	st.b	rD,rS1[rS2]

st.h	rD,rS1,IMM16	st.h	rD,rS1,rS2	st.h	rD,rS1[rS2]
st	rD,rS1,IMM16	st	rD,rS1,rS2	st	rD,rS1[rS2]
st.d	rD,rS1,IMM16	st.d	rD,rS1,rS2	st.d	rD,rS1[rS2]
		st.b.usr	rD,rS1,rS2	st.b.usr	rD,rS1[rS2]
		st.h.usr	rD,rS1,rS2	st.h.usr	rD,rS1[rS2]
		st.usr	rD,rS1,rS2	st.usr	rD,rS1[rS2]
		st.d.usr	rD,rS1,rS2	st.d.usr	rD,rS1[rS2]

Exceptions   Data Access Exception
Misaligned Access Exception (if not masked)
Privilege Violation (.usr option only)

st instruction encoding

Register Indirect with Zero extended Immediate Index

31	28 27	26 25	21 20	16 15	0
0 0 1 0	TY	D	S1	I16	

Register Indirect with Index

31	26 25	21 20	16 15	12 11 10 9	8 7	5 4	0
1 1 1 1 0 1	D	S1	0 0 1 0	TY 0 U	0 0 0	S2	

Register Indirect with Scaled Index

31	26 25	21 20	16 15	12 11 10 9	8 7	5 4	0
1 1 1 1 0 1	D	S1	0 0 1 0	TY 1 U	0 0 0	S2	

D: For **st**, this field specifies the data source to be stored

TY: 00 - Double word

01 - Word

10 - Half word

11 - Byte

S1:   Source 1 Register

I16:   16 bit immediate index

U: 0 - Access determined by MODE bit in PSR

                   1 - Access user space

S2:   Source 2 register

Store to control register

The stcr instruction takes the data contained in whatever general purpose register is specified by the S1 field of the instruction and stores it to the integer unit control register specified by the CRD field.

There is an exception to this one—specifically, privilege violation. This is a privileged instruction. Because the integer unit control registers can be accessed only in supervisor mode, this instruction can only be performed from supervisor mode.

stcr operation   Control Register ⇦ Source Register

Assembler syntax

    stcr   rS1,crD

Exceptions   Privilege Violation

stcr instruction encoding

Control Register

31 26	25 21	20 16	15 11	10 5	4 0
1 0 0 0 0 0	0 0 0 0 0*	S1	1 0 0 0 0	CRD	S2

*These bits are not decoded, but should be assembled as specified for future compatibility.

S1:   Source 1 register
CRD: Control register destination
S2:   Source 2 register
                 Note: S1 and S2 must contain the same value

sub

Integer subtract

The sub instruction subtracts the data contained in the rS2 register from the data contained in the rS1 register, or it subtracts an unsigned zero extended 16-bit immediate operand from rS1. Either way, the result is placed in the rD register.

But, there are options on this one. You can do subtract with borrow operations via the use of the carry bit. A clear carry bit indicates a borrow, a set carry bit indicates no borrow. Subtraction is done by adding the one's complement of the source 2 operand and either a constant one or the carry bit to the source 1 operand. All 32 bits of the operand participate in the addition. The generated carry bit can also be written to the PSR.

There is an exception to this instruction. If the carry out of the sign bit position and the carry into the sign bit are not the same, you will get an overflow exception.

You can also use the sub instruction to implement a "set carry bit" operation. Just write:

```
sub.co r0,r0,r0
```

The instruction subtracts zero from zero (recall that r0 contains 0 by hardware convention), resulting in a one carry bit. Because the instruction specifies r0 as the destination and it is read-only, no register contents are altered as the result.

sub operation   Destination ⇦ Source 1 − Source 2

Assembler syntax

sub	rD,rS1,rS2	subtract without borrow
sub.ci	rD,rS1,rS2	subtract and use borrow in
sub.co	rD,rS1,rS2	subtract and propagate borrow out
sub.cio	rD,rS1,rS2	subtract and propagate borrow in and out
sub	rD,rS1,IMM16	subtract immediate (without borrow)

Exceptions Integer overflow

sub instruction encoding

Register with 16 bit Immediate

31	26	25	21	20	16	15	0
0 1 1 1 0 1		D		S1		IMM16	

Triadic Addressing

31	26	25	21	20	16	15	10	9	8	7	5	4	0
1 1 1 1 0 1		D		S1		0 1 1 1 0 1		I	O	0 0 0		S2	

D:	Destination
S1:	Source 1 register
S2:	Source 2 register
IMM16:	16 bit unsigned Immediate value
I:	0 - Disable Carry In
	1 - Add Carry to result
O:	0 - Disable Carry out
	1 - Generate Carry

subu

Unsigned integer subtract

The subu instruction takes the data contained in the rS2 register and subtracts it from the data contained in the rS1 register. The result is then
placed in the rD register. Just as with sub, the carry bit can be used as an
option to perform subtract with borrow operations.

Subtraction is performed by adding the one's complement of the
source 2 operand and either a constant one or the carry bit to the source 1
operand. All 32 bits of the operand participate in the addition. The generated carry bit can optionally be written to the PSR.

subu operation   Destination ⟻ Source 1 − Source 2

Assembler syntax

subu	rD,rS1,rS2	unsigned subtract without borrow
subu.ci	rD,rS1,rS2	unsigned subtract and use borrow in
subu.co	rD,rS1,rS2	unsigned subtract and propagate borrow out
subu.cio	rD,rS1,rS2	unsigned subtract and propagate borrow in and out
subu	rD,rS1,IMM16	unsigned subtract immediate (without borrow)

Exceptions   None

subu instruction encoding

Register with 16 bit Immediate

31	26 25	21 20	16 15	0
0 1 1 0 0 1	D	S1	IMM16	

Triadic Addressing

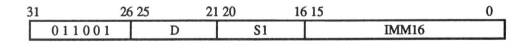

31	26 25	21 20	16 15	10 9	8 7	5 4	0
1 1 1 1 0 1	D	S1	0 1 1 0 0 1	I	O	0 0 0	S2

D:	Destination
S1:	Source 1 register
S2:	Source 2 register
IMM16:	16 bit unsigned Immediate value
I:	0 - Disable Carry In
	1 - Add Carry to result
O:	0 - Disable Carry out
	1 - Generate Carry

Trap on bit clear

This instruction examines the bit in the rS1 register specified by the B5 field. If that bit is clear, then the 88K realizes that it has a trap on its hands, and begins exception processing. The exception vector address is formed by concatenating the upper 20 bits of the vector base register with the 9-bit VEC9 field, followed by a 3-bit field of zeros. (You'll recall the VEC9 is an index into the exception handlers.)

When the tb0 instruction executes, it effectively synchronizes the 88100. That is, everything that it was trying to do before—all the previous operations—are allowed to complete before tb0 executes. The scoreboard register and data unit are cleared. As you will see in chapter 9 on exceptions, you will use this synchronizing capability, via a *trap not taken* used simply to perform synchronization.

There is an exception possible. When the tb0 instruction is executed in the user mode, a trap to a hardware vector (vectors 0 through 127) causes a privilege violation exception whether or not the trap condition was met.

tb0 operation   If bit B5 is clear: Trap VEC9

Assembler syntax

    tb0   B5,rS1,VEC9

Exceptions   Trap VEC9
                  Privilege Violation

tb0 instruction encoding

Triadic Addressing

31 26	25 21	20 16	15 9	8 0
1 1 1 1 0 0	B5	S1	1 1 0 1 0 0 0	VEC9

B5:   5 bit unsigned integer indicating a bit number
S1:   Source 1 register
VEC9:   Vector number in the vector table

Trap on bit set

This is exactly like tb0, except that it responds to a set bit instead of a clear one.

As before, the tb1 instruction examines the bit in the rS1 register specified by the B5 field. If that specified bit is set, then the 88K begins exception processing. The exception vector address is formed by concatenating the upper 20 bits of the vector base register with the 9-bit VEC9 field, followed by a 3-bit field of zeros.

When the tb1 instruction executes, it effectively synchronizes the 88100. That is, everything that it was trying to do before—all the previous operations—are allowed to complete before tb1 executes. The scoreboard register and data unit are cleared.

And, there is an exception. When the tb1 instruction is executed in the user mode, a trap to a hardware vector (vectors 0 through 127) causes a privilege violation exception whether or not the trap condition was met.

tb1 operation   If bit B5 is set: Trap VEC9

Assembler syntax

    tb1   B5,rS1,VEC9

Exceptions   Trap VEC9
                 Privilege Violation

tb1 instruction encoding

Triadic Addressing

31	26	25	21	20	16	15	9	8	0
1 1 1 1 0 0		B5		S1		1 1 0 1 1 0 0		VEC9	

B5:   5 bit unsigned integer indicating a bit number
S1:   Source 1 register
VEC9:   Vector number in the vector table

tbnd

Trap on bounds check

The tbnd instruction causes the data in the rS1 register to be compared either with the data in the rS2 register, or with the zero extended 16-bit immediate operand using unsigned arithmetic. If the source 1 operand is larger (i.e., it is out-of-bounds), then a bounds check trap is taken and the 88K proceeds to exception processing.

And, by definition, here is an exception. Specifically, it's the bounds check exception, which makes sense because the whole point of the instruction is to initialize exception processing in response to an operand being out of bounds.

There is, however, one fact of which you have to be aware. Even though this is a conditional trap instruction, and even though all the other conditional trap type instructions met here so far synchronize the processor—this one doesn't. The tbnd does not clear the 88100 prior to execution.

tbnd operations   If unsigned (S1) > (S2): Trap (bounds check vector)
If unsigned (S1) > (IMM16): Trap (bounds check
vector)

Assembler syntax

    tbnd   rS1,rS2
    tbnd   rS1,IMM16

Exceptions   Bounds Check

tbnd instruction encoding

Register with 16 bit Immediate

31	26	25	21	20	16	15	0
111110		00000*		S1		IMM16	

Triadic

31	26	25	21	20	16	15	5	4	0
111101		00000*		S1		11111000000		S2	

* These bits are not decoded, but should be zero to ensure future compatibility

S1:	Source 1 Register
IMM16:	16 bit zero extended Immediate value
S2:	Source 2 register

tcnd

Conditional trap

The tcnd instruction is a truth trapper. It looks at the data contained in rS1 to discover the value of the sign bit (the most significant bit) and the zero bit (logical NORing of bits $30-0$). These two bits are then concatenated to form an index into the M5 field of the instruction. If the indexed bit is set, then off you go into exception processing. Note: the term "zero bit" differs from "zeroth bit." The *zero bit* is a special CPU bit that, simply put, tells whether or not any of the bits $30-0$ are 1. If any are 1, the zero bit will equal 1; if all are zero, the zero bit will equal zero.

The tcnd instruction allows traps on such conditions as zero, negative, positive, greater than or equal to zero, and less than or equal to zero, without proceeding the trap instruction by a compare instruction. The exception vector address is formed by concatenating the upper 20 bits of the vector base register with the 9-bit VEC9 field followed by a 3-bit field of zeros. The values for the M5 field are:

Condition	25	24	23	22	21
eq0 (equals zero)	0	0	0	1	0
ne0 (not equal to zero)	0	1	1	0	1
gt0 (greater than zero)	0	0	0	0	1
lt0 (less than zero)	0	1	1	0	0
ge0 (greater than/equal to zero)	0	0	0	1	1
le0 (less than/equal to zero)	0	1	1	1	0

As with all the other conditional traps (save tbnd), this one synchronizes the 88100.

There is an exception. In user mode, a trap to a hardware vector (vectors zero through 127) causes a privilege violation exception whether or not the trap condition is met.

tcnd operation   If Condition True: Trap

Assembler syntax

    tcnd   *cc*,rS1,VEC9 (*cc* stands for one of the M5 comparisons
                              codes above)

    tcnd   M5,rS1,VEC9

Exceptions   VEC9
Privilege Violation

tcnd instruction encoding

Register with 16 bit Displacement

31	26	25	21	20	16	15	9	8	0
1 1 1 1 0 0		M5		S1		1 1 1 0 1 0 0		VEC9	

M5:   5 bit field for condition to be matched

Bit 25 - Reserved, must be zero

Bit 24 - Maximum negative number

Bit 23 - Less than zero

Bit 22 - Equal to zero

Bit 21 - Greater than zero

S1:   Source 1 register

VEC9:   Vector number in the vector table

trnc

Truncate floating point to integer

The trnc instructions take the single- or double-precision number specified by the rS2 register and converts it to a 32-bit integer using the IEEE 754 round-to-zero rounding method. The result is then placed in the rD register. .ss instructs trnc to convert a single-precision floating point number to an integer, and .sd to convert a double-precison to integer.

There are three exceptions possible. If the rS2 operand exponent is greater than or equal to 30, the floating point integer conversion overflow exception is taken. If reserved operands turn up someplace, then a floating point reserved operand exception occurs. If r0 is specified as the destination register, or if trnc attempts to execute while the FPU is out of action, then a floating point unimplemented exception is taken.

trnc operation   Destination ⇦ Truncate (Source 2)

Assembler syntax

    trnc.ss
    trnc.sd

Exceptions   Floating Point Reserved Operand
Floating Point Integer Conversion Overflow
Floating Point Unimplemented

trnc instruction encoding

Control Register

31	26 25	21 20	16 15	9 8 7	6 5 4	0
1 0 0 0 0 1	D	0 0 0 0 0	0 1 0 1 1 0 0	T2	0 0	S2

D: Destination register (r0 not allowed)
T2:   Source 2 operand size
              Note: for T2 field,
                    00 - Single precision
                    01 - Double precision
S2:   Source 2 register

Exchange control register

The xcr instruction takes the data in whichever general purpose register is specified by rS1 and copies that data into the control register specified by the Control Register Source and Destination (CRS/D) field. Meanwhile, it takes the contents of the specified control register and loads them into the general purpose register specified by the D field.

xcr is a privileged instruction. If it tries to execute in user mode, you will have a privilege violation.

xcr operations   (temp) ⇦ Source 1
Destination Register ⇦ Control Register
Control Register ⇦ (temp)

Assembler syntax

    xcr   rD,rS1,crS/D

Exceptions   Privilege Violation

xcr instruction encoding

Control Register

31	26	25	21	20	16	15	11	10	5	4	0
1 0 0 0 0 0		D		S1		1 1 0 0 0	CRS/D		S2		

D: Destination register
S1:   Source 1 register
CRS/D: Control register source and destination
S2:   Source 2 register
            Note: S1 and S2 must contain the same value

xmem

Exchange register with memory

This instruction takes the contents of the destination register and exchanges them with some memory location. The rS1 register contains the memory base address to be used. Added to that base is either a zero extended 16-bit immediate index or the unsigned 32-bit word index contained in the rS2 register. The index in the rS2 register can be scaled or unscaled. The contents of the rD register are exchanged (load and store) with the memory location. This destination register is marked "in use" (in the scoreboard register) until the memory fetch completes.

Also, a quick aside on this one. It is *atomic*—in the original Greek meaning of the word. (You'll recall our little lecture on quantum physics.) The memory access generated for the load and store are indivisible. In other words, once this instruction gets started, nothing stops it. It cannot be interrupted by external interrupts, bus arbitration, or imprecise exceptions. The atomicity of xmem is the reason for using it. It is faster to do a load and store, but you can't control the bus that way.

The only potential interruption occurs if the store causes a data access exception after the load has already been performed. After the software handles the exception, the xmem instruction must be executed again to ensure operand consistency.

Moreover, xmem synchronizes the 88100. All previous operations are allowed to complete (effectively clearing the scoreboard register and data unit pipeline) before xmem itself executes.

The xmem instruction with no options specifies a 32-bit operation. However, stick a .bu on its end and you'll specify an unsigned byte (8 bits).

For scaled index modes, the scale factor is determined by the size option of the instruction. Operations that are byte and word in size define scale factors of one and four respectively, when the rS2 field is specified within square brackets—to wit, [ ].

Which memory space is being dealt with here is defined by the value of bit 31—the MODE bit, in the PSR. When it's set, the memory address is in supervisor memory space. When it's clear, the address is in user space. Whether MODE is set or clear is reflected by the DS/$\overline{\text{U}}$ P bus signal. And, as usual, there are ways of changing this. The .usr option specifies that the memory address must be in user space, regardless of what the MODE is or isn't. And, as usual, .usr is itself available only in supervisor mode.

The xmem instruction asserts the $\overline{\text{DLOCK}}$ (bus lock) signal on the P bus to prevent the memory accesses from being interrupted. Bus locking with the xmem instruction is intended for semaphore operations.

xmem operations   (temp) ⇦ Source Register
                      Source Register ⇦ Destination
                      Destination ⇦ (temp)

Assembler syntax

Unscaled Immediate		**Unscaled**		**Scaled**	
xmem.bu	rD,rS1,IMM16	xmem.bu	rD,rS1,rS2	xmem.bu	rD,rS1,[rS2]
xmem	rD,rS1,IMM16	xmem	rD,rS1,rS2	xmem	rD,rS1,[rS2]
		xmem.bu.usr	rD,rS1,rS2	xmem.bu.usr	rD,rS1,[rS2]
		xmem.usr	rD,rS1,rS2	xmem.usr	rD,rS1,[rS2]

Exceptions   Data Access Exception
                Misaligned Access Exception (if not masked)
                Privilege Violation (.usr option only)

Note that, although the current 88000 allows I16 addressing with xmem, this will not be allowed in future versions.

xmem instruction encoding

Register Indirect with Zero extended Immediate Index

31	28 27 26 25	21 20	16 15	0
0 0 0 0	TY	D	S1	I16

Register Indirect with Index

31	26 25	21 20	16 15	12 11 10 9	8	7 5 4	0
1 1 1 1 0 1	D	S1	0 0 0 0	TY 0	U	0 0 0	S2

Register Indirect with Scaled Index

31	26 25	21 20	16 15	12 11 10 9	8	7 5 4	0
1 1 1 1 0 1	D	S1	0 0 0 0	TY 1	U	0 0 0	S2

TY: 00 - Byte
          01 - Word

D:	Destination Register
S1:	Source 1 Register
I16:	16 bit immediate index
S2:	Source 2 register
U:	0 - Access determined by MODE bit in PSR
	1 - Access user space

Logical exclusive OR

The xor instruction has a couple of uses. When it is used via triadic register addressing, it takes the contents of the rS1 register and XORs (XOR stands for Exclusive OR) them with the contents of the rS2 register. The result is then stored in the rD register.

If the .c, for complement, option is used, the source 2 operand is complemented before being XORed. However, when xor is used with immediate addressing, the contents of the rS1 register are logically XORed with the unsigned 16-bit immediate operand, and the upper 16 bits of the rS1 are copied unchanged to rD. If the .u (upper word) option is specified, then the upper 16 bits of the source 1 operand are XORed, and the lower 16 bits of rS1 are copied unchanged to rD. The result is stored into the rD register.

xor operation   Destination $\Leftarrow$ Source 1 $\oplus$ Source 2

Assembler syntax

```
xor     rD,rS1,rS2
xor.c   rD,rS1,rS2
xor     rD,rS1,IMM16
xor.u   rD,rS1,IMM16
```

Exceptions   None

xor instruction encoding

Register with 16 bit Immediate

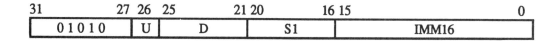

31	27 26	25	21 20	16 15	0
0 1 0 1 0	U	D	S1	IMM16	

Triadic Addressing

31	26 25	21 20	16 15	11 10 9	5 4	0
1 1 1 1 0 1	D	S1	0 1 0 1 0 0	C	0 0 0 0 0	S2

D: Destination
S1:   Source 1 register

S2:	Source 2 register
IMM16:	16 bit unsigned Immediate value
U:	0 - XOR IMM16 to bits 15-0 of S1
	1 - XOR IMM16 to bits 31-16 of S1
C:	0 - S2 not complemented before operation
	1 - S2 complemented before operation

Instruction summaries

This chapter is really a reference rather than light before-bed reading. On the next page is an organization of all the 88K's instructions in various ways to make looking them up simpler, reprinted with permission of Motorola, Inc.

They are first listed by operation type.

Logical instructions

Mnemonic	Encoding																		

Mnemonic	31				27	26	25		21	20		16	15							0
and	0	1	0	0	0	U		D			S1					IMM16				
mask	0	1	0	0	1	U		D			S1					IMM16				
xor	0	1	0	1	0	U		D			S1					IMM16				
or	0	1	0	1	1	U		D			S1					IMM16				

Mnemonic	31					26	25		21	20		16	15				11	10	9				5	4		0
and	1	1	1	1	0	1		D			S1		0	1	0	0	0	C	0	0	0	0	0		S2	
xor	1	1	1	1	0	1		D			S1		0	1	0	1	0	C	0	0	0	0	0		S2	
or	1	1	1	1	0	1		D			S1		0	1	0	1	1	C	0	0	0	0	0		S2	

U: 0 – Apply IMM16 to Bits 15–0 of S1
          1 – Apply IMM16 to Bits 31–16 of S1
D: Destination Register
S1:   Source 1 Register
IMM16: 16-bit Unsigned Immediate Operand
C: 0 – Second operand not complemented before the operation
          1 – Second operand complemented before the operation
S2:   Source 2 Register

Integer instructions

Mnemonic	Encoding			
	31 26	25 21	20 16	15 0
addu	0 1 1 0 0 0	D	S1	IMM16
subu	0 1 1 0 0 1	D	S1	IMM16
divu	0 1 1 0 1 0	D	S1	IMM16
mul	0 1 1 0 1 1	D	S1	IMM16
add	0 1 1 1 0 0	D	S1	IMM16
sub	0 1 1 1 0 1	D	S1	IMM16
div	0 1 1 1 1 0	D	S1	IMM16
cmp	0 1 1 1 1 1	D	S1	IMM16

Mnemonic	Encoding							
	31 26	25 21	20 16	15 10	9	8	7 5	4 0
addu	1 1 1 1 0 1	D	S1	0 1 1 0 0 0	I	O	0 0 0	S2
subu	1 1 1 1 0 1	D	S1	0 1 1 0 0 1	I	O	0 0 0	S2
divu	1 1 1 1 0 1	D	S1	0 1 1 0 1 0	0	0*	0 0 0	S2
mul	1 1 1 1 0 1	D	S1	0 1 1 0 1 1	0	0*	0 0 0	S2
add	1 1 1 1 0 1	D	S1	0 1 1 1 0 0	I	O	0 0 0	S2
sub	1 1 1 1 0 1	D	S1	0 1 1 1 0 1	I	O	0 0 0	S2
div	1 1 1 1 0 1	D	S1	0 1 1 1 1 0	0	0*	0 0 0	S2
cmp	1 1 1 1 0 1	D	S1	0 1 1 1 1 1	0	0*	0 0 0	S2

D: Destination Register
S1:   Source 1 Register
IMM16: 16-bit Unsigned Immediate Operand
I: 0 – Disable Carry In   1 – Add Carry to Result
O: 0 – Disable Carry Out   1 – Generate Carry
S2:   Source 2 Register
*   The MC88100 does not decode these bits; however, assemble as shown to guarantee compatibility with future implementations.

Floating point unit instructions

Mnemonic	Encoding							
	31 ... 26	25 ... 21	20 ... 16	15 ... 11	10 9	8 7	6 5 4	0
fmul	1 0 0 0 0 1	D	S1	0 0 0 0 0	T1	T2	TD	S2
flt	1 0 0 0 0 1	D	0 0 0 0 0	0 0 1 0 0	0 0	0 0	TD	S2
fadd	1 0 0 0 0 1	D	S1	0 0 1 0 1	T1	T2	TD	S2
fsub	1 0 0 0 0 1	D	S1	0 0 1 1 0	T1	T2	TD	S2
fcmp	1 0 0 0 0 1	D	S1	0 0 1 1 1	T1	T2	0 0	S2
int	1 0 0 0 0 1	D	0 0 0 0 0	0 1 0 0 1	0 0	T2	0 0	S2
nint	1 0 0 0 0 1	D	0 0 0 0 0	0 1 0 1 0	0 0	T2	0 0	S2
trnc	1 0 0 0 0 1	D	0 0 0 0 0	0 1 0 1 1	0 0	T2	0 0	S2
fdiv	1 0 0 0 0 1	D	S1	0 1 1 1 0	T1	T2	TD	S2

Mnemonic	31 ... 26	25 ... 21	20 ... 16	15 ... 11	10 ... 5	4 ... 0
fldcr	1 0 0 0 0 0	D	0 0 0 0 0*	0 1 0 0 1	FCRS	0 0 0 0 0*
fstcr	1 0 0 0 0 0	0 0 0 0 0*	S1	1 0 0 0 1	FCRD	S2
fxcr	1 0 0 0 0 0	D	S1	1 1 0 0 1	FCRS/D	S2

D: Destination Register (r0 allowed for **fldcr**, **fstcr**, and **fxcr** only)
S1:   Source 1 Register
T1:   Source 1 Operand Size
T2:   Source 2 Operand Size
TD: Destination Operand Size
      Note: For the T1, T2, and TD Fields:
          00 – Single Precision
          01 – Double Precision
S2:   Source 2 Register
FCRS: Floating-Point Control Register Source
FCRD: Floating-Point Control Destination Register
FCRS/D: Floating-Point Control Source/Destination
*   The MC88100 does not decode these bits; however, assemble as shown to guarantee compatibility with future implementation.

Bit field instructions

Mnemonic	Encoding					
	31 26	25 21	20 16	15 10	9 5	4 0
clr	1 1 1 1 0 0	D	S1	1 0 0 0 0 0	W5	O5
set	1 1 1 1 0 0	D	S1	1 0 0 0 1 0	W5	O5
ext	1 1 1 1 0 0	D	S1	1 0 0 1 0 0	W5	O5
extu	1 1 1 1 0 0	D	S1	1 0 0 1 1 0	W5	O5
mak	1 1 1 1 0 0	D	S1	1 0 1 0 0 0	W5	O5
rot	1 1 1 1 0 0	D	S1	1 0 1 0 1 0	0 0 0 0 0*	O5

Mnemonic	31 26	25 21	20 16	15 5	4 0
clr	1 1 1 1 0 1	D	S1	1 0 0 0 0 0 0 0 0 0 0	S2
set	1 1 1 1 0 1	D	S1	1 0 0 0 1 0 0 0 0 0 0	S2
ext	1 1 1 1 0 1	D	S1	1 0 0 1 0 0 0 0 0 0 0	S2
extu	1 1 1 1 0 1	D	S1	1 0 0 1 1 0 0 0 0 0 0	S2
mak	1 1 1 1 0 1	D	S1	1 0 1 0 0 0 0 0 0 0 0	S2
rot	1 1 1 1 0 1	D	S1	1 0 1 0 1 0 0 0 0 0 0	S2

Mnemonic	31 26	25 21	20 16	15 5	4 0
ff1	1 1 1 1 0 1	D	0 0 0 0 0*	1 1 1 0 1 0 0 0 0 0 0	S2
ff0	1 1 1 1 0 1	D	0 0 0 0 0*	1 1 1 0 1 1 0 0 0 0 0	S2

D: Destination Register
S1:   Source 1 Register
W5:   5-Bit Unsigned Integer Denoting a Bit-Field Width (0 denotes 32 bits)
O5:   5-Bit Unsigned Integer Denoting a Bit-Field Offset
S2:   Source 2 Register
*   The MC88100 does not decode these bits; however, assemble as shown to guarantee compatibility with future implementation.

Load/store/exchange instructions

Mnemonic	Encoding

Bits: 31 30 29 28 27 26 25 ... 21 20 ... 16 15 ... 0

Mnemonic	31	30	29	28	27 26	25 ... 21	20 ... 16	15 ... 0
xmem (imm)	0	0	0	0	TY	D	S1	I16
ld (imm)	0	0	P		TY	D	S1	I16
st (imm)	0	0	1	0	TY	D	S1	I16
lda (imm)	0	0	1	1	TY	D	S1	I16

Bits: 31 ... 26 25 ... 21 20 ... 16 15 ... 11 10 ... 5 4 ... 0

Mnemonic	31 ... 26	25 ... 21	20 ... 16	15 ... 11	10 ... 5	4 ... 0
ldcr	1 0 0 0 0 0	D	0 0 0 0 0*	0 1 0 0 0	CRS	0 0 0 0 0*
stcr	1 0 0 0 0 0	0 0 0 0 0*	S1	1 0 0 0 0	CRD	S2
xcr	1 0 0 0 0 0	D	S1	1 1 0 0 0	CRS/CRD	S2

Bits: 31 ... 26 25 ... 21 20 ... 16 15 14 13 12 11 10 9 8 7 ... 5 4 ... 0

Mnemonic	31 ... 26	25 ... 21	20 ... 16	15 14	13 12	11 10	9	8	7 ... 5	4 ... 0
ld (uns)	1 1 1 1 0 1	D	S1	0 0	P	TY	0	U	0 0 0	S2
ld (scl)	1 1 1 1 0 1	D	S1	0 0	P	TY	1	U	0 0 0	S2

Bits: 31 ... 26 25 ... 21 20 ... 16 15 ... 12 11 10 9 8 7 ... 5 4 ... 0

Mnemonic	31 ... 26	25 ... 21	20 ... 16	15 ... 12	11 10	9	8	7 ... 5	4 ... 0
xmem (uns)	1 1 1 1 0 1	D	S1	0 0 0 0	TY	0	U	0 0 0	S2
xmen (scl)	1 1 1 1 0 1	D	S1	0 0 0 0	TY	1	U	0 0 0	S2
st (uns)	1 1 1 1 0 1	D	S1	0 0 1 0	TY	0	U	0 0 0	S2
st (scl)	1 1 1 1 0 1	D	S1	0 0 1 0	TY	1	U	0 0 0	S2
lda (uns)	1 1 1 1 0 1	D	S1	0 0 1 1	TY	0	0†	0 0 0	S2
lda (scl)	1 1 1 1 0 1	D	S1	0 0 1 1	TY	1	0†	0 0 0	S2

P:	00 – Load Unsigned (byte and half-word only)
	01 – Load Signed
TY:	00 – Double Word
	01 – Word
	10 – Half Word
	00 – Byte
D:	Destination Register (Source for Store Operations)
S1:	Source 1 Register
I16:	16-Bit Immediate Index
U:	0 – Access per User/Supervisor Bit in PSR (normal mode)
	1 – Access User Space Regardless of PSR
S2:	Source 2 Register
CRS:	Control Register Source
CRD:	Control Register Destination
†	Causes privilege violation exception if bit is set and instruction is executed in user mode.
*	The MC88100 does not decode these bits; however, assemble as shown to guarantee compatibility with future implementation.

Flow control instructions

Mnemonic	Encoding
br	`1 1 0 0 0` N | D26
bsr	`1 1 0 0 1` N | D26
bb0	`1 1 0 1 0` N | B5 | S1 | D16
bb1	`1 1 0 1 1` N | B5 | S1 | D16
bcnd	`1 1 1 0 1` N | M5 | S1 | D16
tb0	`1 1 1 1 0 0` | B5 | S1 | `1 1 0 1 0 0 0` | VEC9
tb1	`1 1 1 1 0 0` | B5 | S1 | `1 1 0 1 1 0 0` | VEC9
tcnd	`1 1 1 1 0 0` | M5 | S1 | `1 1 1 0 1 0 0` | VEC9
jmp	`1 1 1 1 0 1` | `0 0 0 0 0 0 0 0 0 0`* | `1 1 0 0 0` | N | `0 0 0 0 0` | S2
jsr	`1 1 1 1 0 1` | `0 0 0 0 0 0 0 0 0 0`* | `1 1 0 0 1` | N | `0 0 0 0 0` | S2
rte	`1 1 1 1 0 1` | `0 0 0 0 0 0 0 0 0 0`* | `1 1 1 1 1 1 0 0 0 0 0 0 0 0 0 0`
tbnd	`1 1 1 1 1 0` | `0 0 0 0 0`* | S1 | IMM16
tbnd	`1 1 1 0 1` | `0 0 0 0 0`* | S1 | `1 1 1 1 1 0 0 0 0 0` | S2

Bit positions: 31, 27, 26, 25, 21, 20, 16, 15, 11, 10, 9, 8, 5, 4, 0

N: 0 – Next sequential instruction suppressed
     1 – Next sequential instruction executed before branch is taken
B5: 5-Bit Integer Denoting a Bit Number in the S1 Operand
S1: Source 1 Register
D16: 16-Bit Sign-Extended Displacement
M5: 5-Bit Condition Match Field:
       Bit 25: reserved, unused by the branch selection logic
       Bit 24: maximum negative number   [Sign and Zero]
       Bit 23: less than zero   [Sign and (not Zero)]
       Bit 22: equal to zero   [(not Sign) and Zero]
       Bit 21: greater than zero   [(not Sign) and (not Zero)]
D26: 26-bit Sign-Extended Displacement
S2: Source 2 Register
VEC9: Vector number from the start of the page address in the vector base register
*   The MC88100 does not decode these bits; however, assemble as shown to guarantee compatibility with future implementation.

Then we list them in numeric order:

Mnemonic	31	30	29	28	27 26	25 ... 21	20 ... 16	15 ... 0
xmem (imm)	0	0	0	0	TY	D	S1	IMM16
ld (imm)	0	0	P		TY	D	S1	IMM16
st (imm)	0	0	1	0	TY	D	S1	IMM16
lda (imm)	0	0	1	1	TY	D	S1	IMM16
and	0	1	0	0	0 U	D	S1	IMM16
mask	0	1	0	0	1 U	D	S1	IMM16
xor	0	1	0	1	0 U	D	S1	IMM16
or	0	1	0	1	1 U	D	S1	IMM16
addu	0	1	1	0	0 0	D	S1	IMM16
subu	0	1	1	0	0 1	D	S1	IMM16
divu	0	1	1	0	1 0	D	S1	IMM16
mul	0	1	1	0	1 1	D	S1	IMM16
add	0	1	1	1	0 0	D	S1	IMM16
sub	0	1	1	1	0 1	D	S1	IMM16
div	0	1	1	1	1 0	D	S1	IMM16
cmp	0	1	1	1	1 1	D	S1	IMM16

Mnemonic	31 ... 26	25 ... 21	20 ... 16	15 ... 11	10 ... 5	4 ... 0
ldcr	1 0 0 0 0 0	D	0 0 0 0 0*	0 1 0 0 0	CRS	0 0 0 0 0*
fldcr	1 0 0 0 0 0	D	0 0 0 0 0*	0 1 0 0 1	FCRS	0 0 0 0 0*
stcr	1 0 0 0 0 0	0 0 0 0 0*	S1	1 0 0 0 0	CRD	S2
fstcr	1 0 0 0 0 0	0 0 0 0 0*	S1	1 0 0 0 1	FCRD	S2
xcr	1 0 0 0 0 0	D	S1	1 1 0 0 0	CRS/CRD	S2
fxcr	1 0 0 0 0 0	D	S1	1 1 0 0 1	FCRS/D	S2

Mnemonic	31 ... 26	25 ... 21	20 ... 16	15 ... 11	10 9	8 7	6 5	4 ... 0
fmul	1 0 0 0 0 1	D	S1	0 0 0 0 0	T1	T2	TD	S2
flt	1 0 0 0 0 1	D	0 0 0 0 0	0 0 1 0 0	0 0	0 0	TD	S2
fadd	1 0 0 0 0 1	D	S1	0 0 1 0 1	T1	T2	TD	S2
fsub	1 0 0 0 0 1	D	S1	0 0 1 1 0	T1	T2	TD	S2
fcmp	1 0 0 0 0 1	D	S1	0 0 1 1 1	T1	T2	0 0	S2
int	1 0 0 0 0 1	D	0 0 0 0 0	0 1 0 0 1	0 0	T2	0 0	S2
nint	1 0 0 0 0 1	D	0 0 0 0 0	0 1 0 1 0	0 0	T2	0 0	S2
trnc	1 0 0 0 0 1	D	0 0 0 0 0	0 1 0 1 1	0 0	T2	0 0	S2
fdiv	1 0 0 0 0 1	D	S1	0 1 1 1 0	T1	T2	TD	S2

Mnemonic	31 ... 27	26	25 ... 0
br	1 1 0 0 0	N	D26
bsr	1 1 0 0 1	N	D26

* The MC88100 does not decode these bits; however, assemble as shown to guarantee compatibility with future implementation.

Mnemonic	Encoding

31 — 27 26 25 — 21 20 — 16 15 — 0

Mnemonic	31–27	26	25–21	20–16	15–0
bb0	1 1 0 1 0	N	B5	S1	D16
bb1	1 1 0 1 1	N	B5	S1	D16
bcnd	1 1 1 0 1	N	M5	S1	D16

31 — 26 25 — 21 20 — 16 15 — 10 9 — 5 4 — 0

Mnemonic	31–26	25–21	20–16	15–10	9–5	4–0
clr	1 1 1 1 0 0	D	S1	1 0 0 0 0 0	W5	O5
set	1 1 1 1 0 0	D	S1	1 0 0 0 1 0	W5	O5
ext	1 1 1 1 0 0	D	S1	1 0 0 1 0 0	W5	O5
extu	1 1 1 1 0 0	D	S1	1 0 0 1 1 0	W5	O5
mak	1 1 1 1 0 0	D	S1	1 0 1 0 0 0	W5	O5
rot	1 1 1 1 0 0	D	S1	1 0 1 0 1 0	0 0 0 0 0*	O5

31 — 26 25 — 21 20 — 16 15 — 9 8 — 0

Mnemonic	31–26	25–21	20–16	15–9	8–0
tb0	1 1 1 1 0 0	B5	S1	1 1 0 1 0 0 0	VEC9
tb1	1 1 1 1 0 0	B5	S1	1 1 0 1 1 0 0	VEC9
tcnd	1 1 1 1 0 0	M5	S1	1 1 1 0 1 0 0	VEC9

31 — 26 25 — 21 20 — 16 15 — 12 11 10 9 8 7 — 5 4 — 0

Mnemonic	31–26	25–21	20–16	15–12	11 10	9	8	7–5	4–0
xmem (uns)	1 1 1 1 0 1	D	S1	0 0 0 0	TY	0	U	0 0 0	S2
xmem (scl)	1 1 1 1 0 1	D	S1	0 0 0 0	TY	1	U	0 0 0	S2
ld (uns)	1 1 1 1 0 1	D	S1	0 0 P	TY	0	U	0 0 0	S2
ld (scl)	1 1 1 1 0 1	D	S1	0 0 P	TY	1	U	0 0 0	S2
st (uns)	1 1 1 1 0 1	D	S1	0 0 1 0	TY	0	U	0 0 0	S2
st (scl)	1 1 1 1 0 1	D	S1	0 0 1 0	TY	1	U	0 0 0	S2
lda (uns)	1 1 1 1 0 1	D	S1	0 0 1 1	TY	0	0‡	0 0 0	S2
lda (scl)	1 1 1 1 0 1	D	S1	0 0 1 1	TY	1	0‡	0 0 0	S2

31 — 26 25 — 21 20 — 16 15 — 11 10 9 — 5 4 — 0

Mnemonic	31–26	25–21	20–16	15–11	10	9–5	4–0
and	1 1 1 1 0 1	D	S1	0 1 0 0 0	C	0 0 0 0 0	S2
xor	1 1 1 1 0 1	D	S1	0 1 0 1 0	C	0 0 0 0 0	S2
or	1 1 1 1 0 1	D	S1	0 1 0 1 1	C	0 0 0 0 0	S2

31 — 26 25 — 21 20 — 16 15 — 10 9 8 7 — 5 4 — 0

Mnemonic	31–26	25–21	20–16	15–10	9	8	7–5	4–0
addu	1 1 1 1 0 1	D	S1	0 1 1 0 0 0	I	O	0 0 0	S2
subu	1 1 1 1 0 1	D	S1	0 1 1 0 0 1	I	O	0 0 0	S2
divu	1 1 1 1 0 1	D	S1	0 1 1 0 1 0	0	0*	0 0 0	S2
mul	1 1 1 1 0 1	D	S1	0 1 1 0 1 1	0	0*	0 0 0	S2
add	1 1 1 1 0 1	D	S1	0 1 1 1 0 0	I	O	0 0 0	S2
sub	1 1 1 1 0 1	D	S1	0 1 1 1 0 1	I	O	0 0 0	S2
div	1 1 1 1 0 1	D	S1	0 1 1 1 1 0	0	0*	0 0 0	S2
cmp	1 1 1 1 0 1	D	S1	0 1 1 1 1 1	0	0*	0 0 0	S2

* The MC88100 does not decode these bits; however, assemble as shown to guarantee compatibility with future implementation.

‡ Causes privilege violation exception if bit is set and instruction is executed in user mode.

Mnemonic	Encoding

First group

	31		26 25		21 20		16 15										5 4		0
clr	1 1 1 1 0 1		D		S1		1	0	0	0	0	0	0	0	0	0	0	S2	
set	1 1 1 1 0 1		D		S1		1	0	0	0	1	0	0	0	0	0	0	S2	
ext	1 1 1 1 0 1		D		S1		1	0	0	1	0	0	0	0	0	0	0	S2	
extu	1 1 1 1 0 1		D		S1		1	0	0	1	1	0	0	0	0	0	0	S2	
mak	1 1 1 1 0 1		D		S1		1	0	1	0	0	0	0	0	0	0	0	S2	
rot	1 1 1 1 0 1		D		S1		1	0	1	0	1	0	0	0	0	0	0	S2	

Second group

	31	26 25										16 15					11 10 9					5 4	0
jmp	1 1 1 1 0 1	0	0	0	0	0	0	0	0	0	0*	1	1	0	0	0	N	0	0	0	0	0	S2
jsr	1 1 1 1 0 1	0	0	0	0	0	0	0	0	0	0*	1	1	0	0	1	N	0	0	0	0	0	S2

Third group

	31	26 25		21 20					16 15										5 4	0
ff1	1 1 1 1 0 1	D		0	0	0	0	0*	1	1	1	0	1	0	0	0	0	0	0	S2
ff0	1 1 1 1 0 1	D		0	0	0	0	0*	1	1	1	0	1	1	0	0	0	0	0	S2
tbnd	1 1 1 1 0 1	0 0 0 0 0*	S1						1	1	1	1	1	0	0	0	0	0	0	S2
rte	1 1 1 1 0 1	0 0 0 0 0		0	0	0	0	0*	1	1	1	1	1	1	0	0	0	0	0	0 0 0 0 0*
tbnd	1 1 1 1 1 0	0 0 0 0 0*	S1						IMM16											

* The MC88100 does not decode these bits; however, assemble as shown to guarantee compatibility with future implementation.

8

Bus operation

The 88K has its own buses—three of them, to be precise. There are two P buses that link the 88100 to its companion 88200s or, in those rarer systems that lack 88200s, directly to memory. There's also an M bus that connects the 88200s to system memory.

Normally, the buses will not concern you overmuch. They'll crank away quite happily by themselves, responding as necessary to software, and doing so more or less without the programmer's input.

Still, it is probably worthwhile to take a look at them, if only on the principle that it is nice to know about the drive shaft even if you don't need to know about it to successfully shift gears.

The P bus

Start with the P bus as it looks from the perspective of the 88100.

P bus features

Normally, there are two P buses for each 88100—one linking the processor to the instruction 88200, and the other linking to the data 88200. (See Fig. 8-1.)

The two P buses have different purposes in life (one does instructions while the other does data), and will carry different types of signals (the signals are detailed in Fig. 8-2), but physically the P buses are very much

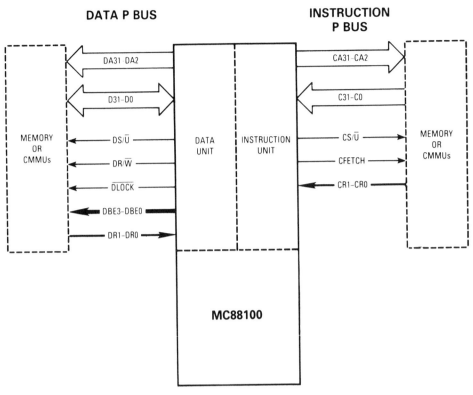

DATA P BUS

INSTRUCTION P BUS

DA31-DA2

CA31-CA2

D31-D0

C31-C0

MEMORY OR CMMUs

DATA UNIT

INSTRUCTION UNIT

MEMORY OR CMMUs

DS/$\overline{\text{U}}$

CS/$\overline{\text{U}}$

DR/$\overline{\text{W}}$

CFETCH

$\overline{\text{DLOCK}}$

CR1-CR0

DBE3-DBE0

DR1-DR0

MC88100

8-1 P buses. (Reprinted with permission of Motorola Inc.)

alike. Both are fully synchronous and both support 32-bit transfers. On the data bus, you can actually break that 32-bit package up a bit. It will support both bytes and half words.

Both boast a peak transfer rate, meanwhile, of one word per clock cycle—which is exactly what you would expect, given that this is a RISC system. Speed of processing gets another boost in that the P bus is as pipelined as just about everything else in 88K. The 88100 can start a new transaction down the P bus before getting back the results of the transaction that came before.

But, regardless of the speed, when the P bus carries data or instructions, they're aligned on word address boundaries, which is also in keeping with the way that the 88K contains and manipulates data elsewhere.

The P buses recognize two types of devices—slave and master. An 88100 is always a master. An 88200 is always a slave. The P bus manages the flow of data and instructions, and replies according to that scheme of

Data P Bus		Instruction P Bus	
Signal	**Description**	**Signal**	**Description**
DA31-DA2	Data Address Bus	CA31-CA2	Code Address Bus
D31-D0	Data Bus	C31-C0	Code Bus
$DS/\overline{U}$	Data Supervisor/User Select	$CS/\overline{U}$	Code Supervisor/User Select
$DR/\overline{W}$	Data Read/Write high for read low for write		
$\overline{DLOCK}$	Data Bus Lock		
DBE3-DBE0	Data Byte Enable DBE0 ➜ D7-D0 DBE1 ➜ D15-D8 DBE2 ➜ D23-D16 DBE3 ➜ D31-D24	CFETCH	Code Fetch
DR1-DR0	Data Reply DR1 DR0 0 0 Reserved 1 0 Success 0 1 Wait 1 1 Fault	CR1-CR0	Code Reply CR1 CR0 0 0 Reserved 1 0 Success 0 1 Wait 1 1 Fault

8-2 P bus signals.

things. It's like a telephone line that happens to be slightly intelligent. It has an idea about which of the two parties in a conversation is the speaker (the 88100) and who is listening (the 88200). It expects the listener to respond, and even to pass considerable information to the speaker, but only in response to the order to do so. It never expects an 88200 to begin a conversation.

The P bus also displays its intelligence during clock cycles in which the process or doesn't need fresh data or instructions. At those times, the P bus itself generates dummy transactions to fill the void. The 88100 simply ignores the null transactions.

Currently, you can have up to eight 88200s connected to one 88100 on the P bus. Motorola has, however, hinted that will change in good time. There have also been hints about future devices, other chips, which could exist on the P bus as either masters or slaves.

The instruction P bus

The *instruction P bus* links the 88100 to one or more 88200s (or location in system memory) that carry instructions. It takes instruction addresses from the 88100, gives them to the 88200s, and then takes the resulting instruction back again to the processor. It is therefore a one-way bus. Instructions go into the processor but not back out again and instruction P bus transactions are reads.

The part of the 88100 to which the instruction P bus links is the instruction unit. You'll recall that the instruction unit prefetches instructions before they're actually needed by the 88100 as a whole. It tries to get one instruction per each clock cycle.

There are times when it can't. Occasionally, for whatever reason, there's a tie-up. In that case, it repeats the attempt until finally it does get through.

There are also three times in its life when the instruction P bus will perform a null transaction—when it gets a reset signal; when it finds that the next instruction pointer (NIP) or fetch instruction pointer (FIP) is marked "not valid"; and when the 88K encounters a memory fault and the 88K takes an exception.

The data P bus

The *data P bus* is a bit more complex in that it does both reads and writes. It takes data from the 88200 to the 88100, and also takes back that data— appropriately modified—to cache, and ultimately to system memory.

During reads, the data P bus looks almost exactly like the instruction P bus. It takes in data in bytes, half words, or words and carries them in much the same way that the instruction P bus deals with instructions. It's even pipelined in much the same way, with requests for information overlapping with the answers to the previous requests.

It's in the writes that things get a bit different. During a write, the 88100 attempts to transfer a word, a byte, or a half word to the data 88200. To do this, it takes the address where it would like the data to be placed and puts that address out on the P bus. The data cache then takes custody of that information and signals its readiness to take the data. The 88100 then shoves the data onto the P bus, where the 88200 can pick it up and, ultimately, put it wherever it needs to go.

Because the data P bus is a two-way street, there are complications. If things were left to themselves, there could be bus contention. But, things aren't left to themselves, and the 88100's data unit constantly monitors the bus chatter. When it perceives that a transaction is complete, it then goes ahead with the next order of business.

Another complication is the xmem instruction. You'll recall that this instruction causes the contents of one general purpose register to be exchanged with that of some piece of system memory. When xmem executes, the 88200 asserts the $\overline{\text{DLOCK}}$ signal, which effectively tells everything else in the system not to access memory until the xmem transaction is finished. That way, nothing gets modified or misplaced while data is getting switched from the register to memory.

However, there are times and places when an instruction might be able to execute before xmem completes its write. Motorola suggests that you place a "trap not taken" instruction just after xmem each time you use it. That way, you can be certain xmem will have time to finish its work. (A trap not taken is simply a trap instruction that you know won't happen. You just want to take advantage of the trap instruction's synchronizing capability. An example of a trap not taken is tb1 0,r0,0. Since r0 can't have any bits set, the trap can't be taken.)

The M bus

The M bus is quite a different beast. It is the synchronous bus that links the 88200 to system memory, as well as other devices. M bus operations are a bit more complex than those of the P bus, which is only what you'd expect. The P bus, after all, links only a limited number of devices—one 88100 and up to eight 88200s—in a relatively straightforward way. There are only slaves and masters on it, and they never change their roles.

The M bus, on the other hand, has to deal with the complexities of multiple 88200 devices that change their very natures according to the task at hand. By default, they are bus slaves. But, when they access memory, they are bus masters.

Here it will be explained, piece by piece.

Bus arbitration

You'll recall that there are M bus masters and M bus slaves, which would be simple if weren't for the fact that sometimes an 88200 is a slave (in fact, that's the default state), but at other times a master. It changes according to the task at hand.

But, because there might be multiple 88200s in a system, as well as other M bus devices, there's always a risk of a conflict between two (or more) of them attempting to be bus masters at the same time. So, whenever an 88200, or other M bus device, wants to become an M bus master, it first tests the waters. It checks the M bus to make certain that someone isn't already using the bus. If everything seems quiet, the 88200 sends out a bus request (BR) signal on the M bus. When an 88200 makes the request, it is said to enter the *contend state*.

Other devices on the M bus then respond. If they don't need the bus, and don't plan to ask for it in the near future, then they'll yield the channel without a fight. If, however, other devices are currently using the M bus, then they'll voice their claim accordingly.

How the various bus masters and would-be bus masters work out ownership of the bus depends on the arbitration scheme in place. If this particular 88K based system is in *fairness mode* (i.e., if the priority arbitration bit of the SCTR is set for fairness), then the contending 88200 enters a *blocked state*, and simply waits its turn. Eventually, it will get to the head of the line, take possession of the M bus, and carry out its assignment.

If, however, the contending 88200 is set to *priority mode* (as it would be in, for example, real time systems), then it makes no pretense of civility. It squeezes itself first in line for the bus, in spite of those already in line, and performs whatever tasks it must.

Thus it is that the M bus's condition always reflects the state of its master. If no 88200 is currently the M bus master, then the bus is said to be *inactive*. If there is a master but it is currently between transactions or otherwise not engaged, then the bus is *idle*. If the master is sending out the addresses for whatever data it might want, then the bus is in *address phase*. And, finally, if the master is receiving or sending data down the M bus, then the bus is in *data* phase.

As a final note on arbitration, the fairness doctrine is implemented within the 88200s—sort of the agreed upon Marquis of Queensberry rules of caches. However, priority is not implemented within them. The SCTR bit signals priority, but external hardware supplied by the system must actually make the priority effective.

M bus reads

The M bus is a two-way street. Data and addresses flow down it to system memory and sometimes, come back again.

An M bus read transaction happens when an 88K based system finds itself in need of data or instructions that happen to reside outside of the 88200's cache.

Once the 88200 in question realizes that it doesn't have some necessary piece of data, and must therefore order out, it attempts to become the M bus master. Once it has that status, it dispatches the address of the requested data down the M bus to whatever it might be—in system memory, in another 88200, or some other M bus device.

Whichever M bus device it is that does have the data decodes the address, and signals with what is known as the "OK signal"—its readiness to transmit. The first 88200—the M bus master—then signals its own readiness to receive. The second device, acting as an M bus slave, then goes ahead and passes the data along the M bus. It tries to do so in burst mode, if it can.

Then, finally, the master 88200 signals that the transaction is complete with the LDT signal.

All of this assumes, of course, that there aren't any errors or glitches along the way. Had there been, master and slave had the option of signalling "error" and "retry." Moreover, the slave has the power to signal the master to insert a few waits into its operations. Normally, an 88200 wants to eat its data in a single clock cycle. If, however, the slave can't decode the addresses, or can't supply the data that quickly, it can ask the master to repeat its current operation until it can catch up. It then sends out an OK and things continue at the normal speed.

M bus writes

The reverse of a read is, of course, a write. And, an M bus write occurs whenever an 88200 needs to put data into some other M bus device—usually system memory, though there's no reason why it can't be anything else that would fit onto the M bus.

In any case, an M bus write is hard to tell from an M bus read, except that data flows in the opposite direction. An 88200 finds it must transfer data elsewhere. Perhaps the data has been modified according to software and is now being returned to system memory. Or perhaps this particular 88200 has been snooping—that is, watching the M bus for transactions that might concern data which it currently holds—and has just spotted a read of that data by another 88200.

If it is the former case, then the 88200 signals its desire to become a bus master. If it is the latter case, then the 88200 blocks the current transaction by signalling "retry," and then attempts to become a bus master.

When it does get ownership of the bus, it puts the address of the place where it wishes the data to go on the M bus. The target M bus device, now acting as a slave, decodes that address and (assuming there aren't any errors along the way) announces its readiness to take the data with an OK signal.

The master 88200 then transfers the data. The slave takes it and (again assuming there are no errors) deals with it accordingly.

The master 88200 sends the data to the slave in chunks of various sizes—byte, half word, word, or double word, depending on the request. After it transfers a unit of data (which it attempts to do in burst mode), it then sends a new address that is the old address incremented by four. It then sends the next chunk of data to that address, and the whole thing begins again. Ultimately, when the master 88200 runs out of material to transfer, it signals the end of the transaction with an LDT signal.

M bus errors

On occasion, an M bus transaction will go wrong. Specifically, you can encounter an M bus error in a snoop copyback, a flush, and a probe. However, because these operations normally don't trouble the processor, they aren't reported as faults. Instead, the 88200 itself makes note of the errors and then the processor or other devices can track down the problem.

For example, if the 88K is doing a probe transaction and then runs across an M bus error, the 88200 will set the BE bit of the SSR as a kind of warning flag to everyone that this probe has been unsuccessful and its result should be considered invalid. Moreover, the 88200 puts the physical address of the fault in its system address register (SAR), so that the 88100 (or whatever) can seek it out later.

Much the same occurs if there is a bus error during a flush under the copyback option. Then, too, the BE bit is set, while the physical address where the error occurred is stored in the system address register (SAR).

There's also bus snooping (which is detailed in the next section). When an 88200 realizes that some other M bus device is about to access data that it has modified in itself, it then rushes to update the system memory. But, in the process of trying to update system memory, it might run across an M bus error. If so, then the 88200 will freeze the transaction and set its copyback error (CE) bit.

Another kind of error that the 88200 can come across is parity error. Like any decent piece of electronics, the 88200 watches itself for errors via parity checking. Motorola says that when an 88200 is an M bus master, it always generates even parity on the M bus address, control signals, and write data. It also always checks parity on read data. However, if it notices something amiss—an odd when there ought to be an even—then it reports the problem to the processor via a fault reply.

When it is operating as an M bus slave the 88200 checks parity on address and write data during access to its internal control registers. It also checks parity on addresses that it encounters while snooping—but, it doesn't check for parity on data.

It does, however, check parity on reads of data bytes when those data bytes have their byte enables asserted. Conversely, during a write, parity is always generated on all data bytes. And, when a slave 88200 is a doing a burst read, and then detects a parity error, it completes the read before alerting the 88100 to the problem.

In any case, regardless of the ways and means of the situation, the CPU must handle parity error as it would any other exception.

M bus snooping

There are, of course, a number of different kinds of transactions that happen on the M bus. All of these are covered in the 88200 manual. But, for our purposes, bus snooping might be the most interesting.

You'll recall that the 88K is designed with the idea of multiprocessing in mind. One of the things that makes this so is that the 88200 is set up to perform bus snooping. Any 88200 that has its snoop enable (SE) register set to 1 is constantly ready to snoop. Once it detects a transaction on the M bus that is marked global, it compares the address of the data that is being requested with the address tags of the data in its cache. If it finds that it does indeed have that data, and that the data has been modified, it signals "retry."

In this way, no one processor in a multiprocessor system will find itself operating on stale data.

Most software folks won't have to plow thru bus operations very often. This chapter has been more primer than full-blown reference—a Berlitz one week course for the occasional traveler, if you will. If you find the need to be fluent, you should refer to the 88100 and 88200 user's manuals. We modestly believe that after reading this chapter, the user's manuals will be more useful to you than had we not included it.

9

Exception handling

This chapter is of necessity quite involved. If you wish only a passing acquaintanceship with exceptions, read only through "Exception priority." However, if you have the need to become intimate with exceptions, the rest of this chapter should provide a number of hours of interesting reading.

In the parlance of Luke Skywalker and Obi Wan, exceptions are disturbances in the force of the normal execution of instructions. An exception would result, for example, when an invalid data item finds its way into a correctly functioning program and causes a math error of divide by zero; or from a physical situation, such as the floppy disk drive needs to inform the system that some process is trying to read from a floppy disk that is not in the drive. These are exceptions, and the 88100 provides methods (albeit complex) for recognizing, correcting and continuing from exceptions.

The four conditions that can cause exceptions are:

- Interrupts (like from the floppy drive) signalled through the INT input
- Externally signalled errors (like a memory access fault)
- Internally recognized errors (like divide by zero)
- Trap instructions

You might hear people talk about interrupts and exceptions interchangeably. Lots of times you'll hear the term interrupt handler used. You can nod knowingly—but for the 88K, strictly speaking, interrupts are a sub-class of exceptions. *Interrupts* are acknowledgment of some external event. *Exceptions* take both external and internal events into account.

The term *handling* derives from the circumstance that normal execution is stopped and special processing is begun to "handle" the exception. Under nearly all conditions, the result is a transfer of execution control to special code known as an *exception handler*.

Exceptions come in two flavors: precise and imprecise. The first, *precise*, describes an exception that occurs when the processor has all the information to define the cause exactly. For instance, a privilege violation. In an imprecise exception, the processor does not have all necessary state information to pinpoint the cause. An example of that latter situation would be a floating point overflow. By the time the exception occurs, the source operands that caused the overflow are not available. It is sufficient to know that the exception occurred along with the intermediate result.

Vectors

Vector is the name given to the method of transferring control to an exception handler when a given exception occurs. There are 512 possible exceptions. Each has an assigned vector address within a 4 Kbyte page pointed to the Vector Base Register (VBR). Whew! A lot of content there in a few words.

Each exception has a unique number associated with it. For example, #5 means that an unimplemented operation was attempted. Associated with exception 5 is a vector of 0x28. This means that the start of the exception handler to deal with an unimplemented opcode exception is 0x28 bytes from the start of the vector base table. That table is a collection of all exception vectors, and can be located anywhere. Often, it is in a portion of system memory that is not subject to translation or any effect that would take up time.

The vector table is loaded, and a pointer to it loaded into the VBR (aka control register 7), both by system software. Each vector in the table is comprised of two instruction words. Universally, one of these must be a branch to another location containing the balance of the exception handler. To gain one cycle, most handlers use the .n (delayed branch) option, and place the first "real" instruction of the handler as the second of the two instruction words.

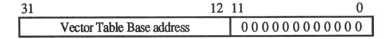

31	12	11	0
Vector Table Base address		0 0 0 0 0 0 0 0 0 0 0 0	

Under some circumstances, it might be appropriate to modify the VBR in flight—for instance, to specify different pages of exception vectors. If this is necessary, it should only be done when interrupts are disabled. Imagine, if you will, a routine that altered the vector table to point to a new set of exception handlers, and was interrupted prior to setting up the pointers to those routines. The processor would be lost in space.

So, a hypothetical vector table might look something like:

Address	Word 1	Word 2
0x0	br.n excp0	st r1,excp0+0x100
0x8	br.n excp1	st r1,excp1+0x100
~		
~		
0x3F8	br.n excp127	st r1,excp127+0x100

where 0x0 is the top of the vector table. There are a couple of sample exception handlers in chapter 11.

In each case, the first word of the vector performs a delayed branch to the exception handler, while the second saves register 1 so that it may be used within the handler and restored when the handler completes. Figure 9-1 is a comprehensive view of the table with the definitions of the vectors.

If you sift through all the "reserved" and "future use" notes, you find that only $0-10$ are needed for the 88100 and $114-115$ for the FPU. Vectors $128-512$ are special cases for trap instructions. You can see some of these specified in chapter 10 on binary interoperability.

Now that you have an understanding of sorts of the vector table, examine the dynamics of its addressing. When an exception occurs, the VBR points to the table. The specific vector is generated by the CPU hardware, and is nine bits in length. The vector is appended to the upper 20 bits of the VBR, and bits $2-0$ set to zero to provide the vector address within the table. Because the vector address is equal to the vector number multiplied by eight, the lower three bits will always be zero. (See Fig. 9-2.)

For example:

VBR=0x400000
Exception 5 occurs vector=0x28
Resulting address=0x400028 for the start of the exception 5 handler.

One note about the VBR: only its upper 20 bits $(31-12)$ are used for the base address. The other bits contain zero in the 88100, but might not contain zero in future versions.

Exception Number	Address (VBR +)	Exception
0	0x0	Reset (VBR cleared before vectoring)
1	0x8	Interrupt
2	0x10	Instruction access
3	0x18	Data access
4	0x20	Misaligned access
5	0x28	Unimplemented opcode
6	0x30	Privilege violation
7	0x38	Bounds check violation
8	0x40	Illegal integer divide
9	0x48	Integer overflow
10	0x50	Error
11-113		Reserved for Supervisor and future hardware use
114	0x390	SFU 1 - Floating point Precise
115	0x398	SFU 1 - Floating point Imprecise
116	0x3A0	SFU 2 - Precise *
117	0x3A8	Reserved
118	0x3B0	SFU 3 - Precise *
119	0x3B8	Reserved
120	0x3C0	SFU 4- Precise *
121	0x3C8	Reserved
122	0x3D0	SFU 5 - Precise *
123	0x3D8	Reserved
124	0x3E0	SFU 6 - Precise *
125	0x3E8	Reserved
126	0x3F0	SFU 7 - Precise *
127	0x3F8	Reserved
128-511		Supervisor call - reserved for trap vectors

* An instruction coded for SFU 2-7 will cause a precise exception, as these SFUs are not currently implemented.

9-1 Exception vectors.

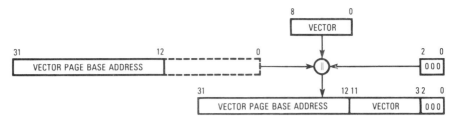

9-2 Exception vector address formation. (Reprinted with permission of Motorola Inc.)

Shadowing

Who knows what evil lurks in the hearts of 88100 processors—the Shadows know! Like the Shadow of the radio era, the shadowing capability of the 88100 provides information that might be otherwise lost.

Shadowing is the term used to refer to maintaining copies of certain control registers so as to have sufficient information to restart after an exception occurs. Shadowing must be explicitly enabled or disabled. As a default, at power up or at reset time, it is frozen (shadow freeze bit in the PSR is set to 1). Typically, it is set by system software via an stcr instruction. As a consequence of returning from handling an exception via rte, if shadowing was enabled prior to the exception, it will be reenabled because the rte will restore the PSR to its pre-exception state.

Although it might look somewhat like a shadow register, the EPSR (Exception time Processor Status Register) is really an exception time register, and is not affected by shadowing.

Exception priority

The world does not always time events in neat, sequential Von Neuman patterns. If multiple exceptions occur simultaneously, the 88100 requires a way to accommodate that. That accommodation is "exception priority." Exceptions with the same priority in Fig. 9-3 cannot occur at the same time.

Exception processing

OK, here is where the rubber meets the road—where when the going gets tough, the smart ones skip to the next chapter. Our apologies if we missed any of your favorite aphorisms.

Exception	Priority
Reset	1
Instruction Access	2
Unimplemented Opcode	3
Privilege violation	4
Misaligned Access Integer overflow Illegal Integer Divide Trap Instruction Bounds check SFU precise exception	5
Interrupt	6
SFU imprecise exception	7
Data Access	8

9-3 Exception priority.

For most exceptions, the 88100 has a standard sequence of processing exceptions. The sequence is:

- Recognize the exception—(Pretty obvious, huh) At this time, the 88100 saves the processor context in the shadow registers (assuming shadowing is enabled) and redirects program execution to the appropriate exception handler.
- Handle the exception—Do something constructive to remedy the exception.
- Return from the exception—restore the processor context as it was before the exception, and redirect execution to the proper program location.

This is a straightforward process. If, however, you want to handle multilple exceptions (often called *nested* exceptions), then you as the systems programmer, must provide that additional complexity. The processor context must be saved to memory—usually in the stack. Then interrupts would be enabled and execution of the first exception handler begun. More on this later.

If there is no software for handling nested exceptions, and a second occurs while the 88100 is in its exception processing state, you have big trouble. The CPU gets totally confused and is fatally injured, resulting in the error exception. Recall at the first of this section, we said "for most exceptions..."? The error exception is one of the exceptions that is not handled with the standard sequence. The only other one is reset.

While in the exception processing state, the CPU will process the trap exceptions. This makes sense, because traps are simply requests for execution of some specific function. That function might be one you want to use within an exception handler.

Exception recognition

According to Motorola, the sequence of events at recognition time with shadowing enabled is:

1. Wait till all pending memory accesses are complete (or till they fail with data access exception). If the latter occurs, it doesn't cause an error even though it is an exception within an exception. In that case, the valid bit is set in DMT0 to identify that a data exception has occurred. The exception handler (we'll get to that part next) would check that bit and take care of that situation as well, before returning to the original program. If the original exception was a data access problem, the CPU doesn't wait for pending access to complete. Instruction prefetching continues although the instructions fetched are discarded. If those fetches cause any errors that would normally result in an exception, those errors are ignored. This simplifies the design of the processor by reducing the complexity required in the prefetch pipeline.

2. The current values in the PSR are copied to the EPSR. Basically, this means that bits $31-28$ (MODE, BO, SER, and C) and $3-0$ (SFD1, MXM, IND, and SFRZ) are copied to the EPSR to save the processor context as it existed at the time of exception.

3. The processor is placed in the exception processing state by:
   - Setting the SFRZ bit in the PSR. This freezes the shadow registers, having the context at the time of exception.
   - Setting the SFU1 disable bit, disabling the FPU and preventing it from writing back any results to the general registers or from signalling any floating point exceptions.

- Setting the interrupt disable bit in the PSR, preventing more external event recognition.
- Setting the MODE bit, placing the 88100 into supervisor state.
- Clearing the register scoreboard so that all the general registers may be used by the exception handler.

Register	State
PSR	Bit 31 & 3, 1, 0 set, all others unchanged
EPSR	Contains the contents of the PSR before exception and after data unit operations have completed (or faulted).
SB	Cleared
SSBR	Contains value in SB before exception
Instruction Pointers	FIP = exception vector address V bits in NIP and XIP cleared marking them invalid
SNIP, SFIP, SXIP	Contain XIP, FIP, and NIP values before exception.
VBR	Unchanged
r1-r31	Unchanged
DMT0-2	For data access exception, contain data on memory transaction that faulted. If not a data access exception, V bits are clear.
DMA0-2	For data access exception, contain address of memory reference that faulted. If not a data access exception, contents are undefined.
DMD0-2	For data access exception, contain data for a store transaction that faulted. Contents are undefined for other exceptions and conditions.
Internal registers	Unchanged
FPU registers	FPCR, and FPSR are unchanged. Others contain data on floating point exceptions as appropriate.

9-4 Register states after exception.

4. The entry point to the exception handler is generated from the VBR and the vector number. Program execution is transferred to that entry point.
5. Prefetch and execute exception handler instructions. (Shadowing remains frozen.)

While all this is going on, the control registers are reacting as well. They'll go to certain predefined states, rather as they do after $\overline{\text{RST}}$. Those states are shown in Fig. 9-4.

Exception handling

The exception is recognized and the 88100 placed it in the exception processing state. Now you need to correct or accommodate the situation that caused the exception. There are two types of exception handling: nested, and non-nested:

Non-nested   The 88100 remains in the exception processing state, with interrupts, FPU and shadowing disabled. All context information is stored in the shadow registers, and all information needed to handle the exception exists in the control registers. Completion of the handler is via an rte instruction, which restores the context. The primary problem with non-nested handlers is the situation in which another exception occurs while in the middle of the handler of the first. In that case, an error exception occurs and the processor enters a loop that can only be exited by a processor reset. See "Error exception" for more detail.

Nested   The handler must save the context to memory, and depending on the exception, this may include the general purpose registers. The handler then reenables shadowing usually via an stcr instruction. Interrupts and the FPU could be reenabled as well. The re-enabling allows another exception to occur without creating an error exception. When a nested handler completes, the shadow registers are frozen, and the context information is loaded into them. Then an rte instruction restores the context to the processor.

The nested approach is more flexible and robust, because multiple exceptions may be accommodated. However, it is considerably more complex as well as difficult to debug.

Recall from "Exception recognition" that if a data access exception occurred while the processor was waiting for accesses to complete, then the exception wasn't taken, and the valid bit was set in DMT0. Exception handlers must check the status of DMT0 and take care of any data access problems. This usually means bringing the missing page of virtual memory from disk and putting it into system memory, and then updating the page tables. This would usually be performed by calling the data access exception handler from within the first exception handler.

Return from exception

Whew! You recognized it, took care of it, and now you are ready to set things up to restart the real stuff you were doing before the exception hit the fan.

Most typically, returning is done by the appropriately named returned-from-exception instruction, or rte. It restores, SNIP, SFIP, SXIP, EPSR, and SSBR to their run time counterparts. (More detailed information on each of the 88100 registers can be found in chapter 5.)

When rte is executed, the control registers are restored to their state prior to the exception.

SSBR

The SSBR shadows the scoreboard register to track register usage. You'll recall that this keeps the pipeline from tripping itself up.

You'll also recall that SSBR isn't a true shadow register—as is SNIP, for example, because scoreboard (SB) register is not copied to it each clock cycle. Instead, individual bits are set or cleared as they are set or cleared in SB. This means that SSBR could be different from SB if SB changed after the SFRZ bit was cleared, disabling shadowing. This does occur during execution of an exception handler, but when SSBR is restored on rte, they both match.

Something to remember is that if SSBR is undefined, it must be explicitly cleared before shadowing is enabled. This synchronizes SB and SSBR, and must be done following a reset.

SNIP/SFIP/SXIP

The SNIP is a shadow of NIP, while SFIP has the same role for the FIP, and SXIP the XIP. When a precise exception occurs, the SFIP points to the next instruction to be fetched, and SNIP to the next instruction to be executed—that's assuming that you come back from the exception via a normal rte.

There are two bits in the two that can change that: the V and E bits. They were discussed in chapter 8, but in short, V is for valid, and E is for exception. If V = 0, the target instruction is treated as a no-op. If E = 1 an instruction access exception is generated when that instruction is reached. The CPU clears V bits under some conditions, and the exception handler can use E bits to avoid execution of an instruction. E bits of SNIP and SFIP are not set by hardware at all.

The SXIP points to the instruction that was executing when the exception occurred. The SXIP also has V and E bits, but their meaning is somewhat different. If V is set, the instruction was attempting to execute; if clear, the instruction was not executed, indicating an invalid instruction. E tells if the instruction was prefetched or not; and is set if NIP had its E bit set when the pipeline advanced.

Because the exception handler runs in supervisor mode, it can examine and alter the contents of SFIP and SNIP. For example, if the handler wants to change instruction flow from the normal return, it can put a new target instruction's address in SNIP and the next sequential address in SFIP and then do an rte. The prefetch of the targets of SNIP and SFIP are from the address space specified by the MODE bit in ESPR. Privilege checking is done on the basis of that MODE bit. Thus if the instruction executing at exception time was a user mode instruction, the SFIP/SNIP fetches will be from user space, and they will be checked for user-only privilege.

rte instruction sequence

The rte can be a bit more comprehensible if stretched out a bit. Look at the sequence of events that follows an rte:

1. SNIP & SFIP are copied to NIP & FIP respectively. Those instructions are prefetched.
2. SSBR is copied to SB
3. EPSR is copied to PSR
4. Execution begins at the instruction pointed to by NIP

If the FPU is enabled with rte (by having SFD1 set in the EPSR), those floating point instructions that were executing at exception time continue. Their destination registers will still be marked correctly in the scoreboard register.

If interrupts are enabled (via IND=0) in EPSR, and an interrupt is pending on return, it will be recognized immediately, and another exception will be taken.

Trap and trap-not-taken

Trap instructions are of course familiar to you from the day-to-day business of programming. However, traps and their kin have uses with 88100 that go beyond what might be expected of them.

A trap instruction synchronizes the 88100 by allowing all previous operations to complete. It clears the scoreboard register and the data unit pipeline. The FPU also is allowed to complete its instructions. This is a useful item, particularly in exception handling, when you want to bring things to a known state. It is so useful that you may use it without intending to take the trap; known as a *trap-not-taken*, it just synchronizes the CPU.

An easy way to do a trap-not-taken is to execute:

```
tb1 0,r0,0
```

This says "trap if the 0th bit is set in r0." Because r0 is always 0, the bit isn't set, and the trap isn't taken. BUT the synchronization still occurs. You'll see reference to trap-not-taken in some of the following discussion. (Note: you can't use tbnd to do this synchronization because it executes without allowing other operations to complete.)

Changing PSR values

Changes to the PSR can be made via rte by modifying EPSR before executing the rte. You can also change PSR through stcr and xcr, but you've got to exercise a bit more care when you take this particular path.

First, SB and SSBR must be equal before shadowing is reenabled. This ensures that register usage is correct. The SSBR can be cleared and a trap-not-taken instruction executed. The trap-not-taken synchronizes the 88100, such that all previous operations complete. This clears the scoreboard register and clears the data unit pipeline. Then shadowing can be enabled.

Second, if the FPU is disabled by clearing SFD1, there must be no floating point instructions "in flight"; otherwise, the SB will show that those registers are in use and prevent them from being used by other instructions. This results in "scoreboard hold"—an indefinite tie-up of the processor. To avoid this unpleasant turn of events, execute a trap or trap-not-taken before the stcr or xcr.

Thirdly, a trap (or trap-not-taken) must be executed before either an stcr or xcr that freezes shadowing. The trap ensures that any instructions in progress get completed, and any resulting exceptions are reported before the big freeze.

The fourth scenario involves the interrupt disable (bit 1 in the PSR). When set, interrupts are disabled following the *subsequent* instruction. So you don't want to freeze shadowing and disable interrupts in the same instruction, lest you get caught by a situation in which an interrupt is received while shadowing is frozen and the shadow registers are unable to provide data to handle the exception. A recommended sequence would be:

```
tb1    0,r0,0   trap not taken
stcr   r1,cr1   r1 contains "10" in bits 1 & 0—disable interrupts
stcr   r2,cr1   r2 contains "01" in bits 1 & 0—freeze shadowing
```

The first stcr sets interrupt disable, but that doesn't occur until after the next instruction, which is the shadow freeze. Note that r1 and r2 would have their other bits set as appropriate. An alternative would be to branch to a routine that modified the EPSR and then did an rte. This would require a short bit of code that did something like:

```
         br     FrzDis
FrzDis   stcr   r1,cr1   r1 contains "11" in bits 1 & 0
                         modify any other registers necessary
         rte             return from FrzDis to the address set in
                         SNIP
```

There is also a one-instruction delay when interrupts are enabled. But, when interrupts are enabled via rte, a pending interrupt is recognized immediately after the return.

The fifth possibility concerns the situation when the FPU is enabled via clearing the SFD1 bit in the PSR with stcr or xcr. When this occurs, the FPU must be empty of in-progress calculations. If there were things in flight, they would require some destination registers that would not be indicated in the scoreboard registers. If the registers aren't scoreboarded, they could be clobbered by another instruction's use of those registers or vice versa.

And, finally, when stcr or xcr change the MODE bit, there are two thoroughly nasty snags that can crop up—either the privilege check for the subsequent instruction might not be correct, or the next couple of instructions might have been prefetched from the wrong space.

To give an example of the first, say that you were in supervisor space and changed to user mode via an stcr. If the next instruction were a supervisor instruction, then the privilege patrol would cite you for a violation of user privileges. In the second case, if you hadn't sorted out the SNIP correctly, you could get charged with a space violation as well.

Completing FPU instructions

The 88100 exception processing disables the FPU to avoid the grim scenario in which the FPU writes to general registers *and* continues executing.

We can allow the FPU to complete by executing an rte that returned control to a trap-not-taken. The rte restores the SB (from the SSBR) and would enable the FPU. The trap-not-taken would politely wait till the FPU had completed before continuing.

Clearing SSBR

SSBR and SB don't always match after a reset. That's a problem because shadowing isn't enabled until they do. So, to bring the two into line, the SSBR must be cleared at initialization time, by executing:

```
stcr r0,cr3
```

This stores zeros into the SSBR.

Interrupt latency

Interrupt latency has to do with the length of time taken by the 88000 between signalling an interrupt and beginning processing. This is of critical importance in real time systems where the amount of time that passes between an input and the system's response to it has to be both reasonably short, and absolutely predictable. (It is one of the interesting ironies of real time systems design that oft times the shorter, but less predictable response time is less preferable to one which might be a bit longer, but which never varies.)

The interrupt latency for any 88K system is based on:

- 1 clock cycle for internal synchronization of the interrupt
- 0−4 times the maximum data memory access latency to clear the data unit

- 1−2 times the maximum instruction memory access latency for clearing and prefetching instructions
- 1 cycle to decode the first exception handler instruction
- 1 cycle for instruction execution

The memory access latency (maxmem) times are affected by CMMUs. If some or all of the addresses result in cache hits, each of the accesses will require only one cycle. The 88100 often has less than four accesses pending, further reducing the time for data latency.

Max latency $= 3 +$ maximum of $(4 \times \text{maxmem}_d, \text{maxmem}_i) + \text{maxmem}_i$

The three cycles are for synchronization, decoding, and execution. Clearing the data unit will probably take longer than completing the prefetch in process so the $4 \times \text{maxmem}_d$ will likely be the larger of the two values. The maxmem_i represents the exception handler instruction fetch time.

So far, exceptions have been discussed generically—what happens regarding priority, how the vector table works . . . and so on. Now, though, explicit exceptions will be looked at. They are organized by their functional type:

Instruction unit

This cheery little fellow is the heart of the 88100. It recognizes the instructions that are fed into it, and tries its best to execute them flawlessly. When it can't, it is courteous enough to advise you of that unhappy event.

Interrupt exception (Vector offset 0x8)

These exceptions are generally external events. Something that you should know about outside the 88100 has happened, and you must recognize that and take some action. The communication facility that lets you know about an interrupt is the INT signal.

Recall that you can disable or enable the interrupts, essentially ignore them, by the value of the IND bit (bit 1) in the PSR. When you do enable interrupts, take care that shadowing is not frozen. If an interrupt takes place with shadowing frozen, the dreaded error exception occurs. This will be seen later, but basically the error exception is the 88100's way of saying "something has happened, and you have me in such a state that I can't do anything constructive about it."

The 88100 has only the one INT signal. Other processors have multiple interrupt signals, usually called *levels*. 88000 systems will usually have external hardware called an *interrupt controller*, to map multiple external events into the single INT signal. The interrupt controller will sort out priority of the various events. The exception handler is directed by the vector table offset of 0x8 to handle interrupts; however, the interrupt controller can write a vector number on the data bus and the 88100 can use that vector from within the interrupt exception to compute the address of the specific device interrupt handler. This allows mapping many devices onto the single INT signal.

Misaligned access exception (Vector offset 0x20)

When a memory accessing instruction such as load or store is attempted to an address that is not consistent with the access sizes, a misaligned access exception occurs—for example, when a word access is made to a half-word address. Misaligned access is a precise exception. You may recall from earlier in the chapter that a precise exception is one in which the cause can be exactly determined. In this case, the condition is discovered before the memory access is sent to the data unit. So, like the supercop on the beat, it detected the crime before it happened.

When this exception does occur, the SXIP points to the guilty instruction. For an instruction involving a destination register, such as ld, the relevant scoreboard bit is set. This scoreboard bit must be cleared by the exception handler if the instruction is aborted. This exception can be masked off, or avoided, by setting the MXM bit (bit 2) in the PSR. If MXM is set and a misaligned access occurs, the 88100 rounds *down* to a consistent address. Thus, if you tried to access 0x507 on a half-word access, the 88100 would pat you on the shoulder for a good try and actually access 0x506.

Unimplemented opcode exception (Vector offset 0x28)

This exception strikes when you tell the 88100 to do something it has no idea how to, or even maybe what it is we're asking. There are instruction combinations that are possible as bit patterns, but which are not currently valid instructions. If some such jabberwocky is fed to the CPU, it responds with this exception. Again, this is a precise exception and SXIP points to the offender. If an unimplemented SFU instruction is attempted, this exception would **not** take place. Instead, an SFU exception would take place.

Although, within the exception handler, you could handle the pseudo instruction in software, the result would not necessarily be binary portable, and this sort of thing is prohibited by the 88000 BCS.

However, this exception can be used to emulate non-88100 instructions. For example, when (no promises you understand) Motorola introduces the next member of the 88000 processor family, and it offers some really spiffy instruction, you could emulate that functionality on an 88100 from within the unimplemented opcode exception handler.

Privilege violation exception (Vector offset 0x30)

This exception chances by when a privileged operation is undertaken while in user mode. It happens if you do any of three things:

- Access a control register other than FPCR or FPSR
- Employ a .usr option
- Specify exception vectors 0 − 127 in a trap instruction

Each of these are fine so long as you're in supervisor mode. If this exception does occur, it is precise. The SXIP points to the embarrased instruction and the privileged instruction is NOT performed. For instructions, such as ld or xmem via .usr, that specify a destination register, the bit will be set in the scoreboard and must be cleared by the exception handler.

Trap instruction exceptions (Vector offset 0x400 − 0x7F8)

(tcnd, tb1, tb0)

Earlier in this chapter it was said that traps, whether taken or not, allow completion of previous instructions before starting the exception processing. Each of these three trap instruction (tbnd is next) can initiate any exception handler. There is the proviso that traps to 0 − 127 be performed only when in supervisor mode.

The error exception, you'll recall, occurs when an exception takes place while shadowing is frozen. If a trap instruction is executed while shadowing is frozen, then the dreaded error exception does not occur.

Traps are useful critters when writing exception handlers, and this conveniently allows that use. All that happens is that the PSR is updated as with any exception, and execution continues. None of the exception or shadow registers are affected.

Bounds check violation exception (Vector offset 0x38)

This is another trap instruction, tbnd, but one that detects limits being exceeded. The instruction performs a comparison between two registers or one register and an immediate value and traps if rS1 is larger. There is a key difference between tbnd and the other traps. *The 88100 is not synchronized before the trap executes!*

If you want immediate response to a trap condition, such as in a serious error, you would use tbnd. If you wanted to allow operations to complete, you would trap with *tcnd*, *tb1*, or tb0.

Integer overflow exception (Vector offset 0x38)

The integer unit has only one exception—which is a pleasant change. It's nice to know so little can go wrong.

But, when this one happens, it does so when the result of an integer arithmetic operation can't be expressed in a 32-bit signed number. For example $2^{31} + 137$. Because the limit of signed integers is 2^{31}, you can't exceed that and would get back an integer overflow exception. The SXIP as usual points to the instruction that caused the exception. The scoreboard bit for the destination register must be cleared by the exception handler, but neither destination register itself nor the carry bit are affected by an instruction that ends with this exception.

Data unit exceptions

These exceptions take place between the 88100 and 88200 in most systems. The 88200 sees the problem and reports it to the 88100 which takes exception to the fault. There are four ways that data unit exceptions can happen:

- load, store, xmem, or instruction prefetch refers to an invalid address

- load, store, or instruction prefetch refers to a segment or page not currently in system memory
- load, store, or instruction prefetch violation of access privilege or write protection
- An error caught by hardware (usually a bus error)

Instruction access exception (Vector offset 0x10)

The title describes this exception well. It is also a relatively common exception in virtual memory systems, because it occurs when reference is required to an instruction that exists in virtual but not system memory. As that instruction was prefetched, the 88200 sent "transaction fault" (CR0−CR1 = 11); and as execution was attempted, the 88100 takes the exception. Both XIP and SXIP contain the faulted address.

The hardware of the memory system must intervene here and indicate the cause of the fault. CR0−CR1 simply indicate that a memory transaction fault occurred. It could be for a variety of reasons. When using CMMU's in the memory system, the PFSR (P bus Fault Status Register) provides this information. In the case of this exception, it indicates:

- Bus Error (some hardware problem)
- Segment fault
- Page fault
- Supervisor violation
- Write violation

It was mentioned earlier that memory access exceptions were treated somewhat differently—that data accesses in progress aren't allowed to complete before the exception is taken. Instruction Access Exceptions have the following recognition process:

1. The FIP holds the address of the instruction causing the exception.
2. The FIP value moves to NIP after the fetch has begun but before it is complete.
3. The contents of NIP propagate to XIP where the 88100 sets the E bit. This bit flags the processor to force an instruction access fault if execution is tried. From that point, processing is the same as earlier described in Exception Recognition.

The exception handler must figure out what caused the exception and might retry the fetch. If the cause was merely a page fault, then it would certainly retry after the indicated page was brought into system memory. But if the data pipeline is full, and things are in process then you must back up and restart after the page fault is satisfied.

The exception handler does the following:

1. The execution context is saved to memory (EPSR, SXIP, SNIP, and SFIP)
2. Shadowing is enabled (SFRZ bit cleared in PSR)
3. Corrects the condition causing the exception.
4. Clear E bits in SXIP and SNIP saved to memory in 1.
5. Freeze shadowing (SFRZ bit set)
6. Restore saved context.
   Saved EPSR ⇨ EPSR
   Saved SXIP ⇨ SNIP
   Saved SNIP ⇨ SFIP
7. rte to the task running at exception time.

Data access exception (Vector offset 0x18)

These are recoverable, but imprecise. That is, there is no guaranteed pointer to the offending instruction. But, that's OK. You can manage without it. Like the instruction access exception, the 88100 merely gets a signal that indicates a problem with the access. Something in the memory system must contain the cause. For the 88200, the cause is contained in the PFSR. The exception handler reads the status and takes action based on the cause.

Remember, the data unit is a pipeline, and it has a set of nine shadow registers to tell what is going on inside. The nine are divided into three sets: DMT0−2, DMD0−2, and DMA0−2. The 0th set contains information on stage 0, the 1st on stage 1, etc. DMTx holds information about the memory access in progress.

DMDx contains the data at each stage, while DMAx has the address. The transaction shadowed by stage 0 is the access that caused the exception. Stage 1 is the next memory access queued up. The address phase of the stage 1 transaction started but got cancelled when stage 0 had the exception. Stage 2 hasn't started anything yet. Either of Stage 1 or 2 could be a part of a double word access or half of an xmem.

Returning from a data access exception isn't as simple as restoring the shadow registers and doing an rte. The DMXx shadow registers aren't restored automatically and the flight picked up where it left off. The exception handler must use the contents of the data unit shadow registers to emulate the instructions that were in the pipeline. (Emulation of these instructions is quite sophisticated, and is beyond the scope of this book.) The shadow scoreboard register references related to the data unit pipeline must be cleared. When these little details are complete, then an rte will return.

Following is a description of the handler operations:

1. Save execution context (EPSR, SNIP, SFIP, SXIP, SSBR, and DMXx)
2. Enable shadowing (clear SFRZ)
3. Correct the cause of the exception.
4. Emulate the instructions that were in the pipeline.
5. Freeze shadowing (set SFRZ)
6. rte

Floating point unit exceptions

Like other execution units in the 88100, the FPU can have both precise and imprecise exceptions. The data representation, the exceptions, and the response to them within the FPU are governed by the IEEE 754 standard on floating point numbers. For a sure cure for insomnia, IEEE 754 is a superb bedtime volume. Like most standards, there is a burden on the developer to comply, but an enormous benefit to the end user in consistent performance across products.

The FPU has two exception vectors, one each for its precise (Vector 0x390) and imprecise (Vector 0x398) flavors. When either is received, the instruction unit swings into action and saves the execution context to the shadow and exception time registers. The data really needed to handle the exception is saved into the Floating point control registers (fcr0 − fcr8, and fcr62 − 63). The information in the FPU registers relates only to the FPU instruction that caused the problem.

As a part of the 88100 process of FPU exceptions, the FPU is disabled and the offending instruction purged from the pipeline. Anything else in the pipeline is frozen. When this is complete, the 88100 branches to the appropriate vector. The complete sequence is:

1. FPU signals the instruction unit of an exception
2. FPU sets the exception cause bit in FPECR
3. Disables the FPU by setting SFD1 bit in the PSR
4. Removes the instruction that caused the exception from the FPU pipeline

In the first paragraph, it is stated that FPU exceptions are governed by IEEE 754. That compliance is a combination of the 88000 hardware and the software of the exception handler. Motorola supplies a default exception handler that does comply, but you have the latitude to change it. If you do so, either be sure that your changes don't affect compliance, or that *you realize that portability of software and data may be lost!* Better you should use the default versions unless you are intimate with 754 *and* have an outstanding reason for the change. If you have the technical skills and reasons for change, we would like to be able to use you as a technical reference— you know more about it than we do.

If you do provide a user exception handler, then for each of the following exceptions you must enable your handler by setting the appropriate bit in the FPCR:

- EFINV—Invalid operation
- EFDVZ—Divide by zero
- EFUNF—Underflow
- EFOVF—Overflow
- EFINX—Inexact

In some situations, the exception handler might need to give results indicating that valid results are not possible. There are two IEEE 754 data representations called $\pm$NAN (Not A Number). Their values are:

- Single precision + NAN = 0x7FSxxxxx, where S has its high bit on, and xxxxx is non-zero. A valid +NAN single is 0x7FFFFFFF
- Single precision − NAN = 0xFFSxxxxx, where S has its high bit on, and xxxxx is non-zero. A valid −NAN single is 0xFFFFFFFF
- Double precision + NAN = 0x7FFxxxxx xxxxxxxx, where any bit in the x's area is non-zero. A valid +NAN double is 0x7FFFFFFF 00000000
- Double precision −NAN = 0xFFFxxxxx xxxxxxxx, where any bit in the x's area is non-zero. A valid −NAN double is 0xFFFFFFFF 00000000

NANs are two of the IEEE 754 reserved values. There are a total of 6.

$$\pm\text{NAN} \quad \pm\text{Infinity} \quad \pm\text{Denormalized}$$

Chapter 5 covered the FPU's registers in excruciating detail, but it seems useful to recap them here. fcr0−fcr8 have information on the exception,

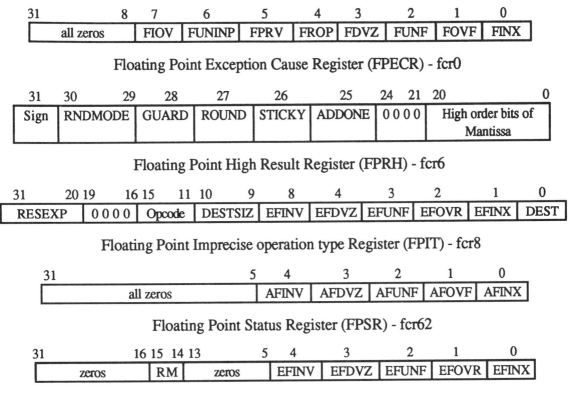

31		8	7	6	5	4	3	2	1	0
	all zeros		FIOV	FUNINP	FPRV	FROP	FDVZ	FUNF	FOVF	FINX

Floating Point Exception Cause Register (FPECR) - fcr0

31	30	29	28	27	26	25	24 21	20	0
Sign	RNDMODE	GUARD	ROUND	STICKY	ADDONE		0 0 0 0	High order bits of Mantissa	

Floating Point High Result Register (FPRH) - fcr6

31	20 19	16 15	11	10	9	8	4	3	2	1	0
RESEXP	0 0 0 0	Opcode	DESTSIZ		EFINV	EFDVZ	EFUNF	EFOVR	EFINX	DEST	

Floating Point Imprecise operation type Register (FPIT) - fcr8

31		5	4	3	2	1	0
	all zeros		AFINV	AFDVZ	AFUNF	AFOVF	AFINX

Floating Point Status Register (FPSR) - fcr62

31	16 15	14 13		5	4	3	2	1	0
zeros	RM	zeros		EFINV	EFDVZ	EFUNF	EFOVR	EFINX	

Floating Point Control Register (FPCR) - fcr63

9-5 Floating point control registers.

but are available only in supervisor mode. The other two, fcr62−63 may be read in user mode. (See Fig. 9-5.)

While the FPU is disabled and its pipeline frozen, its control registers may still be read, but it will only execute the fldstr, fstcr, and fxcr instructions. When exception handling is complete and the FPU restarted via rte, the remaining instructions in the FPU pipeline resume execution. The exceptioned instruction must be either completed by the exception handler, or discarded. Any relevant scoreboard register bits must be cleared by the handler as well. The following are the floating point exceptions:

Integer-divide error exception (Vector offset 0x40)

In the spirit of cooperation, the FPU is kind enough to use its powers to perform integer divides and multiplies for the integer unit. Sort of "divides are hard, and you already know how, would you do them for me?" Same sort of thing you hear from your kids about algebra homework. The FPU is a sucker for this, but that means it must deal with the exceptions as well.

The exception occurs when you div or divu by zero, or when either operand is negative in a div. SXIP points to the instruction that caused the problem, and the scoreboard bit is set for the destination register, even though that register isn't affected. fcr2 has the dividend and fcr4 has the divisor, while fcr5 has the destination register number along with the opcode and operand size data. The opcode information alone isn't sufficient to tell directly whether the div or divu instruction was used. However, process of elimination will narrow things down a bit. If fcr4 (the divisor) = 0 it doesn't matter—you have to solve that for either. If fcr4 ≠ 0 and either fcr4 or fcr2 has the bit 31 set, then the instruction was a div. Had it been divu no error would have occurred.

For a zero divisor situation, the exception handler could return 0x7FF-FFFFF into the destination register. That is the maximum signed integer value. For negative operands, the handler could make the numbers positive, perform the operation again, and set the sign bit on the result before returning. See the example of signed multiply in chapter 11.

Floating point precise exceptions (Vector offset 0x390)

There are 6 possible FPU precise exceptions. None of the instructions causing them are executed. In all six, the scoreboard bit or bits are set for the destination register prior to exception recognition. So, you must clear them before doing the rte. Remember that these don't have separate vectors. The precise exception vector is taken, and that exception handler does the cause finding.

FPU disabled

This one is simple: an FPU instruction was tried when the FPU was asleep. This means no floating point, no conversion, and no integer divides and multiplies. Because the FPU was disabled, the FPECR is not valid. The exception handler must test the SFD1 bit (bit 3) of the PSR to see of this was the cause. If it is clear, then the cause must be one of the other precise floating point exceptions.

Floating point to integer conversion overflow

This one is a sort of imprecise precise exception. You know what its cause was and "who done it," but the result only *might* overflow. If the floating point exponent is ≥ 30, the exception occurs, as the result might overflow an integer. It is up to the exception handler to figure out if it really would overflow. If not, the handler must perform the conversion and place the result in the destination. Because floats (as floating point numbers are known to their close friends) are signed, the resulting integer is signed. That being so, you know that the range of possible integer values is $2^{31} - 1$ to -2^{31}.

When the precise exception handler gets control, it can identify this exception from the FIOV (bit 7) bit in the FPECR. To have a user-supplied handler receive control, the EFINV bit (bit 4) would have been set in the FPCR. The default handler would set AFINV (bit 4) in the FPSR and write $\pm$ NAN to the destination. The AFINV bit would tell the program that caused the exception that an invalid operation occurred.

Floating point unimplemented opcode

This exception is peculiar. For each FP instruction, it was said that if you attempt execution while the FPU is disabled, then the Floating Point Unimplemented exception is taken. Yet earlier the FPU disabled exception was described. Well, yeah, but . . .

What happens is that when the FPU is disabled, the precise exception handler first checks to see if the FPU is disabled via the PSR—because, if so, the FPECR is not valid. So even though the FP instructions try to go to exception via FP Unimplemented, they really are correctly pigeonholed by the handler. However, it is possible to attempt execution of an FP opcode that isn't implemented in the FPU. If that happens, the FUNIMP bit (bit 6) would be set in FPECR, while SFD1 would show the FPU was enabled. This exception can't have a user-supplied exception handler. But there might be a very smart system exception handler for FUNIMP. Such a handler could emulate an unimplemented operation.

For just a moment, look at the FP instruction opcode. FPU instructions are a subset of the SFU instructions. Never mind that it is the only SFU, that will change in time. Bits $31 - 26$ are 100001 for all FPU instructions, and there is a sub opcode in bits $15 - 10$. That is 6 bits, and $2^6 = 64$. Well, there are but nine "real" 88100 FP instructions. The 55 unimplemented opcodes can be used for things like trigonometric functions. If provided, they would be performed by exception handler software.

Back to our regularly scheduled program.

If the exception occurred as the intentional result of a pseudo-opcode, then the handler would take care of it. If not, the instruction can be discarded. As the instruction doesn't get decoded, nothing gets set in the scoreboard.

Floating point privilege violation

Somebody tried a no-no. Either an fldcr, fstcr, or fxcr instruction was tried to control registers fcr0−8 while in user mode. Use of those three instructions is allowed from user mode, but only with FPCR and FPSR. The FPRV bit (bit 5) is set in the FPECR. The instruction doesn't set anything in the scoreboard, and you can't have a user handler for the exception.

Floating point reserved operand

Back in "Floating point unit exceptions," the start of this section, NANs were discussed. Six IEEE 754 reserved values were also listed. This exception means that one of them was used.

FROP (bit 4) is set in FPECR. What the exception handler does with the exception is specified by IEEE 754 for most situations. This allows the software to take care of operands that are valid, but that can't be used by the FPU. If the operands aren't covered by the standard then control is passed to the user-supplied handler, if any. If there is one, remember that EFINV must be set in the FPCR. Whether a user-supplied handler is invoked or not, the AFINV bit is set in FPSR.

Floating point divide by zero

It can't be done for integers and it can't be done for floats either. The cause is a ±zero divisor. User-supplied handlers can be invoked, but there are two choices:

If the operation is ±zero divided by ±zero, and EFINV is set in FPCR, then AFINV is set in the FPSR and the invalid operation user handler is invoked.

If the numerator is non-zero, and EFDVZ is set in FPCR, then AFDVZ is set in FPSR and the divide-by-zero user handler is invoked. The handler must clear the appropriate bits in the scoreboard.

Floating point imprecise exceptions (Vector offset 0x398)

All of the above were nice, mild-mannered precise exceptions. They're predictable. You know what caused them, and how to get back from them. But, there are other kinds of exceptions—wild exceptions, not-so-nice exceptions, imprecise exceptions—whose exact cause might not be known.

You can see the effects of this unruly bunch on the scoreboard register, which reflects their imprecision. The relevant SB bit is cleared for a single-precision result and for the first register of a double-precision result. Thus the exception might have left the SB in a confused state. The exception handler must clear the bit for the second register of a double-precision result to correct the confusion.

Floating point underflow

Underflow occurs when a floating point result is too small to be a "normalized" float. IEEE 754 calls this "tininess" (as in tiny-ness). FUNF (bit 2) is set in FPECR. If EFUNF is set in the FPCR, control is passed to the user handler. If not, the default handler checks the data for loss of accuracy.

Loss of accuracy comes in two flavors: inexact result, and denormalization loss. The first is found by the FPU hardware when significant bits were lost in the process of rounding. The second is detected by software when signficant bits were lost when the result was denormalized.

First, to define a denormalized number: The official, IEEE-approved definition states that a *denormalized number* is a representation of a number that can't be represented as a normalized number.

Huh?

Admittedly, this sounds like the authors took a quick trip to Washington D.C. to study Bureaucratese. But, believe it or not, there's meaning here. What it says is that if there appears a number that cannot be represented according to the rules set down by the various standards for this sort of thing, then the 88K does its best to represent it in some other fashion.

If a loss of accuracy exists, AFUNF and AFINX are set in the FPSR. Then the FPCR is checked to see if the EFINX is set; if so the user inexact exception handler is invoked. If there isn't a user handler than the default is taken, to write the denormalized result to the destination and rte.

Floating point overflow

This is sort of the inverse of the underflow case. The FPU determines that the rounded result is larger than can be represented. The FOVF bit (bit 1) is set in the FPECR. If EFOVF is set in FPCR, the user overflow handler is invoked. If not then AFOVF is set in FPSR and the EFINX bit is checked to see if a user inexact handler is available. If so, control transfers to it. If not, AFINX is set in FPSR and the exception ignored; while $\pm$ Infinity is written to the destination.

Floating point inexact

This happens when rounding the calculated result causes a loss of accuracy. The result is in fcr6−8, with the rounding, guard, and sticky bits of the result in fcr6. Processing inexact exceptions is tied to the over/underflow exception. If bits will be lost in underflow, then an inexact exception occurs in addition to the underflow exception. If there is no overflow user handler; e.g. EFOVF is not set, then the overflow exception will not occur, and the inexact exception will be taken.

When inexact is signalled by the FPU, EFINX is checked. If set, the exception is taken, FINX (bit 0) is set in the FPECR, and control is passed to the user handler. If EFINX is clear, then the exception is not taken and AFINX is set in FPSR. Yep, this means that the choice of whether or not this exception is taken is under software control.

FPU registers after exceptions

The table in Fig. 9-6 depicts the state of each of the FPU control registers after an exception occurs.

RESET (Vector offset 0x0)

RESET is a special exception triggered by the $\overline{RST}$ signal. This is discussed at length in chapter 5, but RESET forces the 88100 to a known state. All inflight transactions are aborted, VBR is cleared, and the processor goes to the following state, shown in Fig. 9-7.

Register	State
FPECR	Bits 7-0 indicate which exception occurred. If more than one bit is set, the priority is from 7 high to 0 low.
FP Source operand registers	For precise exceptions, they contain the source operands of the faulted instruction. For imprecise exceptions, they are undefined.
FPPT	For precise exceptions, it contains opcode, size fields and destination register of the faulted instruction. Undefined for imprecise exceptions.
FPIT	For precise exceptions, it is undefined. For imprecise exceptions, it contains opcode, size fields, result exponent, user exception handler information, and destination register of the faulted instruction.
Floating point result registers	For precise exceptions, they are undefined. For imprecise, they contain the partial result and rounding information.
FPCR and FPSR	Both contain the values they had before the exception.

9-6 FPU register states after exception.

9.21 Error exception (Vector offset 0x50)

Recall that this character was mentioned earlier. It occurs if shadowing is frozen and an exception other than a trap takes place. With its shadow registers frozen, the 88100 has no mechanism to save the information necessary to process the incoming exception. It quietly gives up with this exception. The error exception can also occur if there is an error in fetching an exception vector. The situations are similar. In the first, data must be saved to process the exception but there's no place to put it. In the second, the data was saved, but there's no place to go to process it. If the error exception vector can't be fetched, it puts the 88100 into an infinite loop.

Avoiding error exceptions means that exception handlers should execute without exceptions, and that interrupts are masked off; or that the handlers enable shadowing. The latter case requires that the context information in the shadow registers be saved to memory.

It also requires that the vector table and at least the first part of all handlers are locked in main memory. If they weren't, it is possible that the exception handler you needed got paged out; and when that exception occurred, an instruction access exception would occur while shadowing was frozen. Then you'd end up here in the error exception.

Thanks for bearing through all this. Exceptions are complex, no way around it. If you must delve into them, this chapter won't solve all your problems, but we hope it illluminates the swamp a bit.

Register	State
PSR	Bit 31 & 9-0 set all others clear (0x800003FF)
EPSR	Undefined
SB	Cleared
SSBR	Undefined
Instruction Pointers	FIP = 0x0 (physical) V bits in NIP and XIP clear
SNIP, SFIP, SXIP	Undefined
VBR	Cleared
r1-r31	Undefined
DMT0-2	Bit 0 cleared other bits undefined
DMA0-2	Undefined
DMD0-2	Undefined
Internal registers	Undefined
FPU registers	FPECR, FPCR, FPSR cleared, others undefined

9-7 Register states following Reset.

10

Programming for binary interoperability

We disscussed 88open's Binary Compatibility Standard (BCS) in chapter 2. Let's go into a bit more depth on what is required in order to have truly binary portable software. Only a bit more, though, because this is a subject on which whole books can be written—and indeed, have been. The 88open Consortium Ltd. has, in fact, published an entire volume on just the subject of binary compatibility.

The information in this chapter is provided through the courtesy of the 88open Consortium. It reproduces much of the BCS Standard Release 1.1. But, where 88open had many pages to fill, only a few are shown here. Therefore, this chapter is highly condensed. It should be considered a reference work only. Its purpose is not to examine the BCS in exhaustive detail, but to give a quick and handy guide to those elements of UNIX System V.3 that are involved in making application software portable between 88000-based systems. Start by looking at the data used within a system.

Data types

This section specifies the sizes and types of data objects that are used to interface with a conforming system. It does not specify interfaces within an application.

Size and format of primitive data types

The sizes of primitive data types used for communications between the system and the application are defined as:

Type	# of 8-bit bytes	Format	Aligned on byte multiples of
char	1		1
short	2		2
int	4		4
long	4		4
float	4	IEEE	4
double	8	IEEE	8

The size of a pointer to any data type or structure is four bytes; and it is aligned on a four-byte boundary. All data is stored in "Big Endian" order, with the most significant values stored at the lowest address.

Alignment of data within structures

Alignment of data within structures passed between application programs and the system are specified as follows: the table lists data types and restrictions on the addresses of each type within a structure.

Type	Aligned on byte multiples of
char	1
short	2
int	4
long	4
float	4
double	8

Structures and unions shall be aligned to the alignment of their most restrictive data type. The sizes of structures and unions shall be multiples of their alignments. Within a structure or union, the alignment of arrays shall be the same as their constituent members.

For example, the structure

```
struct {
    char c;
    short  s;
```

```
double   d;
char c1;
int i;
char *p;
}
```

shall have members at the following addresses (relative to the beginning of the structure):

Variable	Address (relative)
c	0
s	2
d	8
c1	16
i	20
p	24

The example structure is padded at the end to be 32 bytes long.

The special notation to show explicit padding between structure members is: " *<pad>* ." The contents of *<pad>* fields are *unspecified*.

Symbolic data types

The following table gives definitions for POSIX, SVID, and X3.159-1989 (C Standard) implementation-specific data types used in the BCS standard.

Type	Derived From	Primitive Definition
clock_t	POSIX	*unsigned long*
dev_t	POSIX	*unsigned long*
gid_t	POSIX	*unsigned long*
ino_t	POSIX	*unsigned long*
key_t	SVID	*long*
mode_t	POSIX	*unsigned long*
nlink_t	POSIX	*unsigned long*
off_t	POSIX	*long*
pid_t	POSIX	*long*
sigset_t	POSIX	*struct {unsigned long s[2]}*
tcflag_t	POSIX	*unsigned long*
time_t	X3.159	*long*
uid_t	POSIX	*unsigned long*

The sigset_t type is a 64-bit quantity where signal numbers are mapped to bit numbers, as shown below:

	Word 0												Word 1		
Signal #	1	2	3	...		31	32	33	34	35				63	64
Bit #	31	30	29	...		1	0	31	30	29		...		1	0

Common Object File Format (COFF)

A conforming system shall support "demand paged—type 0413" executable files in Common Object File Format (COFF).

File structure

An executable COFF file shall consist of at least four parts that will always be found in the same order. Some of these parts are ignored (or not specified) for binary standard executable files. The file parts shall follow each other in this order:

1. File header
2. Optional header
   Note: Despite its name, this section is not optional in a conforming application.
   See "Optional Header."
3. Section
4. Raw section data
5. Relocation information (ignored by the exec( ) functions)
6. Line numbers (ignored by the exec( ) functions)
7. Symbol table (ignored by the exec( ) functions)
8. String table (ignored by the exec( ) functions)

The sections numbered 1 through 4 above shall always appear; numbers 5 through 8 are optional, although they will appear in the order stated. Other optional sections may follow the sections shown. The following describes the contents of these sections in a binary standard executable file.

File header

The file header is a data structure that describes how the other parts of the file fit together. The header starts at byte 0 of the executable file. It contains the following fields:

Name	Size	Offset	Description
f_magic	2	0	magic number: MC88MAGIC = 0555 (0x016D)
f_nscns	2	2	Shall be $> 3 - .text, .data,$ and $.bss$
f_timdat	4	4	(Ignored by the *exec*( ) functions)
f_symptr	4	8	(Ignored by the *exec*( ) functions)
f_nsyms	4	12	(Ignored by the *exec*( ) functions)
f_opthdr	2	16	Size (in bytes) of Optional Header, always 28
f_flags	2	18	Flags (see below)

The length of the section is 20 bytes.

The f_flags field contains the following bits:

F_AR16WR (0x0080) (PDP byte order) and F_AR32WR (0x0100) (VAX byte order) shall be off; i.e., ((f_flags & 0x0180)==0)

F_EXEC (0x0002) and F_AR32W (0x0200) shall be on; i.e., ((f_flags & 0x0202)==0x0202)

The upper five bits shall be set off; i.e., ((f_flags & 0xf800)==0)

Note: An implementation should use additional section headers to define different actions that are implementation-specific, rather than defining different f_flags.

Additional flags shall be implementation-defined.

Optional header

Despite its name, this section is required.

The size of the optional header is provided in the f_opthdr field in the file header. The size of this header is 28 bytes. A conforming application shall specify the fields magic and entry. All other fields shall be implementation defined. This header has the fields shown below.

Name	Size	Offset	Description
magic	2	0	Magic number-shall be 0413
vstamp	2	2	(Ignored by the exec( ) functions)
tsize	4	4	(Ignored by the exec( ) functions)
dsize	4	8	(Ignored by the exec( ) functions)

bsize	4	12	(Ignored by the exec( ) functions)
entry	4	16	Process entry point
text_start	4	20	(Ignored by the exec( ) functions)
data_start	4	24	(Ignored by the exec( ) functions)

Note: Type 407 files that allow the free mixing of text and data are not allowed. The nature of the instruction and data caches on the M88000 could add excessive overhead if type 407 files were allowed. The memctl( ) function can be used to explicitly control the execution of data.

Section headers

There are a number of section headers in the file; the actual number is provided in the f_nscns field in the file header. The section header layout is shown below.

Name	Size	Offset	Description
s_name	8	0	Section name, padded with null bytes
s_paddr	4	8	(Ignored by the exec( ) functions)
s_vaddr	4	12	Virtual address at which the section will be loaded (see "Memory Map" for calculation of this address, aligned for an 8-byte boundary)
s_size	4	16	Section size in bytes (this shall always be a multiple of 8 bytes)
s_scnptr	4	20	The byte offset into the COFF file of the start of the raw data to be loaded (on an 8-byte boundary)
s_relptr	4	24	(Ignored by the exec( ) functions)
s_lnnoptr	4	28	(Ignored by the exec( ) functions)
s_nreloc	4	32	(Ignored by the exec( ) functions; Note: this field is defined as 2 bytes in SVR3)
s_nlnno	4	36	(Ignored by the exec( ) functions)
s_flags	4	40	(See table below)

The length of the section header is 44 bytes. Raw section data shall always be aligned to an 8-byte boundary.

A conforming application shall provide exactly one of each of the following three sections. Any other sections (e.g., comment, line numbers) provided by an application are not guaranteed or required to be supported by a conforming system, except as noted below.

s_name	s_flags	s_scnptr
.text	STYP_TEXT (0x0020)	
.data	STYP_DATA (0x0040)	
.bss	STYP_BSS (0x0080)	0

A conforming system shall support these three sections.

A conforming system shall be prepared to receive zero or more of the following optional sections, used for vendor-specific extensions. The actions to be taken when these sections are present are implementation-defined.

s_name	s_flags
< vendor stamp >	STYP_VENDOR (0x1000)

The name of the vendor section encodes the vendor stamp. A vendor section name shall consist of the character "$" followed by the seven-digit hexadecimal representation of the vendor stamp, padded with leading zeros. For example, the vendor section for vendor stamp 4164072 is named $03f89e8.

The presence or absence of vendor sections in a conforming application shall not limit the correct execution of the application on a conforming system.

The vendor sections allow a conforming system access to information that only that conforming system uses without requiring all conforming systems to use that information, and without sacrificing the ability of the conforming application to execute on other conforming systems.

Raw section data

This part of the file contains the raw loadable data for sections whose section headers have sizes that are greater than zero. The data is located at byte offsets given in the corresponding section header's s_scnptr fields. Each set of section data is of the size given in its header's s_size field and is a multiple of eight bytes in length and is aligned on an eight-byte boundary. Sections with an s_scnptr field of zero have no corresponding section data and are loaded with their address space filled with zeros.

Relocation information, line numbers, symbol table, & string tablesections

Are all ignored by the exec( ) functions.

Memory map

The BCS defines all executables to have an optional COFF system header magic number (the field magic in the Optional Header) of 0413. These executables are linked so that the .text and .data/.bss sections load into separate regions attached on protection boundaries in the process virtual address space. The protection boundary for conforming applications shall be 4 megabytes.

The following restrictions shall apply to the choice of a section's virtual address:

1. The .text, .data, and .bss sections shall not overlap. A conforming application shall use a single address space.
2. The .bss section shall always immediately follow the .data section (i.e., the virtual address of .bss is exactly equal to the .data section's s_vaddr field plus its s_size field).
3. The .text section shall always be present. It shall be possible to map the .text section to a non-zero virtual address that meets the data alignment restrictions and fits in the memory map. Note: This is so that zero references can be caught by the hardware.
4. The .text section shall be readable and executable, but not writable. A conforming application shall not make write accesses to the .text section, except after using the memctl( ) system call.
5. The .data and .bss sections shall be readable and writable, but not executable. Code can be executed from such a section only after using the memctl( ) system call.
6. The linker shall assign the virtual address of each section according to the following formula:
   (virtual address of first byte in section) modulo (65536)
   = (file offset of section data) modula (65536)

This formula allows an operating system with a page size and a disk block size that are both evenly divisible into 65536 (64K) to directly page blocks from the program file into main memory.

A conforming system shall support a per-process address space of at least 4 megabytes (MB) .text, 4MB .data/.bss, and 4MB stack. The application shall specify any requirements for an address space greater than this.

The stack segment is a valid range of address space that monotonically increases in size. Its upper bound is the stack base which is 0xf0000000; its lower bound is the stack top. The stack top is the value held in r31 when the stack was last extended; a conforming application shall ensure that r31 always points to an address aligned to an 8-byte boundary. The stack is extended to the value of r31 when a reference is made to an invalid region between the stack top and r31. If such extension would result in the overlap of another segment, a SIGSEGV signal is generated. The stack segment may be safely extended (i.e., segment overlap is guaranteed to generate a SIGSEGV signal) if the stack is always extended by an amount no more than 4 megabytes. A conforming system shall support a 4-megabyte minimum stack segment size.

A conforming BCS application is allowed to change the address of its stack to some other region (such as .data or .bss) provided that region is both readable and writable. When using such a region for a stack, automatic stack expansion is not guaranteed.

Note: The implications of this are:

1. The conforming system will maintain an invalid region of at least 4 megabytes at the stack limit.
2. Secure stacks are implemented by stack probing at 4-megabyte intervals. A system with a 4K page size will allocate every 1024th page.
3. The conforming system may or may not put the argument block, created by execve( ), at the stack base.

A conforming application shall not use the address space above the stack base (> 0xf0000000).

Note: This upper 256 megabytes is reserved for a possible shared library region in a future version of this standard.

Entry to user process

When a process is first entered (from an exec( ) system call), registers are initialized as follows:

r1	is implementation-defined.
r2	contains argc, the number of arguments
r3	contains argv, a pointer to the array of argument pointers in the stack. The array is immediately followed by a NULL pointer.
r4	contains envp, a pointer to the array of environment pointers in the stack. The array is immediately followed by a NULL pointer. If no environment exists, r4 shall point to a NULL pointer.
r5 − r13	are reserved for future versions of this standard; the values are undefined.
r14 − r30	are implementation-defined.
r31	is the initial stack pointer, aligned to an 8-byte boundary.
FPSR	is the floating point user status register. This register is initially cleared.
FPCR	is the floating point user control register. This register is set to round to nearest mode and all the user exception handlers are disabled. Individual processes may change the register contents if desired.
PSR	is the Processor Status Register; it contains 0x3f0, which corresponds to:

- Big-Endian byte ordering
- concurrent operation allowed
- carry bit clear
- SFU1 enabled
- SFU2 − SFU7 disabled
- misaligned accesses cause an exception
- interrupts enabled
- shadow registers enabled

Individual object modules might need to manipulate the stacked data and register contents at startup before control passes to the main section of the program. These manipulations can be accomplished via a user library startup routine (typically crt0.o).

Note: Typically, for a C language process, crt0.o merely needs to create a homing area on the stack, initialize the floating point unit, and then call main( ). Some applications or languages may use a different startup procedure. For the sake of binary compatibility, all application-dependent startup code should be placed into the user startup routine rather than the kernel. (See Fig. 10-1.)

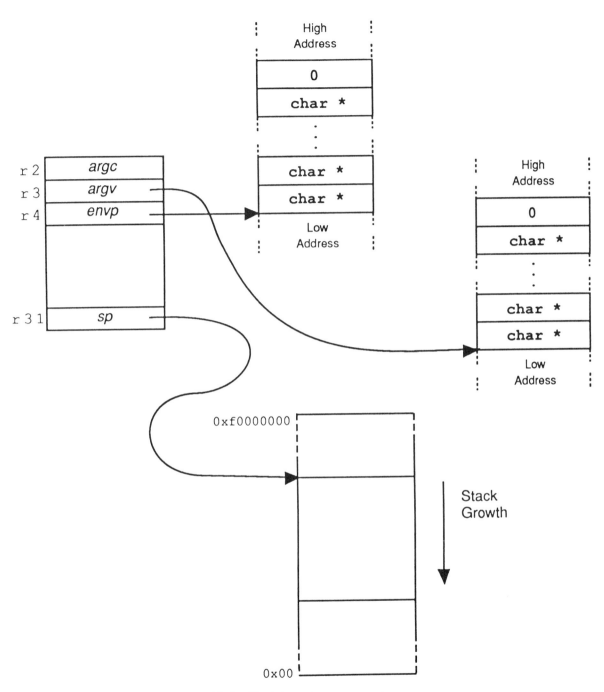

10-1 Registers at process entry.

Signal handling

When a signal is delivered to a user process, the system builds a data structure on the user stack and returns to an address in user space previously specified by one of the signal support system calls. The system returns control to the signal interface code linked into the user program. This signal interface code then generally calls the appropriate signal handling routine in the user program. The user signal handler can use one of three methods to complete:

1. Use the _exit( ) call to terminate the process.
2. Restore the context of the user process to a point where it had previously been saved in anticipation of signal handling. The user process context save and restore are generally performed using routines equivalent to sigsetjmp( ) and siglongjmp( ) defined in ANSI/IEEE Std 1003.1-1988 (POSIX).
3. Return to its caller. If the user signal handler is to return to its caller it will return to the signal handler interface code linked into the program. This code will perform a sigret( ) systemcall to return. Typically this call will be made from the /usr/lib/libc signal interface, making it transparent to the user program.

Location of Signal Frame

When a signal is delivered to a conforming application, a conforming system shall place a signal frame (see below) on the application's stack. If insufficient writable address space exists on the application's stack, or the stack reference itself is invalid, the application shall be terminated. Its exit status shall indicate that the process was killed by a SIGSEGV signal.

Signal frame format

When a signal is delivered to a conforming application a conforming system shall place the structure on the user's stack (see Fig. 10-2).

Note 1: Including the value of the user stack pointer at the time the signal was caught allows kernel implementations to add additional information between the signal frame specified in Fig. 10-2 and the previous top of the user stack.

Note 2: These words can be modified by the application before calling sigret( ).

An exception block is arranged as shown in Fig. 10-3.

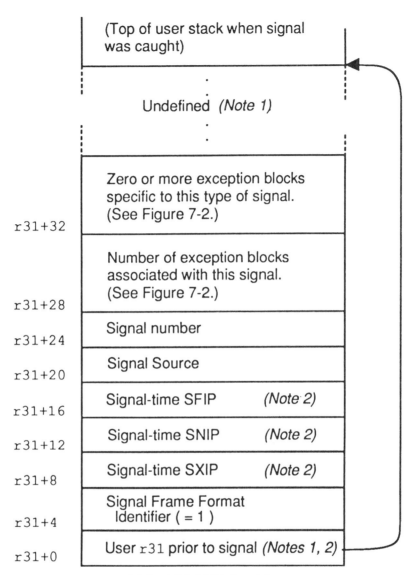

(Top of user stack when signal was caught)

Undefined *(Note 1)*

r31+32	Zero or more exception blocks specific to this type of signal. (See Figure 7-2.)
r31+28	Number of exception blocks associated with this signal. (See Figure 7-2.)
r31+24	Signal number
r31+20	Signal Source
r31+16	Signal-time SFIP *(Note 2)*
r31+12	Signal-time SNIP *(Note 2)*
r31+8	Signal-time SXIP *(Note 2)*
r31+4	Signal Frame Format Identifier (= 1)
r31+0	User r31 prior to signal *(Notes 1, 2)*

10-2 MC88100 signal frame.

Signal source

The signal source encodes the origin of the signal as follows:

1. Signal was generated by a hardware exception (e.g. SIGILL); all of the signals that can be generated in this manner are described in "Relationship Between Signals and Exceptions."
2. Signal was generated by the kernel (e.g. SIGPIPE).
3. Signal was generated by a call to kill( ).

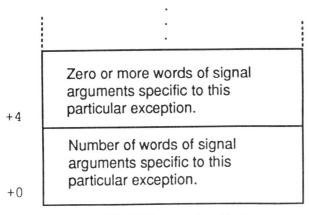

10-3 MC88100 exception block.

Concurrent exceptions

Due to the nature of the MC88100, several instructions may be executing concurrently. These instructions might generate imprecise exceptions, and these exceptions might generate signals with information indicating the cause of the exception. These instructions might also generate precise exceptions that occur at the same time as the imprecise exceptions. Thus, multiple exceptions might exist when a signal is taken.

With the signal frame format in Fig. 10-2, a conforming system shall treat multiple instances of a particular type of exception (generated as the result of entering the system with multiple exceptions) as a single signal.

The information associated with each separate exception shall be placed on the user's stack. Note: The signal interface code linked into the user program may then parse this information and call the user's signal handler, as appropriate.

Signal representations in traditional UNIX systems cannot distinguish between multiple instances of a particular signal. Signals are represented by a flag that indicates that a particular signal has been received by an application. This conveys no information about how many such signals were received, only that at least one was received, and is therefore outstanding. The signal scheme described above makes the process's signal state more visible. Conforming systems interpret signals in the traditional UNIX system manner (a flag that indicates the receipt of at least one instance of a particular signal). All concurrent imprecise exceptions shall generate exactly one signal of each type generated by the exceptions. Each such signal represents one or more exceptions, as appropriate.

There is a distinction between a set of exceptions and a signal generated by the kill( ) system call. Each of these is treated as the occurrence of one signal—the first with multiple exception blocks, and the second with zero exception blocks.

Process state

The three signal instruction pointer values SXIP, SNIP, and SFIP on the stack (at r31+8, r31+12, and r31+16, respectively) shall point to instructions in user space. Upon entry to the signal interface code, the PSR, FPSR, FPCR, and the general registers, except for r31, shall contain the values they would have contained if the application had reached that instruction indicated by SXIP. r31 shall be ANDed with 0xfffffff8 and shall point to the top of the stack, and the value stored at r31+0 shall be the value which r31 would have contained had the application reached the instruction at SXIP.

If the signal is sent in response to a precise exception taken by a conforming application, SXIP shall point to the instruction which caused the exception. If the signal is sent in response to an imprecise exception, SXIP points to the last instruction executed by the Integer Unit, or dispatched to the Floating Point Unit or Data Unit.

An application might experience multiple imprecise exceptions before the signal associated with a particular precise or imprecise exception can be delivered. It is then impossible to select register values consistent with serial execution up to any particular instruction. In this case, each exception shall cause a separate exception block to be generated. The order of the exception blocks for the set of exceptions constituting a signal is unspecified. At most one signal of each type (e.g., SIGSEGV or SIGFPE) shall be sent to the process for the entire set of exceptions (see previous section). The signals associated with these exceptions may be delivered in an unspecified order, and the value of registers (including the FPSR) affected by the faulting, but as-yet incomplete, instructions shall have the values they had before these instructions were dispatched.

Returning from signals

A signal handler in a conforming application may choose to return to the signal interface code that may execute the sigret( ).

Relationship between signals and exceptions

A conforming system shall handle exceptions caused by the execution of a conforming application by completing the faulted operation in a manner transparent to the application or by delivering a signal to the application. The arguments shown are only valid when the "Signal Source" is 1 or 2. Exceptions correspond to signal values as described below:

Exception	Signal	Arguments	Remarks
Code access	SIGSEGV	0x01	See Note 1
Data access	SIGSEGV DMA0 DMT0 DMD0	0x02	See Note 2
Misaligned data access	SIGBUS	0x01	See Note 3
Protection violation	SIGBUS DMA0 DMT0 DMD0	0x02	
Unimplemented opcode	SIGILL	0x01	See Note 11
Privileged instruction violation	SIGILL	0x02	
Integer overflow	SIGFPE	0x80000001	
Integer divide	SIGFPE	0x80000002 or 0x80000001	See Note 4
Bounds check trap	SIGFPE	0x80000003	
Trap on fork( ) system call	SIGTRAP	-1	See fork( )
Trap on execve( ) system call	SIGTRAP	-2	See execve( )
Trap to vectors 504-511	SIGTRAP	vector number	
Floating point inexact	SIGFPE FPRH FPRL FPIT	0x01	See Note 5
Floating point overflow	SIGFPE FPRH FPRL FPIT	0x02 or 0x01	See Note 6
Floating point underflow	SIGFPE FPRH FPRL FPIT	0x04 or 0x01	See Note 7
Floating point divide by zero	SIGFPE	0x08 or 0x10	See Note 8

Floating point reserved operand	SIGFPE	0x10 or 0x80	See Note 9
Floating point integer conversion overflow	SIGFPE	0x10	See Note 10
Floating point privilege violation	SIGFPE	0x20	
Floating point unimplemented opcode	SIGFPE	0x40	

Notes:

1. Code access exceptions caused by demand paging within the text segment and areas made executable with the memctl( ) call shall be handled transparently to the application.
2. Data access exceptions caused by references to the stack segment shall be handled by extending the stack in a manner transparent to the application. Data access exceptions caused by demand paging shall be handled transparently to the application.
3. This exception can be disabled by setting the MXM bit of the Processor Status Register, via setpsr( ).
4. If the faulting instruction is DIV, the dividend is the most negative integer and the divisor is -1, then the SIGFPE signal shall be sent with 0x80000001 as the first argument. If the divisor is zero, the SIGFPE signal shall be sent with 0x80000002 as the first argument. Otherwise, the faulting instruction must be DIV and one or both operands is negative. In this case, the system shall complete the operation in a manner transparent to the application.
5. This exception can be disabled by clearing bit 0 (EFINX) of the Floating Point Control Register.
6. If bit 1 (EFOV) of the FPCR is set, the SIGFPE signal shall be sent with 0x02 as the first argument. Otherwise, bit 1 (AFOVF) of the FPSR shall be set, and if bit 0 (EFINX) of the FPCR is set, the SIGFPE signal shall be sent with 0x01 as the first argument. If bit 0 of the FPCR is also clear, then bit 0 (AFINX) of the FPSR shall be set and the system shall complete the operation in a manner transparent to the application and consistent with IEEE Std 754-1985 and the MC88100 user's manual.
7. If bit 2 (EFUNF) of the FPCR is set, the SIGFPE signal shall be sent with 0x04 as the first argument. If there has been a loss of accuracy, bit 2 (AFUNF) of the FPSR shall be set. In this case, if bit 0 (EFINX) of the FPCR is set, the SIGFPE signal shall be sent

with 0x01 as the first argument; if it is clear, then bit 0 (AFINX) of the FPSR shall be set. If no signal is sent, the system shall complete the operation in a manner transparent to the application and consistent with IEEE Std 754-1985 and the MC88100 user's manual.

8. If the numerator is zero, the exception shall be handled as a floating point reserved operand exception. Otherwise, if bit 3 (EFDVZ) of the FPCR is set, the SIGFPE signal shall be sent with 0x08 as the first argument. If bit 3 of the FPCR is clear, then the system shall set bit 8 (AFDVZ) of the FPSR and complete the operation in a manner transparent to the application and consistent with IEEE Std 754-1985 and the MC88100 user's manual.

9. If the operation is the subtraction of two infinities, the multiplication of infinity and zero, or the division of one infinity by another, and bit 4 (EFINV) of the FPCR is set, then the SIGFPE signal shall be sent with 0x10 as the first argument; otherwise bit 4 (AFINV) of the FPSR shall be set. If either operand is a signalling NaN and bit 4 of the FPCR is set, then the SIGFPE signal shall be sent with 0x80 as the first argument; otherwise bit 4 of the FPSR shall be set. If no signal is sent, the system shall complete the operation in a manner transparent to the application and consistent with IEEE Std 754-1985 and the MC88100 user's manual.

10. If the operand can be converted to an integer without overflow, the system shall complete the operation in a manner transparent to the application. If it cannot, and bit 4 (EFINV) of the FPCR is set, then the SIGFPE signal shall be sent. If bit 4 of the FPCR is clear, then bit 4 (AFINV) of the FPSR shall be set and the system shall complete the operation in a manner transparent to the application and consistent with IEEE Std 754-1985.

11. Conforming applications shall not use unimplemented opcodes. Rationale: It is possible that some currently unimplemented opcodes may eventually be used for other functions in future chip revisions. Therefore, conforming applications must assume that such opcodes are undefined and avoid their use, e.g., as a means of generating an exception.

Core file description

When a signal causes the creation of a core file, it shall have the format shown in Fig. 10-3. Note: This standard does not mandate that signals create core files, nor does it mandate the use of the name core.

Common header file values

Symbolic values

This section describes symbolic values usually found in a <limits.h> or <unistd.h> and the values they shall be given on conforming systems.

The following constants shall be defined in the headers as shown:

Constant	Value	Description
{CHAR_BIT}	8	The number of bits per byte.
{NGROUPS_MAX}	0	Multilple groups are not supported by default; use sysconf( ) at run-time to determine if this option is installed.
{_POSIX_SAVED_IDS}	1	Saved-set-user/group-IDs are supported.
{_POSIX_VERSION}	198808L	Version of POSIX standard.

The constant {CHAR_BIT} may be used by a BCS conforming application at compile time. For the constants {_POSIX_SAVED_IDS} and {_POSIX _VERSION}, the sysconf( ) call shall return exactly the values shown in the preceding table. For {NGROUPS_MAX}, the sysconf( ) call may return a number greater than zero if the POSIX multiple groups option is supported.

The following table contains values that are not defined in the headers, but represent values that must be queried by the application at run-time, using the sysconf( ) system call. The values shown in the Description column are the most restrictive values supported by conforming BCS systems and may be used by conforming BCS applications without resorting to the run-time call.

Constant	Description
{ARG_MAX}	Maximum length for the arguments to the execve( ) call is $\geq$ 5120. Note: This is greater than the corresponding POSIX minimum value, 4096.
{CHILD_MAX}	Maximum number of simultaneous processes per real user ID is $\geq$ 25. Note: This is greater than the corresponding POSIX minimum value, 6.
{OPEN_MAX}	Maximum number of open files per process is $\geq$ 25. Note: This is greater than the corresponding POSIX minimum value, 16.

{_POSIX_JOB_CONTROL} Job control is supported by default; use sys-conf( ) at run-time to determine if this option is installed

The following table contains values that are not defined in the headers, but represent values that must be queried by the application at run-time, using the pathconf( ) (or fpathconf( )) system call on the file in question. The values shown in the Description column are the most restrictive values supported by conforming BCS systems on any local file system. In a networking environment, values less than these most restrictive values could be returned by a remote file system. Therefore, the application should use either the pathconf( ) return value or the stated POSIX minimum value for each file that could be remotely mounted.

Constant	Description
{LINK_MAX}	Maximum of a file's link count is ≥ 1024. Note: This is greater than the corresponding POSIX minimum value, 8.
{MAX_CANON}	Maximum number of bytes in a terminal canonical input queue is ≥ 255.
{MAX_INPUT}	Maximum number of bytes for which space will be available in a terminal input queue is ≥ 255.
{NAME_MAX}	Maximum filename length is ≥ 14.
{PATH_MAX}	Maximum pathname length is ≥ 255.
{PIPE_BUF}	Maximum atomic write to pipe is ≥ 5120. Note: This is greater than the corresponding POSIX minimum value, 512.
{_POSIX_CHOWN_RESTRICTED}	It must be determined at run-time whether changing file ownership requires appropriate privileges.
{_POSIX_NO_TRUNC}	It must be determined at run-time whether filenames longer than {NAME_MAX} generate an error.

{_POSIX_VDISABLE}   Terminal special characters defined in <termios.h> can be individually disabled using the value returned by pathconf( ) on a per-file basis.

The values for {NGROUPS_MAX}, {_POSIX_CHOWN_RE-STRICTED}, and {_POSIX_NO_TRUNC} do not meet the requirements of the POSIX FIPS, NIST Publication 151; they should be ≥ 8, 1, and 1, respectively. All of these values can be interrogated by the application at run-time to see if it's actually running on a FIPS-conforming system.

Error return values

The following is a table of symbolic error return values usually found in <errno.h> and the values they shall be given on conforming systems. Error return values in the range 1 to 255 are reserved for use by this standard.

Constant	Value	Constant	Value
[EPERM]	1	[EISDIR]	21
[ENOENT]	2	[EINVAL]	22
[ESRCH]	3	[ENFILE]	23
[EINTR]	4	[EMFILE]	24
[EIO]	5	[ENOTTY]	25
[ENXIO]	6	[EFBIG]	27
[E2BIG]	7	[ENOSPC]	28
[ENOEXEC]	8	[ESPIPE]	29
[EBADF]	9	[EROFS]	30
[ECHILD]	10	[EMLINK]	31
[EAGAIN]	11	[EPIPE]	32
[ENOMEM]	12	[EDOM]	33
[EACCES]	13	[ERANGE]	34
[EFAULT]	14	[ENOMSG]	35
[ENOTBLK]	15	[EIDRM]	36
[EBUSY]	16	[EDEADLK]	45
[EEXIST]	17	[ENOLCK]	46
[EXDEV]	18	[ENAMETOOLONG]	78
[ENODEV]	19	[ENOSYS]	89
[ENOTDIR]	20	[ENOTEMPTY]	158

The following table lists error return values that are commonly used in implementation-defined extensions. This standard does not require that any of these values be returned. However, if extensions are implemented that use these symbols, the associated values should be used.

Optional	Value	Optional	Value
[ETXTBSY]	26	[ELIBSCN]	85
[ECHRNG]	37	[ELIBMAX]	86
[EL2NSYNC]	38	[ELIBEXEC]	87
[EL3HLT]	39	[ELOOP]	90
[EL3RST]	40	[ERESTART]	91
[ELNRNG]	41	[EINPROGRESS]	128
[EUNATCH]	42	[EALREADY]	129
[ENOCSI]	43	[ENOTSOCK]	130
[EL2HLT]	44	[EDESTADDRREQ]	131
[EWOULDBLOCK]	[EAGAIN]	[EMSGSIZE]	132
[EBADE]	50	[EPROTOTYPE]	133
[EBADR]	51	[ENOPROTOOPT]	134
[EXFULL]	52	[EPROTONOSUPPORT]	135
[ENOANO]	53	[ESOCKTNOSUPPORT]	136
[EBADRQC]	54	[EOPNOTSUPP]	137
[EBADSLT]	55	[EPFNOSUPPORT]	138
[EDEADLOCK]	56	[EAFNOSUPPORT]	139
[EBFONT]	57	[EADDRINUSE]	140
[ENOSTR]	60	[EADDRNOTAVAIL]	141
[ENODATA]	61	[ENETDOWN]	142
[ETIME]	62	[ENETUNREACH]	143
[ENOSR]	63	[ENETRESET]	144
[ENONET]	64	[ECONNABORTED]	145
[ENOPKG]	65	[ECONNRESET]	146
[EREMOTE]	66	[ENOBUFS]	147
[ENOLINK]	67	[EISCONN]	148
[EADV]	68	[ENOTCONN]	149
[ESRMNT]	69	[ESHUTDOWN]	150
[ECOMM]	70	[ETOOMANYREFS]	151
[EPROTO]	71	[ETIMEDOUT]	152
[EMULTIHOP]	74	[ECONNREFUSED]	153
[EDOTDOT]	76	[EHOSTDOWN]	156
[EBADMSG]	77	[EHOSTUNREACH]	157
[ENOTUNIQ]	80	[EPROCLIM]	159
[EBADFD]	81	[EUSERS]	160
[EREMCHG]	82	[EDQUOT]	161
[ELIBACC]	83	[ESTALE]	162
[ELIBBAD]	84	[EPOWERFAIL]	163

Signal constants

The following is a table of symbolic signal number values usually found in <signal.h> and the values they shall be given on conforming systems. Signal values in the range 1 to 43 are reserved for use by this standard.

Constant	Value	Constant	Value
SIGHUP	1	SIGSEGV	11
SIGINT	2	SIGSYS	12
SIGQUIT	3	SIGPIPE	13
SIGILL	4	SIGALRM	14
SIGTRAP	5	SIGTERM	15
SIGABRT	6	SIGUSR1	16
SIGFPE	8	SIGUSR2	17
SIGKILL	9	SIGCLD	18
SIGBUS	10		

The following table lists signal values that shall be provided by systems that implement the POSIX job control option.

Constant	Value
SIGCHLD	[SIGCLD]
SIGSTOP	23
SIGTSTP	24
SIGCONT	25
SIGTTIN	26
SIGTTOU	27

Implementation note: Because the value for SIGTSTP was selected to be a higher value than SIGCHLD, implementors should check for nonportable behavior by some utility programs; for example, some older versions of the C Shell are coded to rely on SIGTSTP being delivered prior to SIGCHLD. In many historical implementations, the signals are delivered in numerical order. This behavior is specifically not guaranteed by POSIX or by this standard.

The following table lists signal values that are commonly used in implementation-defined extensions. This standard does not require that any of these values be returned. However, if extensions or options are implemented that use these symbols, the associated values should be used.

Constant	Value
SIGIOT	[SIGABRT]
SIGEMT	7
SIGPWR	19
SIGWINCH	20
SIGPOLL	22
SIGURG	33
SIGIO	34
SIGXCPU	35
SIGXFSZ	36
SIGVTALRM	37
SIGPROF	38
SIGLOST	40

File modes

The following table contains the symbolic file mode values usually found in
< sys/stat.h > and the values they shall be given on conforming systems.

Constant	Value	Description
S_IRUSR	0x0100	
S_IREAD	0x0100	
S_IWUSR	0x0080	
S_IWRITE	0x0080	
S_IXUSR	0x0040	
S_IEXEC	0x0040	
S_IRGRP	0x0020	
S_IWGRP	0x0010	
S_IXGRP	0x0008	
S_IROTH	0x0004	
S_IWOTH	0x0002	
S_IXOTH	0x0001	
S_ISUID	0x0800	
S_ISGID	0x0400	
S_ENFMT	[S_IGID]	Note: Defined in SVID Vol III
S_ISVTX	0x0200	Note: Defined in SVR3.

File types

The following table contains the symbolic file type values usually found in
< sys/stat.h > and the values they shall be given on conforming systems.
The values S_IFLNK and S_IFSOCK represent common extensions that
are not supported on all conforming systems.

Constant	Value	Description
S_IFMT	0xf000	
S_IFIFO	0x1000	Passed to the mknod( ) system call for the POSIX mkfifo( ) function.
S_IFDIR	0x4000	
S_IFCHR	0x2000	
S_IFBLK	0x6000	
S_IFREG	0x8000	
S_IFLNK	0xa000	Symbolic link.
S_IFSOCK	0xc000	Socket.

Seek values

The following table contains the symbolic values for lseek( ) and related functions, and the values they shall be given on conforming systems.

Constant	Value
SEEK_SET	0
SEEK_CUR	1
SEEK_END	2

System calls

Information used in describing each system call has been taken from ANSI/ IEEE Std 1003.1-1988. The exceptions to this involve system calls that are part of SVID but are not included in POSIX. In these cases the information used in describing the system call has been taken from SVID (first) or SVR3 (second).

Note: In order for an application to be portable at a binary level, application programs need information about all structures and values that can be passed between the program and the kernel. As such, data structures and constants necessary to implement each system call have been defined. Names for fields in the structure have been chosen to match those specified in POSIX.

System calls (except sys_local( ) and sigret( )) shall be made using the MC88100 instruction:

```
tb0   0, r0, 450
```

The system call number is passed in register r9 as indicated in the code fragments below. Parameters to system calls are passed (in order) in registers starting with register r2 followed by r3, r4, r5, r6, r7, and r8.

Parameters and results of short and unsigned short types must be expanded to 32 bits. That is, the parameter/result resides in bits $0-15$ of the register, and bits $16-31$ must either match bit 15 (for the short type) or all be zero (for the unsigned short type). The extension of parameters is the responsibility of the application; the extension of results is the responsibility of the system.

Return values, if any, shall be in registers r2 and r3. All registers not used for return values shall be unchanged by the system call. If an error occurred during a system call, the system shall return control to the first instruction following the tb0, with errno returned in r2. Otherwise, if no error occurred during the system call, control will return to the second instruction following the tb0.

Note: Careful coordination between the C compiler subroutine calling sequence and the system interface routines may allow the registers used by the C compiler for passing parameters to be the same registers used by the system to receive parameters. For example the read( ) system call has three parameters. A call to the library routine would look like:

```
ld     r2, r0, fd
ld     r3, r0, buf
ld     r4, r0, count
bsr    read
```

and the read( ) routine in the library could contain:

```
read:
or     r9, r0, 40   # 40 = = read( )
tb0    0, r0, 450
br     cerror
jmp    r1
```

Vector numbers $504-511$ shall always deliver a SIGTRAP signal with an argument of the vector number (see "Relationship between signals and exceptions"). Vector number 511 shall always be used as the breakpoint trap vector by a conforming application.

Vectors $0-127$ are reserved for hardware. Vectors $128-447$ shall deliver the SIGSYS signal to the calling process unless an implementation-defined sys_local( ) system call is performed to enable these vectors. Vectors 448, 449, 450 are used for system calls defined in this standard: sigret ( ) (448); sys_local( ) (449); and 450 for all others.

Vectors $451-502$ are reserved for future versions of the BCS and the results of their use are undefined.

Note: The following table summarizes the vectors used for system calls:

Vectors	**Usage**
0-127	Reserved for hardware.
128-447	Returns a SIGSYS signal unless enabled by an implementation-defined sys_local( )
448	sigret( )
449	sys_local( )
450	All other system calls defined by this versionof the BCS.
451-502	Reserved for future version of the BCS.
503	Software-detected divide-by-zero. This trap shall produce the same action as a hardware-detected divide-by-zero. The SXIP shall point to the tb0 instruction.
504-511	SIGTRAP.

Only the following system calls are allowed within the BCS. The number prefixing the name/description is that of the BCS reference number for that call. These calls represent the minimum set necessary to implement all of the functions as defined in POSIX and SVID.

9.1   access—File Accessibility
9.2   brk—Change Data Segment Space Allocation
9.3   chdir—Change Current Working Directory
9.4   chmod—Change Files Modes
9.5   lchown—Change Owner and Group of a File
9.6   chroot—Change Root Directory...
9.7   close—Close a File
9.8   execve—Execute a File
9.9   exit—Terminate a Process
9.10   fcntl—File Control
9.11   fork—Process Creation
9.12   fpathconf—Get Configurable Pathname Variables

This chapter has been incredibly brief. The BCS is more than 200 pages of turgid, exciting prose. We can hardly do justice to it in a single chapter. However, where we trimmed down the most was in the descriptions of the system calls themselves.

The description of COFF, and signal handling, etc. is directly from the BCS, and should prove very useful in writing portable binary code.

11

Programming examples

Sigh! Unfortunately, this chapter must begin with a disclaimer. Because we are providing real world code from various sources, we and they need protection from the ravages of our litigious (read "too many attorneys") society. The examples that you are about to see are for your information and education. You are free to make use of them as you will.

However . . .

The information in this document is provided AS IS and without warranty. There are no restrictions on the use of any computer instructions herein. IN NO EVENT SHALL THE AUTHORS OF THIS BOOK OR THE AUTHORS OF THE CONTRIBUTED CODE BE LIABLE FOR INCIDENTAL OR CONSEQUENTIAL DAMAGES ARISING FROM THE USE OF ANY OF THE FOLLOWING MATERIAL. This disclaimer is in lieu of all warranties, implied, expressed, or statutory, including implied warranties of fitness for a particular purpose.

Well, that nasty little paragraph is out of the way, let's proceed. We have a collection of software that should prove both useful and instructive as examples of 88000 code.

Before starting to plow through the assembly language, look at a couple of programming practices. First, if you get involved in writing user exception handlers or the system exception handlers, you might start from the default exception handlers provided by Motorola. If you ask your Motorola sales representative, they can provide you with ordering information. Included here are two of the default handlers fpup.s and FPunderflow.s. The .s simply means that this code is in assembly language. You might encounter .c for C code or .m4 for the M4 macro preprocessor.

FPU conventions

When the 88100 takes a floating point exception, it will vector to either the precise or imprecise exception handler. Included among the following examples is the precise handler, known affectionately as fpup. When either of them get control after an exception, they examine the situation and vector off to the specific handler that can deal with the cause of the exception. Both fpup and fpui (the imprecise general handler) obey some conventions regarding registers. The floating point control registers are loaded into the general registers as shown in Fig. 11-1.

Recall that the scoreboard is cleared after it was saved to the SSBR, freeing up the registers for use within the exception handling process. In fact, if you look at the code for fpup, you will see that much of the first part of the routine simply saves away the current context and sets up the context for FPU exceptions. Only then does it vector off the specific handler.

r1	return address
r2	FPSR
r3	FPCR
r4	FPECR
r5	FPHS1 (for precise exceptions)
r6	FPLS1 (for precise exceptions)
r7	FPHS2 (for precise exceptions)
r8	FPLS2 (for precise exceptions)
r9	FPPT (for precise exceptions)
r10	FPRH (for imprecise exceptions)
r11	FPRL (for imprecise exceptions)
r12	FPIT (for imprecise exceptions)
r31	exception stack pointer

11-1 FPU register mapping during exception.

User exception handler

For some of the FPU exceptions, it is possible to provide a user-level exception handler. A sample sequence for an integer overflow exception might be:

- FPU precise exception—vector to fpup

- fpup determines that the cause is integer overflow and calls FPintover
- FPintover runs and calls the user handler
- User handler runs and returns to FPintover
- FPintover returns to fpup
- fpup performs an rte to the process that had the exception

Sample user exception handler

Before the user handler is called, it must tell UNIX that it wants to deal with floating point exceptions and where it is located. The assembly code to communicate these little details is:

```
or      r2,r0,8

             ;indicate floating point exception handler

lda     r3,r0,_userhand

             ;load address of user handler

bsr     _signal

             ;tell operating system the address of the handler
```

The user handler will come to life with a stack pointer, and a pointer (in register 2) to the floating point exception values. The latter will be sequentially in memory from the pointer in the following order:

1. FPSR
2. FPCR
3. FPECR
4. FPHS1 for precise, and FPRH for imprecise
5. FPLS1 for precise, and FPRL for imprecise
6. FPHS2 for precise, and FPIT for imprecise
7. FPLS2 for precise
8. FPPT for imprecise

The user handler must use the same pointer and store FPSR, FPCR, and the high and low words of the result. Only the low word is required for single-precision. The results are returned in the following sequence:

1. FPSR
2. FPCR
3. high word of result
4. low word of result

The user handler for divide by zero might look like:

```
            global      _userhand
            text
_userhand   ld      r3,r2,0             ;fetch, modify and store FPSR
            or      r3,r3,0x1f
            st      r3,r2,0
            ld      r4,r2,4             ;fetch FPCR
            or.u    r5,r0,0x7ff0        ;form and store high word of result
            st      r5,r2,8
            or      r6,r0,0             ;form and store low word of result
            st      r6,r2,12
            tb0     0,r0,134            ;return to the operating system
            jmp     r1                  ;not really executed, but good
                                        ;programming practice
            data
```

Memory performance benchmark program

Contributed by: Tom Horsley - Harris Computer Corp.

This is a simple benchmark designed to assess how well the memory system works on an 88000 system. It has three assembler routines (which should not be modified if the results are to be comparable on different 88k systems).

The timer1 routine is a two-instruction loop that does no memory references. It establishes a base time for the machine with no memory references.

The timer2 routine is a memory referencing loop, but it references a region small enough that it should always be in the cache, even with the minimum number of 88200 chips. The time for this should be very similar to the time for timer1.

The timer3 routine is identical to the timer2 routine, but it references an area of memory too large to fit in the cache, even with the maximum number of 88200's. Comparing the time for this routine to the time for the others will provide information about 88k system performance during cache misses.

(Each of the routines prints an effective clock rate to be compared between routines.)

This is by no means the whole story. There is price to think about as well as performance. Many applications might not fall out of even a small cache (and very few applications will fall out of the cache as badly as the timer3 routine), but this is a significant measure of one important aspect of an 88k system, so the numbers should be interesting.

The following are the numbers for this benchmark:

- timer3 inner loop will get 33,554,432 cache misses.
- for zero wait memory that should give 33,554,432*5 = 167,772,160 extra cycles.
- best time for timer3 should be 805,314,567 + 167,772,160 = 973,086,727 cycles

(This is based on the position that a cache miss takes five cycles as it loads an entire line of four words, so a miss will occur on every fourth instruction in the loop.)

```
# Makefile for the simple memory timer benchmark.
#
# This is a CPU bound benchmark dominated by time spent in 3 assembler
# routines so no flags on the compiler should make any measurable
difference
# in time.
#
# On a BCS compliant system, no flags should be needed. If your system
does
# not support the sysconf() system service, then please include a
# -DHZ=<ticks per second> definition in CFLAGS.
#
```

```
# This also uses the times() system service as documented in the BCS and
# POSIX descriptions. If you don't support times(), you will need to come
# up with a different definition for the elapsed_time routine.
#
# If your assembler does not accept the format defined in the OCS document,
# then you will have to translate the assembler by hand (and preferably
# shoot whomever developed your assembler :-).


RESULTS: timer
        ./timer > RESULTS


timer: timer.c timer-asm.s
        $(CC) $(CFLAGS) -o timer timer.c timer-asm.s


shar:
        rm -f Part01
        makekit -m


clean:
        rm -f timer timer.o timer-asm.o
```

timer-.asm.s Code

```
; timer1 is a routine that executes a known:
;
; 2 + 200,000,001 * 2 + 2 = 400000006 cycles
;
; It is used to establish the clock rate of the system.
;
        text
        global      _timer1
_timer1:
        or.u   r2,r0,hi16(200000000)
```

```
        or      r2,r2,lo16(200000000)
@L1:
        bcnd.n      ne0,r2,@L1
        subu    r2,r2,1
        jmp     r1
;
; timer2 is a routine that executes repetitive memory references over
; an 8k region. These should all fit in even the smallest cache and so
; this routine should also have a known execution time based soley on
; cycle count.
;
; 2 + 65536 * 2 + 65536 * 2048 * 6 + 65536 * 2 + 2 = 805568516
;
        global      _timer2
_timer2:
        subu    r31,r31,8224
        or      r2,r0,65535
@L2:
        or      r3,r0,2047
        addu    r4,r31,32
@L3:
        ld      r5,r4[r3]
        or      r5,r5,r0
        bcnd.n      ne0,r3,@L3
        subu    r3,r3,1
        bcnd.n      ne0,r2,@L2
        subu    r2,r2,1
        addu    r31,r31,8224
        jmp     r1
;
; timer3 is like timer2 except it diddles with a 256k chunk of memory
; (much bigger than any cache likely to be on a system using 88200
```

```
; chips).
;
; 4 + 2048 * 2 + 2048 * 65536 * 6 + 2048 * 2 + 3 = 805314567
       global      _timer3
_timer3:
       or.u  r6,r0,hi16(262176)
       or    r6,r6,lo16(262176)
       subu  r31,r31,r6
       or    r2,r0,2047
@L4:
       or    r3,r0,65535
       addu  r4,r31,32
@L5:
       ld    r5,r4[r3]
       or    r5,r5,r0
       bcnd.n      ne0,r3,@L5
       subu  r3,r3,1
       bcnd.n      ne0,r2,@L4
       subu  r2,r2,1
       addu  r31,r31,r6
       jmp   r1
```

timer.c Code

```c
#include <stdio.h>
#include <sys/types.h>
#include <sys/times.h>

#ifndef HZ
#define HZ sysconf(3)
#endif

extern void timer1(), timer2(), timer3();

static int hertz;
```

```
#define ticks_to_ms(t) \
    (((10000 * (t)) + 5) / (hertz * 10))


/* Return user, system, and clock time elapsed since last call in
milliseconds */
static void
elapsed_time(userp, sysp, clockp)
    unsigned long * userp;
    unsigned long * sysp;
    unsigned long * clockp;
{
    static long        last_clock = 0;
    long               this_clock;
    static struct tms last_usersys;
    struct tms         this_usersys;

    this_clock = times(&this_usersys);
    * userp = (unsigned long)
        ticks_to_ms((this_usersys.tms_utime + this_usersys.tms_cutime) -
                    (last_usersys.tms_utime + last_usersys.tms_cutime));
    * sysp = (unsigned long)
        ticks_to_ms((this_usersys.tms_stime + this_usersys.tms_cstime) -
                    (last_usersys.tms_stime + last_usersys.tms_cstime));
    * clockp = (unsigned long) ticks_to_ms(this_clock - last_clock);
    last_usersys = this_usersys;
    last_clock = this_clock;
}


static void
analyze_time(name, cycles, user_ms, sys_ms, clock_ms)
    char * name;
    unsigned long cycles, user_ms, sys_ms, clock_ms;
{
```

```
    double    mega_user, mega_both, mega_wall;


    mega_user = (double)(cycles) / (1000.0 * (double)user_ms);
    mega_both = (double)(cycles) / (1000.0 * (double)(user_ms + sys_ms));
    mega_wall = (double)(cycles) / (1000.0 * (double)clock_ms);
    printf("\
times for %s (%d theoretical cycles):\n\
            user = %6d milliseconds => %6.3f megahertz\n\
    user + system = %6d milliseconds => %6.3f megahertz\n\
            wall = %6d milliseconds => %6.3f megahertz\n",
        name, cycles, user_ms, mega_user, user_ms + sys_ms, mega_both,
        clock_ms, mega_wall);
}


main()
{
    unsigned long tuser, tsys, treal;


    hertz = HZ;
    elapsed_time(&tuser, &tsys, &treal);
    timer1();
    elapsed_time(&tuser, &tsys, &treal);
    analyze_time("timer1", 400000006, tuser, tsys, treal);
    timer2();
    elapsed_time(&tuser, &tsys, &treal);
timer2();
elapsed_time(&tuser, &tsys, &treal);
analyze_time("timer2", 805568516, tuser, tsys, treal);
timer2();
elapsed_time(&tuser, &tsys, &treal);
timer3();
elapsed_time(&tuser, &tsys, &treal);
analyze_time("timer3", 805314567, tuser, tsys, treal);
```

Signed multiply

The mul instruction saves the least significant 32 bits of a multiply result. This routine, contributed by Motorola, performs signed 64-bit integer multiple. Review of this example should be useful if you want to modify the exception handler so as to perform signed divides.

```
;Multiply Signed 32 x 32 = 64
;Operands in r2 and r3
;Result returned in r2 and r3
;Uses 6 temporary registers
;Executes in about 34 clock cycles


define(AH,r28)
define(BH,r27)
define(T3,r26)
define(T2,r25)
define(T1,r24)
define(SIGN,r23)


text


muls:
    xor     SIGN,r2,r3
    bcnd    ge0,r2,@L1      ; Take absolute value of A
    subu    r2,r0,r2
@L1:
    bcnd    ge0,r3,@L2      ; Take absolute value of B
    subu    r3,r0,r3
@L2:
    extu    AH,r2,0<16>     ; AH = Hi 16 of A
    extu    BH,r3,0<16>     ; BH = Hi 16 of B
    extu    r2,r2,16<0>     ; AL = Lo 16 of A
    extu    r3,r3,16<0>     ; BL = Lo 16 of B
```

```
                               ; Multiply each 16-bit part by both
                               ; parts of the other operand
    mul       T2,r2,BH         ; T2 = AL * BH
    mul       T3,AH,r3         ; T3 = AH * BL
    mul       r3,r2,r3         ; BL = AL * BL
    mul       r2,AH,BH         ; AL = AH * BH
    mak       T1,T2,0<16>      ; T1 = Lo 16 of AL*BH
    addu.co   r3,r3,T1         ; Accumulate Lo
    extu      T1,T2,0<16>      ; T1 = Hi 16 of AL*BH
    addu.ci   r2,r2,T1         ; Accumulate Hi
    mak       T1,T3,0<16>      ; T1 = Lo 16 of AH*BL
    addu.co   r3,r3,T1         ; Accumulate Lo
    extu      T1,T3,0<16>      ; T1 = Hi 16 of AH*BL
    bb0.n     31,SIGN,@L3      ; Was one operand negative?
    addu.ci   r2,r2,T1         ; Accumulate Hi
    subu.co   r3,r0,r3
    subu.ci   r2,r0,r2         ; Complement result
@L3:
    jmp       r1
```

Linpack loop

Linpacks are a common performance measurement method. Motorola provided the following code which is the inner loop for a Linpack. Because it is single-precision, all the floating point operations are of the .sss form. In the subroutines L262 and L256, notice that an instruction is loaded into the delay shadow of branch.

```
;This is the inner loop for single precision Linpack.  It performs
;dy(i) = dy(i) + (dx(i) * A) until 4 can evenly divide into i, at
;that point, we can successfully "unroll" the operation by 4.  Note
;that this loop executes at most 3 times.
;R2 is the loop counter i
;R3 is a constant A
;R4 is a pointer to array Dx
```

```
;R6 is a pointer to array Dy
;One pass through the inner loop (@L2001:) takes 27 clock cycles
@L262:
        ld          r11,r4[r2]      ; load dx(i)
        and         r10,r2,3        ; Is (i mod 4) = 0 yet??
        bcnd        eq0,r10,@L256   ; If yes, branch to "unrolled" loop
        fmul.sss    r11,r11,r3      ; dx(i) = dx(i) * A
        ld          r12,r6[r2]      ; Load dy(i)
        fadd.sss    r12,r12,r11     ; dy(i) = dy(i) + dx(i) * A
        st          r12,r6[r2]      ; Store dy(i)
        br.n        @L262           ; Repeat loop
        subu        r2,r2,1         ; Decrement loop counter
@L256:
        ld          r7,r4,8         ; Load dx(2)
        ld          r8,r4,12        ; Load dx(3)
        or          r5,r0,r6        ; r5<-&dy
        ld          r6,r4,4         ; Load dx(1)
        bcnd.n      ne0,r2,@L2001   ; Test if i = 0
        ld          r9,r4,16        ; Load dx(4)
        jmp         r1              ; If i = 0 then we leave.
@L2001:
        fmul.sss    r6,r3,r6        ; dx(1) = dx(1) * A
        fmul.sss    r7,r3,r7        ; dx(2) = dx(2) * A
        fmul.sss    r8,r3,r8        ; dx(3) = dx(3) * A
        fmul.sss    r9,r3,r9        ; dx(4) = dx(4) * A
        ld          r10,r5,4        ; Load dy(1)
        ld          r11,r5,8        ; Load dy(2)
        ld          r12,r5,12       ; Load dy(3)
        ld          r13,r5,16       ; Load dy(4)
        add         r4,r4,16        ; Increment pointer to dx
        sub         r2,r2,4         ; decrement loop counter
        fadd.sss    r10,r10,r6      ; dy(1) = dy(1) + dx(1) * A
        fadd.sss    r11,r11,r7      ; dy(2) = dy(2) + dx(2) * A
```

```
        fadd.sss   r12,r12,r8       ; dy(3) = dy(3) + dx(3) * A

        fadd.sss   r13,r13,r9       ; dy(4) = dy(4) + dx(4) * A

        ld         r6,r4,4          ; Load dx(1)

        st         r10,r5,4         ; Store dy(1)

        ld         r7,r4,8          ; Load dx(2)

        st         r11,r5,8         ; Store dy(2)

        ld         r8,r4,12         ; Load dx(3)

        st         r12,r5,12        ; Store dy(3)

        ld         r9,r4,16         ; Load dx(4)

        st         r13,r5,16        ; Store dy(4)

        bcnd.n     gt0,r2,@L2001    ; Test if i = 0

        add        r5,r5,16         ; Increment pointer to dy

        jmp        r1               ; If i = 0 then we leave
```

Square root subroutine

The following sample takes the square root of the input double-precision
number in register 2 and 3 and returns it in the same registers.

```
;
;       This is a complete rewrite of the sqrt function, it is more than
;       twice as fast as the previous one
;
;       Copyright (c) 1989, Tektronix Inc.
;
;

#include "m88math.h"
        text
        align 4
_sqrt:
        MCOUNT
          fcmp.sds r5,r2,r0
;       .bf:  ;
        extu   r12,r2,11<20>                 ;r12 contains biased exponent
        extu   r8,r12,1<0>
                        ;extract low order bit, later we
                        ;check to see if the exponent was odd
```

```
        bb1.n    le,r5,x_le_zero
or       r10,r0,r2              ;r10 = original x
or       r11,r0,r3
clr      r2,r2,11<20>
or.u     r2,r2,hi16(0x3fe00000)
                        ;x is now in the range [.5,1], exponent
                        ;is -1


;this is a 4th degree polynomial which approximates
;the sqrt with 14 bits of precision, the argument must
;be in the range [.5,1]

;p4(x) = a0 + a1*x + a2*x^2 + a3*x^3 + a4*x^4

  fadd.ssd r4,r0,r2                          ; SP x
  or.u     r5,r0,hi16(0x3fa67c53)
                                    ; a1 = float 1.30067
  or       r5,r5,lo16(0x3fa67c53)
  fmul.ssd r5,r5,r2                       ; a1*x
  fmul.sss r3,r4,r4                       ; x^2
  or.u     r2,r0,hi16(0x3e6a9150)
                                    ; a0 = float 0.229070
  or       r2,r2,lo16(0x3e6a9150)
  or.u     r6,r0,hi16(0xbf68c944)
                                    ; a2 = float -0.909321
  fadd.sss r5,r5,r2                    ; a0+a1*x
  or       r6,r6,lo16(0xbf68c944)
  fmul.sss r2,r3,r6                       ; a2*x^2
  fmul.sss r4,r3,r4                       ; x^3
  fmul.sss r3,r3,r3                       ; x^4
  or.u     r6,r0,hi16(0x3f00444b)
                                ; a3 = float 0.501042
  or       r6,r6,lo16(0x3f00444b)
  fadd.sss r5,r5,r2       ; a0+a1*x+a2*x^2
  fmul.sss r4,r6,r4       ; a3*x^3
  or.u     r2,r0,hi16(0xbdf8c46a)
                                ; a4 = float -0.121468
  or       r2,r2,lo16(0xbdf8c46a)
  fmul.sss r3,r2,r3       ; a4*x^4
  fadd.sss r5,r5,r4       ; a0+a1*x+a2*x^2+a3*x^3
  fadd.dss r2,r5,r3       ; a0+a1*x+a2*x^2+a3*x^3+a4*x^4
```

```
                    ;put number back together, multiply by 2^((oldexp +1)/2)


        subu   r12,r12,1021              ;exponent + 1
        ext    r12,r12,1         ;divide exponent by 2
        mak    r12,r12,12<20>
        bcnd.n        eq0,r8,@even_exponent
                               ;if we have an odd
                               ;exponent then we must
                               ;multiply result by sqrt(2)/2
        addu   r2,r2,r12        ;multiply by 2^newexp
        or.u   r4,r0,hi16(0x3fe6a09e)
        or     r4,r4,lo16(0x3fe6a09e)
        or.u   r5,r0,hi16(0x667f3bcd)
        or     r5,r5,lo16(0x667f3bcd)
        fmul.ddd r2,r2,r4
@even_exponent:

        ;two steps of Heron's method combined (saves 1 multiply)
        ;this should give 56 bits of precision in the mantissa

        fdiv.ddd      r4,r10,r2
        fadd.ddd      r6,r4,r2
        or.u   r2,r0,0x0020      ;multiply by .25 by subtracting
        subu   r12,r6,r2         ;2 from the exponent
        or     r13,r0,r7
        fdiv.ddd      r4,r10,r6


;       .ef:   ;
        jmp.n r1
        fadd.ddd      r2,r4,r12
x_le_zero:
        bb1    eq,r5,return
#ifdef ATT_COMPATIBILITY
        subu      r31,r31,STKSIZE
        st        r1,r31,RTNREG
        st.d      r2,r31,EX_ARG1
        or        r4,r0,DOMAIN
        st        r4,r31,EX_TYPE
        or.u      r4,r0,hi16(SQRT)
        or        r4,r4,lo16(SQRT)
        st        r4,r31,EX_NAME
        or        r4,r0,0                    ;ex.retval = 0.0
```

```
                or      r5,r0,0
                st.d    r4,r31,EX_RETVAL
                addu    r2,r31,EX_START
                bsr     _matherr
                cmp     r10,r2,r0
                bb1     ne,r10,MATHERR_RTN
                or      r2,r0,STDERR
                or.u    r3,r0,hi16(SQRT_ERR)
                or      r3,r3,lo16(SQRT_ERR)
                or      r4,r0,SQRT_ERRLEN
                bsr     _write
                or      r10,r0,EDOM
                or.u    r13,r0,hi16(_errno)
                st      r10,r13,lo16(_errno)
MATHERR_RTN:
                ld.d    r2,r31,EX_RETVAL
                ld      r1,r31,RTNREG
                addu    r31,r31,STKSIZE
#else
                or      r12,r0,EDOM              ;errno = EDOM
                or.u    r13,r0,hi16(_errno)
                st      r12,r13,lo16(_errno)
#endif
return:
                jmp     r1
                align 4
                data
SQRT:           string  "sqrt\0"
SQRT_ERR:       string  "sqrt: DOMAIN error\n\0"
                global  _sqrt
                text
```

FPU precise exception handler

```
;********************************************************************;*
;           M88000 FLOATING POINT EXCEPTION HANDLERS
;*          Warranty Disclaimers, and Limitation on liability
;*
;*
;*    Motorola provides the M88K Floating Point Exception Handler
;*  Software (SOFTWARE) to Motorola customers free of charge.
;*  Since Motorola imposes no restrictions upon the use of the SOFTWARE,
```

```
;function fpup --

            global _Xsfu1pr
            text


;Check the sfulfull location 10 the u_block to see if there are exceptions
;already on the stack.  If there are no other exceptions, then grab the
;0 stack pointer and load the 0 information onto the first
;frame.  Clear the word 10 each of the remaining frames which tells whether
;the frame is 1 or not.  If there are already 0 frames on the
;stack, then find the first empty frame.  If there are no more 0
;frames, then kill the user process.

_Xsfu1pr:   stcr  r31,cr20     ;store original scratch pointer
                               ;into cr20
            or.u  r31,r0,hi16(__U + 0x4) ;get hi address of sfulfull
            or    r31,r31,lo16(__U + 0x4) ;get lo address of sfulfull
            stcr  r1,cr18       ;exchange r1 with cr18
            ld    r1,r31,0      ;get contents
```

```
                bcnd   ne0,r1,findframe   ;1 flag already set

firstframe: set    r1,r0,1<1>   ;set up r1 to write to the boolean
                                ;sfulfull and the 1 bit 10 stkstate
            st     r1,r31,0     ;set boolean sfulfull
            or.u   r31,r0,hi16(__U + 0x8) ;get upper half-word of SSP
            or     r31,r31,lo16(__U + 0x8) ;get lower half-word of SSP
            st     r1,r31,196   ;set 1 bit 10 stkstate
            st     r2,r31,8     ;get extra variable

;Now clear all the 1 bits for the remaining frames
            or     r1,r0,1             ;start counter at 1
clearcmp:   cmp    r2,r1,10
            bb1    2,r2,pointadjust    ;1 bits are all clear
            add    r1,r1,1             ;increment r1
            addu   r31,r31,200 ;increment stack pointer
            br.n   clearcmp     ;branch to compare again
            st     r0,r31,196   ;clear 1 bit
pointadjust:        subu   r31,r31,(10 - 1)*200 ;readjust stack pointer
                                      ;to first frame
            br.n   storereg     ;branch to store registers
            ld     r2,r31,8     ;reload r2 so that the program can store
                                ;the correct value into it later

;If necessary, find the next empty frame
findframe:  or.u   r31,r0,hi16(__U + 0x8) ;get address of bottom of stack
            or     r31,r31,lo16(__U + 0x8)
findincr:   addu   r31,r31,200 ;increment point by a frame
            or.u   r1,r0,hi16(__U + 0x8) ;get address of bottom of stack
            or     r1,r1,lo16(__U + 0x8)
            addu   r1,r1,10*200 ;form address of top of stack
            cmp    r1,r31,r1    ;has the stack overflowed?
            bb1    7,r1,_sigkill       ;overflowed stack
            ld     r1,r31,196   ;load 10 word with 1 information
            bb1    1,r1,findincr;1 frame, check next frame
            set    r1,r0,1<1>   ;indicate frame is now 1
            st     r1,r31,196
;Save the user registers which will
;be used during the 0 handling.  Load some integer and floating
;point unit (FPU) control registers into the general purpose registers,
;and also save these control registers onto the stack before the FPU
;is cleaned out.
```

```
storereg:    fldcr r1,cr62          ;save FPSR before FP is enabled
             st    r1,r31,128
             fldcr r1,cr63          ;save FPCR before FP is enabled
             st    r1,r31,132
             fldcr r1,cr0       ;save FPECR before FP is enabled
             st    r1,r31,136
             fldcr r1,cr1           ;save S1HI before FP is enabled
             st    r1,r31,140
             fldcr r1,cr2           ;save S2LO before FP is enabled
             st    r1,r31,144
             fldcr r1,cr3           ;save S2HI before FP is enabled
             st    r1,r31,148
             fldcr r1,cr4           ;save S2LO before FP is enabled
             st    r1,r31,152
             ldcr  r1,cr5           ;load SNIP
             st    r1,r31,168 ;save SNIP before FP is enabled
             ldcr  r1,cr6           ;load SFIP
             st    r1,r31,172 ;save SFIP before FP is enabled
             ldcr  r1,cr2           ;load SPSR
             st    r1,r31,160 ;save SPSR before FP is enabled
             fldcr r1,cr5           ;save PCR before FP is enabled
             st    r1,r31,156


             st    r2,r31,8   ;need another register
             ldcr  r2,cr3           ;load shadow scoreboard
             bb1.n 5,r1,SSBdoub;destination is double
             extu  r1,r1,5<0> ;get low number of destination register
SSBsing:     set   r1,r1,1<5> ;set width field of 1
             br.n  SSBload            ;load the shadow scoreboard
             clr   r2,r2,r1   ;clear the bit 10 the shadow scoreboard
SSBdoub:     set   r1,r1,1<6> ;set width field of 2
             clr   r2,r2,r1   ;clear the bit 10 the shadow scoreboard
SSBload:     stcr  r2,cr3            ;store modified shadow scoreboard
             ld    r2,r31,8   ;restore to serialize

;check for data access 0
             ldcr  r1,cr8           ;load DMT0
             bb0   0,r1,serialization;if no dacc 0, then serialize
;data 0 handler will preserve this copy of the shadow scoreboard
;If the SPSR has the supervisor bit set, then the data 0 handler will
;think that r31 contains the master stack value, which it does not.
;The data 0 handler thinks that r1 is stored 10 cr18, so store
```

```
;the real value of r1 out into memory and preserve fpup's stack pointer 10
;cr18.
                ldcr    r1,cr18         ;save original r1
                st      r1,r31,4
                ldcr    r1,cr20         ;save original r31
                st      r1,r31,124
                stcr    r31,cr18        ;preserve stack pointer from the
                                        ;data 0 handler
                bsr     _getmsps        ;branch to save registers, call dacchand
                                        ;dacchand will clear shadow scoreboard
                                                ;bits for data access faults

                bsr     _getrs          ;branch to restore registers
                ldcr    r31,cr18        ;restore stack pointer from the
                                        ;data 0 handler
                ld      r1,r31,4
                stcr    r1,cr18         ;save original r1
                ld      r1,r31,124
                stcr    r1,cr20         ;save original r31
```

```
;Load the instruction pointer except and the following instruction
;into SNIP and SFIP so that these will be the next instructions executed
;after cleaning out the FPU.  Set the 1 bits.
;In the SPSR, enable exceptions, the FPU, and serialization.  RTE
;to clean out the floating point unit.
```

```
serialization:  stcr    r0,cr5
                or.u    r1,r0,hi16(except)      ;load instruction pointer
                or      r1,r1,lo16(except)
                set     r1,r1,1<1>      ;set 1 bit of instruction pointer
                stcr    r1,cr6
                ldcr    r1,cr1                  ;load PSR
                and     r1,r1,0xfff4
                stcr    r1,cr2
                ldcr    r1,cr18
                ldcr    r31,cr20
                rte                     ;clear SFU 1 and begin executing
                                        ;instruction at except
```

```
;After the floating point unit is flushed out, then we will be at this
;location
```

```
except:              tbl   0,r0,0              ;force all FPU instructions to
                                              ;complete

          stcr  r1,cr18      ;exchange USP with cr20
          stcr  r31,cr20     ;exchange r1 with cr18


;Find the last 1 0 frame.

exceptframe:         or.u  r31,r0,hi16(__U + 0x8) ;get address of bottom of stack
          or    r31,r31,lo16(__U + 0x8)
exceptincr: ld   r1,r31,196  ;load 10 word with 1 bit
          bb1   1,r1,nextframe
          br.n  reenable     ;1 bit clear, last frame was 1
                             ;branch to rest of 0 processing
          subu  r31,r31,200  ;set pointer to last 1 frame


nextframe: addu  r31,r31,200  ;increment point by a frame
          or.u  r1,r0,hi16(__U + 0x8)  ;get address of bottom of stack
          or    r1,r1,lo16(__U + 0x8)
          addu  r1,r1,10*200  ;form address of top of stack
          cmp   r1,r31,r1     ;has the stack overflowed?
          bb1   6,r1,exceptincr   ;not last frame of stack
          subu  r31,r31,200   ;go to last frame of stack


;Store the user values of the registers that are needed for the rest of the
;code.  Load the values of the control registers.

reenable:  ldcr  r1,cr18      ;retrieve original r1
          st    r1,r31,4     ;save r1 and r2 into supervisor memory
          ldcr  r1,cr20      ;load r1 with original stack pointer
          st    r1,r31,124   ;save original stack pointer into memory
          st    r2,r31,8
          st    r3,r31,12    ;save needed general purpose registers
          st    r4,r31,16
          st    r5,r31,20
          st    r6,r31,24
          st    r7,r31,28
          st    r8,r31,32
          st    r9,r31,36
          st    r10,r31,40
          st    r11,r31,44
          st    r12,r31,48
          st    r13,r31,52   ;save r13 into memory, get extra reg.
```

```
            ld      r1,r31,160   ;get SPSR for unimp/FPU disable check
            ld      r2,r31,128   ;load control registers after cleaning
            ld      r3,r31,132   ;out FPU during the RTE
            ld      r4,r31,136
            ld      r5,r31,140
            ld      r6,r31,144
            ld      r7,r31,148
            ld      r8,r31,152
            ld      r9,r31,156
```

```
;Load into r1 the return address for the 0 handlers.  Looking
;at FPECR, branch to the appropriate 0 handler.  However,
;if none of the 0 bits are enabled, then a floating point
;instruction was issued with the floating point unit disabled.  This
;will cause an unimplemented opcode 0.
```

```
            or.u   r1,r0,hi16(wrapup) ;load return address of function
            bb1.n  3,r1,_FPunimp      ;branch to FPunimp if
                                      ;FPU disabled
            or     r1,r1,lo16(wrapup)

            bb1    6,r4,_FPunimp    ;branch to FPunimp if bit set
            bb1    7,r4,_FPintover  ;branch to FPintover if bit set
            bb1    5,r4,_FPpriviol  ;branch to FPpriviol if bit set
            bb1    4,r4,_FPresoper  ;branch to FPresoper if bit set
            bb1    3,r4,_FPdivzero  ;branch to FPdivzero if bit set
```

```
;To write back the results to the user registers, disable exceptions
;and the floating point unit.  Write FPSR and FPCR and load the SNIP
;and SFIP.
;r5 will contain the upper word of the result
;r6 will contain the lower word of the result
```

```
wrapup:         ld     r11,r31,168
            ld     r12,r31,172
            ldcr   r10,cr1           ;load the PSR
            tb1    0,r0,0            ;make sure all floating point operations
                                     ;have finished
            or     r10,r10,0x2 ;disable interrupts
            stcr   r10,cr1
            or     r10,r10,0x9 ;set disable bit, disable exceptions
```

```
                              ;set SFU 1 disable bit, disable SFU 1
        stcr  r10,cr1
        ld    r10,r31,160  ;load control registers from stack
        fstcr r2,cr62            ;write revised value of FPSR
        fstcr r3,cr63            ;write revised value of FPCR
        stcr  r10,cr2       ;store control registers
        stcr  r11,cr5
        stcr  r12,cr6
```

```
;If the destination is double, then execute both the "writedouble" and
;"writesingle" code, but if it is single, then only execute the
;"writesingle code.  If the destination registers is r1 - r12, r31, then
;write to the portion 10 memory where that register value is stored.  If
;the destination register is r13 - r30, then write to the registers
;directly.  The shadow scoreboard bit is cleared for that particular
;destination register after it is written.  Unimplemented opcodes and
;privilage violations will not write back through this routine.
```

```
               ;writeback routine

               bb0.n  5,r9,writesingle ;branch if destination is single
               extu   r2,r9,5<0>     ;get 5 bits of destination register
writedouble: cmp     r3,r2,13       ;see if destination register is 13 or
                                    ;less
               bb1    5,r3,loadmemd  ;load the memory directly
               cmp    r8,r2,31       ;see if destination register is the SP
               bb1    3,r8,loadregd  ;not stack pointer, then write to
                                    ; registers
loadmemd:    br.n   increment      ;branch to increment destination register
               st     r5,r31[r2]     ;write high word
loadregd:    or.u   r4,r0,hi16(regtable)   ;load address of register table
               or     r4,r4,lo16(regtable)
               sub    r2,r2,14       ;adjust address 10 jump table
               lda.d  r11,r4[r2]     ;modify address 10 register table
               or.u   r1,r0,hi16(moddestd)  ;load r1 with return address
                                    ; moddestd
               or     r1,r1,lo16(moddestd)
               jmp.n  r11            ;jump to load register value
               or     r7,r0,r5       ;place high word 10 r7
moddestd:    add    r2,r2,14       ;readjust desination for low result
```

```
increment:   add    r2,r2,1               ;for double, the low word is the
                                          ;unspecified register
             clr    r2,r2,27<5>           ;perform equivalent of mod 32
writesingle: cmp    r3,r2,13              ;see if destination register is 12 or
                                          ;less
             bb1    5,r3,loadmems         ;load the results into memory
             cmp    r8,r2,31              ;see if destination register is the SP
             bb1    3,r8,loadregs         ;not stack pointer, then write to
                                          ;registers
loadmems:    br.n   endwrite              ;branch since write back is done
             st     r6,r31[r2]            ;write low word into memory
loadregs:    or.u   r4,r0,hi16(regtable)     ;load address of register table
             or     r4,r4,lo16(regtable)
             sub    r2,r2,14              ;adjust address 10 jump table
             lda.d  r11,r4[r2]            ;modify address 10 register table
             or.u   r1,r0,hi16(endwrite)    ;load r1 with return address
                                             ; endwrite
             or     r1,r1,lo16(endwrite)
             jmp.n  r11                   ;jump to load register value
             or     r7,r0,r6              ;place low word 10 r7


;The register table is used for directly writing the result to the
;destination register.

regtable:    jmp.n r1               ;load register with result
             or    r14,r0,r7
             jmp.n r1
             or    r15,r0,r7
             jmp.n r1
             or    r16,r0,r7
             jmp.n r1
             or    r17,r0,r7
             jmp.n r1
             or    r18,r0,r7
             jmp.n r1
             or    r19,r0,r7
             jmp.n r1
             or    r20,r0,r7
             jmp.n r1
             or    r21,r0,r7
             jmp.n r1
```

```
          or     r22,r0,r7
          jmp.n r1
          or     r23,r0,r7
          jmp.n r1
          or     r24,r0,r7
          jmp.n r1
          or     r25,r0,r7
          jmp.n r1
          or     r26,r0,r7
          jmp.n r1
          or     r27,r0,r7
          jmp.n r1
          or     r28,r0,r7
          jmp.n r1
          or     r29,r0,r7
          jmp.n r1
          or     r30,r0,r7


;Load the user register values from memory.

endwrite:  ld     r2,r31,8     ;load registers 2 - 13 from memory
           ld     r3,r31,12
           ld     r4,r31,16
           ld     r5,r31,20
           ld     r6,r31,24
           ld     r7,r31,28
           ld     r8,r31,32
           ld     r9,r31,36
           ld     r10,r31,40
           ld     r11,r31,44
           ld     r12,r31,48
           ld     r13,r31,52

;Clear the 196 1 bit
           ld     r1,r31,196
           clr    r1,r1,1<1>   ;clear the 1 bit
           st     r1,r31,196

;Clear the sfulfull boolean 10 case the user gets any more exceptions during
;this process.  Only clear when this frame is the first one.
           or.u   r1,r0,hi16(__U + 0x8) ;get upper half-word of
```

```
                                ;first frame pointer
        or    r1,r1,lo16(__U + 0x8) ;get lower half-word of
                                    ;first frame pointer
        cmp   r1,r31,r1   ;see if the frame is first frame
        bb1   3,r1,switch ;do no clear bit 10 u_block

        or.u  r1,r0,hi16(__U + 0x4) ;get hi address of sfu1full
        or    r1,r1,lo16(__U + 0x4) ;get lo address of sfu1full
        st    r0,r1,0
```

;Now do check to see if the user's time has run out. If the time
;clock is zero, then make sure that the SPSR indicates user 31 before
;branching to _fptrap.

```
switch:          or.u  r1,r0,hi16(_runrun)      ;get contents of _runrun
           ld    r1,r1,lo16(_runrun)
           bcnd  ne0,r1,return     ;process still has time remaining
           ldcr  r1,cr2            ;grab original SPSR
           bb1   31,r31,return     ;supervisor caused 0, so
                          ;return even though clock has run out
           or.u  r1,r0,hi16(__U + 0x0ff0)      ;load top of system stack onto
           or    r1,r1,lo16(__U + 0x0ff0)      ;r1 since we are going to
                          ;destroy r1 with the bsr
;Decrement and save registers.  Since the process will not need to do
;this operation again with the current data still stored on the stack,
;do not worry about losing your stack pointer.  When the code returns,
;this routine will just grab it again.
           subu  r1,r1,128;allow space for saving registers
           st    r2,r1,8     ;save registers
           st    r3,r1,12
           st    r4,r1,16
           st    r5,r1,20
           st    r6,r1,24
           st    r7,r1,28
           st    r8,r1,32
           st    r9,r1,36
           st    r10,r1,40
           st    r11,r1,44
           st    r12,r1,48
           st    r13,r1,52
           st    r14,r1,56
           st    r15,r1,60
```

```
st      r16,r1,64
st      r17,r1,68
st      r18,r1,72
st      r19,r1,76
st      r20,r1,80
st      r21,r1,84
st      r22,r1,88
st      r23,r1,92
st      r24,r1,96
st      r25,r1,100
st      r26,r1,104
st      r27,r1,108
st      r28,r1,112
st      r29,r1,116
st      r30,r1,120
bsr.n   _ftrap              ;jump to operating system routine to
                            ;switch users
st      r31,r1,124  ;worked hard to get this pointer to
                            ;the 0 stack, so save it
or.u    r1,r0,hi16(__U + 0x0ff0)        ;load top of system stack onto
or      r1,r1,lo16(__U + 0x0ff0)        ;r1 to retrieve old register
                            ;values
subu    r1,r1,128;allow space for saving registers
ld      r2,r1,8     ;save registers
ld      r3,r1,12
ld      r4,r1,16
ld      r5,r1,20
ld      r6,r1,24
ld      r7,r1,28
ld      r8,r1,32
ld      r9,r1,36
ld      r10,r1,40
ld      r11,r1,44
ld      r12,r1,48
ld      r13,r1,52
ld      r14,r1,56
ld      r15,r1,60
ld      r16,r1,64
ld      r17,r1,68
ld      r18,r1,72
ld      r19,r1,76
ld      r20,r1,80
```

```
            ld      r21,r1,84
            ld      r22,r1,88
            ld      r23,r1,92
            ld      r24,r1,96
            ld      r25,r1,100
            ld      r26,r1,104
            ld      r27,r1,108
            ld      r28,r1,112
            ld      r29,r1,116
            ld      r30,r1,120
            ld      r31,r1,124;load pointer to 0 frame


   ;Using r1, retrieve the original stack pointer.
   ;RTE to the user code
   ;where the 0 occurred.

   return:          ld    r1,r31,124  ;load value of original stack pointer
                 stcr  r1,cr20      ;store orig. stack pointer 10 cr20
                 ld    r1,r31,4     ;load real value of r1
                 ldcr  r31,cr20     ;get original stack pointer
                 rte                ;return to normal operation
```

Floating point underflow exception handler

```
;********************************************************************************
***
;*          "M88000 FLOATING POINT EXCEPTION HANDLERS              *
;*             Warranty Disclaimers, and Limitation on liability
      *
;*                                                            *
;*                                                            *
;*    Motorola provides the M88K Floating Point Exception Handler      *
;*  Software (SOFTWARE) to Motorola customers free of charge.  Since Motorola
      *
;*  imposes no restrictions upon the use of the SOFTWARE, the SOFTWARE is
      *
;*  provided on an "AS IS" basis and without warranty.  Accordingly, Motorola
      *
```

```
;function _FPunderflow --
;The documentation for this release give an overall description of this code.

              global _FPunderflow
              text


;First check for an 2 user handler.  If there is not one, then
;branch to the routine to make a denormalized number.  Before branching
;to the 2 user handler, add 192 to a single precision exponent
;and 1536 to a double precision exponent.

 _FPunderflow:   bb0.n 7,r12,denorm ;jump to default procedure
                 st    r1,r31,176 ;save return address
                 bb1.n 10,r12,doubleprec ;double precision destination
```

```
                set     r2,r2,1<2>    ;set 2 flag 10 FPSR
singleprec:     or.u    r6,r0,0x0c00  ;load exponent adjust 192
                br.n    callundhand   ;branch to call handler for user handler
                add     r12,r6,r12    ;adjust single precision exponent
doubleprec:     or.u    r6,r0,0x6000  ;load exponent adjust 1536
                add     r12,r6,r12    ;adjust double precision exponent
callundhand:    bsr     _handler      ;call handler for user handler
                br      return        ;return from subroutine
```

```
;Now the floating point number, which has an exponent smaller than what
;IEEE allows, must be denormalized.  Denormalization is done by calculating
;the difference between a denormalized exponent and an 2 exponent and
;shifting the mantissa by that amount.  A one may need to be subtracted from
;the LSB if a one was added during rounding.
;r9 is used to contain the guard, round, sticky, and an inaccuracy bit 10
;case some bits were shifted off the mantissa during denormalization.
;r9 will contain: bit 4 -- new addone if one added during rounding
;                               after denormalization
;                 bit 3 -- inaccuracy flag caused by denormalization
;                     or pre-denormalization inexactness
;                 bit 2 -- guard bit of result
;                 bit 1 -- round bit of result
;                 bit 0 -- sticky bit of result
```

```
denorm:         bb1.n 10,r12,double ;denorm for double
                extu  r9,r10,3<26>    ;load r9 with grs
single:         mak   r5,r10,21<3> ;extract high 21 bits of mantissa
                extu  r6,r11,3<29> ;extract low 3 bits of mantissa
                or    r11,r5,r6      ;form 24 bits of mantissa
```

```
;See if the addone bit is set and unround if it is.
                bb0.n 25,r10,nounrounds ;do not unround if addone bit clear
                extu  r6,r12,12<20>   ;extract signed exponent from IMPCR
unrounds:       subu  r11,r11,1       ;subtract 1 from mantissa
;If the hidden bit is cleared after subtracting the one, then the one added
;during the rounding must have propagated through the mantissa.  The exponent
;will need to be decremented.
                bb1   23,r11,nounrounds ;if hidden bit is set,then exponent
                                        ;does
                                        ;not need to be decremented
    decexps:        sub   r6,r6,1      ;decrement exponent 1
```

```
                set     r11,r11,1<23>  ;set the hidden bit
```

;For both single and double precision, there are cases where it is easier
;and quicker to make a special case. Examples of this are if the
;amount is only 1 or 2, or all the mantissa is shifted off, or all the
;mantissa is shifted off and it is still shifting, or, 10 the case of
;doubles, if the amount is around the boundary of MANTLO and MANTHI.

```
nounrounds:     or      r8,r0,lo16(0x00000f81)  ;load r8 with -127 10 decimal
                                        ;for lowest 12 bits
                sub     r7,r8,r6        ;find difference between two exponents,
                                        ;this amount is the  amount
                cmp     r6,r7,3         ;check to see if r7 contains 3 or more
                bb1     7,r6,threesing  ;br to code that handles shifts of >=3
                cmp     r6,r7,2         ;check to see if r7 contains 2
                bb1     2,r6,twosing    ;br to code that handles shifts of 2
one:            rot     r9,r9,0<1>      ;rotate roundoff register once, this places
                                        ;guard 10 round and round 10 sticky
                bb0     31,r9,nosticky1s;do not or round and sticky if sticky is
                                        ;0, this lost bit will be cleared later
                set     r9,r9,1<0>      ;or round and sticky
nosticky1s:     bb0     0,r11,guardclr1s ;do not set guard bit if LSB = 0
                set     r9,r9,1<2>      ;set guard bit
guardclr1s:     extu    r11,r11,31<1>  ; mantissa right 1
                br.n    round           ;round result
                mak     r9,r9,3<0>      ;clear bits lost during rotation

twosing:        rot     r9,r9,0<2>      ;rotate roundff register twice, this places
                                        ;guard 10 sticky
                bb0     30,r9,nosticky2s ;do not or guard and sticky if stick is
                                        ;0
                                        ;this lost bit will be cleared later
                br.n    noround2s       ;skip or old guard and old round if old
                                        ;sticky set
                set     r9,r9,1<0>      ;or guard and sticky
nosticky2s:     bb0     31,r9,noround2s ;do not or guard and round if round is 0
                                        ;this lost bit will be cleared later
                set     r9,r9,1<0>      ;or guard and round
noround2s:      bb0     0,r11,roundclr2s ;do not set round bit if LSB = 0
                set     r9,r9,1<1>      ;set round bit
roundclr2s:     bb0     1,r11,guardclr2s ;do not set guard bit if LSB + 1 = 0
                set     r9,r9,1<2>      ;set guard bit
```

```
guardclr2s:        extu  r11,r11,30<2>  ; mantissa right 2
                   br.n  round            ;round result
                   mak   r9,r9,3<0>      ;clear bits lost during rotation


threesing:         bb1   0,r9,noguard3s ;check sticky initially
                                         ;sticky is set, forget most of the oring
nosticky3s:        bb0   1,r9,noround3s  ;check round initially, do not set
                                         ; sticky
                   br.n  noguard3s        ;forget most of the rest of oring
                   set   r9,r9,1<0>        ;if round is clear,set sticky if round
                                           ;set
   noround3s:      bb0.n 2,r9,noguard3s  ;check guard initially, do not set
                                         ; sticky
                   clr   r9,r9,2<1>   ;clear the original guard and round for
                                         ; when
                                         ;you get to round section
                   set   r9,r9,1<0>        ;if guard is clear,set sticky if guard
                                           ; set
   noguard3s:      cmp   r6,r7,23    ;check if # of shifts is <=23
                   bb1   4,r6,s24    ;branch to see if shifts = 24
                   sub   r6,r7,2     ;get number of bits to check for sticky
                   mak   r6,r6,5<5>  ; width into width field
                   mak   r8,r11,r6     ;mask off shifted bits -2
                   ff1   r8,r8       ;see if r8 has any ones
                   bb1   5,r8,nostky23 ;do not set sticky if no ones found
                   set   r9,r9,1<0>  ;set sticky bit
nostky23:          or    r8,r0,34    ;start code to get new mantissa plus two
                                       ;extra bits for new round and new guard
                                       ; bits
                   subu  r8,r8,r7
                   mak   r8,r8,5<5>  ; field width into second five bits
                   extu  r6,r6,5<5>  ; previous shifted -2 into offset field
                   or    r6,r6,r8    ;complete field
                   extu  r11,r11,r6    ;form new mantissa with two extra bits

                   bb0   0,r11,nornd3s ;do not set new round bit
                   set   r9,r9,1<1>  ;set new round bit
nornd3s:           bb0   1,r11,nogrd3s ;do not set new guard bit
                   set   r9,r9,1<2>  ;set new guard bit
nogrd3s:           br.n  round            ;round mantissa
                   extu  r11,r11,30<2>  ; off remaining two bits
```

Floating point underflow exception handler   **351**

```
s24:            cmp     r6,r7,24        ;check to see if # of shifts is 24
                bb1     4,r6,s25        ;branch to see if shifts = 25
                bb1     0,r9,nostky24   ;skip checking if old sticky set
                extu    r8,r11,22<0>    ;prepare to check bits that will be
                                        ;shifted
                                        ;into the sticky
                ff1     r8,r8           ;see if there are any 1's
                bb1     5,r8,nostky24   ;do not set sticky if no ones found
                set     r9,r9,1<0>      ;set sticky bit
nostky24:       bb0     22,r11,nornd24  ;do not set new round bit
                set     r9,r9,1<1>      ;set new round bit
nornd24:        set     r9,r9,1<2>      ;set new guard bit,this is hidden bit
                br.n    round           ;round mantissa
                or      r11,r0,r0       ;clear r11, all of mantissa shifted off

s25:            cmp     r6,r7,25        ;check to see if # of shifts is 25
                bb1     4,r6,s26        ;branch to execute for shifts => 26
                bb1     0,r9,nostky25   ;skip checking if old sticky set
                extu    r8,r11,23<0>    ;prepare to check bits that will be shifted
                                        ;into the sticky
                ff1     r8,r8           ;see if there are any 1's
                bb1     5,r8,nostky25   ;do not set sticky if no ones found
                set     r9,r9,1<0>      ;set sticky bit
nostky25:       set     r9,r9,1<1>      ;set new round bit,this is hidden bit
                clr     r9,r9,1<2>      ;clear guard bit since nothing shifted 10
                br.n    round           ;round and assemble result
                or      r11,r0,r0       ;clear r11, all of mantissa shifted off

s26:            set     r9,r9,1<0>      ;set sticky bit,this contains hidden bit
                clr     r9,r9,2<1>      ;clear guard and round bits since nothing
                                        ;shifted 10
                br.n    round           ;round and assemble result
                or      r11,r0,r0       ;clear mantissa

double:         mak     r5,r10,21<0>    ;extract upper bits of mantissa
                bb0.n   25,r10,nounroundd ;do not unround if addone bit clear
                extu    r6,r12,12<20>   ;extract signed exponenet from IMPCR
unroundd:       or      r8,r0,1
          subu.co  r11,r11,r8           ;subtract 1 from mantissa
            subu.ci  r5,r5,r0           ;subtract borrow from upper word
                bb1     20,r5,nounroundd ;if hidden bit is set, then exponent
                                        ;does
```

```
                                             ;not need to be decremented
decexpd:        sub    r6,r6,1        ;decrement exponent 1
                set    r5,r5,1<20>    ;set the hidden bit
nounroundd:     or     r8,r0,lo16(0x00000c01) ;load r8 with -1023 10 decimal
                                      ;for lowest 12 bits
                sub    r7,r8,r6       ;find difference between two exponents,
                                      ;this amount is the  amount
                cmp    r6,r7,3        ;check to see if r7 contains 3 or more
                bb1    7,r6,threedoub ;br to code that handles shifts of >=3
                cmp    r6,r7,2        ;check to see if r7 contains 2
                bb1    2,r6,twodoub   ;br to code that handles shifts of 2


onedoub:        rot    r9,r9,0<1>     ;rotate roundoff register once, this places
                                      ;guard 10 round and round 10 sticky
                bb0    31,r9,nosticky1d;do not or round and sticky if sticky is
0
                                      ;this lost bit will be cleared later
                set    r9,r9,1<0>     ;or old round and old sticky into new
                                      ; sticky
nosticky1d:     bb0    0,r11,guardclr1d ;do not set new guard bit if old LSB =
                                         ;0
                set    r9,r9,1<2>     ;set new guard bit
guardclr1d:     extu   r11,r11,31<1>  ; lower mantissa over 1
                mak    r6,r5,1<31>    ; off low bit of high mantissa
                or     r11,r6,r11     ;load high bit onto lower mantissa
                extu   r5,r5,20<1>    ; right once upper 20 bits of mantissa
                br.n   round          ;round mantissa and assemble result
                mak    r9,r9,3<0>     ;clear bits lost during rotation


twodoub:        rot    r9,r9,0<2>     ;rotate roundoff register twice, this
                                      ; places
                                      ;old guard into sticky
                bb0    30,r9,nosticky2d ;do not or old guard and old sticky if
                                         ;old sticky is 0
                br.n   noround2d      ;skip or of old guard and old round if old
                                      ;sticky set
                set    r9,r9,1<0>     ;or old guard and old sticky into new
                                      ; sticky
nosticky2d:     bb0    31,r9,noround2d ;do not or old guard and old round if
                                        ;old round is 0
                set    r9,r9,1<0>     ;or old guard and old round into new sticky
noround2d:      bb0    0,r11,roundclr2d ;do not set round bit if old LSB = 0
```

```
                 set   r9,r9,1<1>    ;set new round bit
roundclr2d:      bb0   1,r11,guardclr2d ;do not set guard bit if old LSB + 1 =
                                       ; 0
                 set   r9,r9,1<2>    ;set new guard bit
guardclr2d:      extu  r11,r11,30<2> ; lower mantissa over 2
                 mak   r6,r5,2<30>   ; off low bits of high mantissa
                 or    r11,r6,r11    ;load high bit onto lower mantissa
                 extu  r5,r5,19<2>   ; right twice upper 19 bits of mantissa
                 br.n  round         ;round mantissa and assemble result
                 mak   r9,r9,3<0>    ;clear bits lost during rotation


threedoub:       bb1   0,r9,noguard3d ;checky sticky initially
                                      ;sticky is set, forget most of rest of
                                      ; oring
nosticky3d:      bb0   1,r9,noround3d ;check old round, do not set sticky if
                                      ;old round is clear, set otherwise
                 br.n  noguard3d      ;sticky is set, forget most of rest of
                                      ; oring
                 set   r9,r9,1<0>    ;set sticky if old round is set
noround3d:       bb0   2,r9,noguard3d ;check old guard, do not set sticky if 0
                 clr   r9,r9,2<1>    ;clear the original guard and round for
                                     ;when
                                        ;you get to round section
                 set   r9,r9,1<0>    ;set sticky if old guard is set
noguard3d:       cmp   r6,r7,32      ;do I need to work with a 1 or 2 word mant.
                                     ;when forming sticky, round and guard
                 bb1   4,r6,d33      ;jump to code that handles 2 word mantissas
                 sub   r6,r7,2       ;get number of bits to check for sticky
                 mak   r6,r6,5<5>    ; width into width field
                 mak   r8,r11,r6     ;mask off shifted bits -2
                 ff1   r8,r8         ;see if r8 has any ones
                 bb1   5,r8,nostky32 ;do not set sticky if no ones found
                 set   r9,r9,1<0>    ;set sticky bit
nostky32:        or    r8,r0,34      ;start code to get new mantissa plus two
                                     ;extra bits for new round and new guard
                                     ; bits,
                                     ;the upper word bits will be shifted after
                                     ;the round and guard bits are handled
                 subu  r8,r8,r7
                 mak   r8,r8,5<5>    ; field width into second five bits
                 extu  r6,r6,5<5>    ; previous shifted -2 into offset field
                 or    r6,r6,r8      ;complete bit field
```

```
                  extu   r11,r11,r6    ;partially form new low mantissa with 2
                                       ; more
                                       ;bits
                  bb0    0,r11,nornd32d ;do not set new round bit
                  set    r9,r9,1<1>    ;set new round bit
   nornd32d:      bb0    1,r11,nogrd32d ;do not set new guard bit
                  set    r9,r9,1<2>    ;set new guard bit
   nogrd32d:      extu   r11,r11,30<2> ; off remaining two bits
                  mak    r6,r7,5<5>    ; field width into second 5 bits, if the
                                       ;width is 32, then these bits will be 0
                  or     r8,r0,32      ;load word length into r8

                  sub    r8,r8,r7      ;form offset for high bits moved to low
                                       ; word
                  or     r6,r6,r8      ;form complete bit field
                  mak    r6,r5,r6      ;get shifted bits of high word
                  or     r11,r6,r11    ;form new low word of mantissa
                  bcnd   ne0,r8,regular33 ;do not adjust for special case of r8
                  br.n   round         ;containing zeros, which would cause
                  or     r5,r0,r0      ;all of the bits to be extracted under
                                       ;the regular method
   regular33:     mak    r6,r7,5<0>    ;place lower 5 bits of  into r6
                  mak    r8,r8,5<5>    ; r8 into width field
                  or     r6,r6,r8      ;form field for shifting of upper bits
                  br.n   round         ;round and assemble result
                  extu   r5,r5,r6      ;form new high word mantissa

   d33:           cmp    r6,r7,33      ;is the number of bits to be shifted is 33?
                  bb1    4,r6,d34      ;check to see if # of bits is 34
                  bb1    0,r9,nostky33 ;skip checking if old sticky set
                  mak    r6,r11,31<0>  ;check bits that will be shifted into
                                       ;sticky
                  ff1    r8,r8         ;check for ones
                  bb1    5,r8,nostky33 ;do not set sticky if there are no ones
                  set    r9,r9,1<0>    ;set new sticky bit
   nostky33:      bb0    31,r11,nornd33 ;do not set round if bit is not a 1
                  set    r9,r9,1<1>    ;set new round bit
   nornd33:       bb0    0,r5,nogrd33  ;do not set guard bit if bit is not a 1
                  set    r9,r9,1<2>    ;set new guard bit
   nogrd33:       extu   r11,r5,31<1>  ; high bits into low word
                  br.n   round         ;round and assemble result
                  or     r5,r0,r0      ;clear high word
```

```
d34:            cmp    r6,r7,34        ;is the number of bits to be shifted 34?
                bb1    4,r6,d35        ;check to see if # of bits is >= 35
                bb1    0,r9,nostky34   ;skip checking if old sticky set
                ff1    r8,r11          ;check bits that will be shifted into
                                       ;sticky
                bb1    5,r8,nostky34   ;do not set sticky if there are no ones
                set    r9,r9,1<0>      ;set new sticky bit
nostky34:       bb0    0,r5,nornd34    ;do not set round if bit is not a 1
                set    r9,r9,1<1>      ;set new round bit
nornd34:        bb0    1,r5,nogrd34    ;do not set guard bit if bit is not a 1
                set    r9,r9,1<2>      ;set new guard bit
nogrd34:        extu   r11,r5,30<2>    ; high bits into low word
                br.n   round           ;round and assemble result
                or     r5,r0,r0        ;clear high word
d35:            cmp    r6,r7,52        ;see if # of shifts is 35 <= X <= 52
                bb1    4,r6,d53        ;check to see if # of shifts is 52
                bb1.n  0,r9,nostky35   ;skip checking if old sticky set
                sub    r7,r7,34        ;subtract 32 from # of shifts so that
                                       ; opera-
                                       ;tions can be done on the upper word, and
                                       ;then subtract two more checking guard and
                                       ;sticky bits
                ff1    r8,r11          ;see if lower word has a bit for sticky
                bb1    5,r8,stkycheck35 ;see if upper word has any sticky bits
                br.n   nostky35        ;quit checking for sticky
                set    r9,r9,1<0>      ;set sticky bit
stkycheck35:    mak    r6,r7,5<5>      ;place width into width field
                mak    r8,r5,r6        ;mask off shifted bits - 2
                ff1    r8,r8           ;see if r8 has any ones
                bb1    5,r8,nostky35   ;do not set sticky if no ones found
                set    r9,r9,1<0>      ;set sticky bit
nostky35:       or     r8,r0,32        ;look at what does not get shifted off plus
                                       ;round and sticky, remember that the r7
                                       ; value
                                       ;was adjusted so that it did not
                                       ;new round or new sticky 10 shifted off
                                       ; bits
                subu   r8,r8,r7        ;complement width
                mak    r8,r8,5<5>      ; width into width field
                or     r8,r7,r8        ;add offset field
                extu   r11,r5,r8       ;extract upper bits into low word
                bb0    0,r11,nornd35   ;do not set new round bit
```

```
                 set    r9,r9,1<1>    ;set new round bit
nornd35:         bb0    1,r11,nogrd35 ;do not set new guard bit
                 set    r9,r9,1<2>    ;set new guard bit
nogrd35:         extu   r11,r11,30<2> ; off remaining guard and round bits
                 br.n   round         ;round and assemble result
                 or     r5,r0,r0      ;clear high word

d53:             cmp    r6,r7,53      ;check to see if # of shifts is 53
                 bb1    4,r6,d54      ;branch to see if shifts = 54
                 bb1    0,r9,nostky53 ;skip checking if old sticky set
                 ff1    r8,r11        ;see if lower word has a bit for sticky
                 bb1    5,r8,stkycheck53 ;see if upper word has any sticky bits
                 br.n   nostky53      ;quit checking for sticky
                 set    r9,r9,1<0>    ;set sticky bit
stkycheck53:     mak    r6,r5,19<0>   ;check bits that are shifted into sticky
                 ff1    r8,r6         ;see if r6 has any ones
                 bb1    5,r8,nostky53 ;do not set sticky if no ones found
                 set    r9,r9,1<0>    ;set sticky bit

nostky53:        bb0    19,r5,nornd53 ;do not set new round bit
                 set    r9,r9,1<1>    ;set new round bit
nornd53:         set    r9,r9,1<2>    ;set new guard bit,this is hidden bit
                 or     r5,r0,r0      ;clear high word
                 br.n   round         ;round and assemble result
                 or     r11,r0,r0     ;clear low word

d54:             cmp    r6,r7,54      ;check to see if # of shifts is 54
                 bb1    4,r6,d55      ;branch to execute for shifts =>55
                 bb1    0,r9,nostky54 ;skip checking if old sticky set
                 ff1    r8,r11        ;see if lower word has a bit for sticky
                 bb1    5,r8,stkycheck54 ;see if upper word has any sticky bits
                 br.n   nostky54      ;quit checking for sticky
                 set    r9,r9,1<0>    ;set sticky bit
stkycheck54:     mak    r6,r5,20<0>   ;check bits that are shifted into sticky
                 ff1    r8,r6         ;see if r6 has any ones
                 bb1    5,r8,nostky54 ;do not set sticky if no ones found
                 set    r9,r9,1<0>    ;set sticky bit
nostky54:        set    r9,r9,1<1>    ;set new round bit,this is hidden bit
                 clr    r9,r9,1<2>    ;clear guard bit since nothing shifted 10
                 or     r5,r0,r0      ;clear high word
                 br.n   round         ;round and assemble result
                 or     r11,r0,r0     ;clear low word
```

```
u55:            set   r9,r9,1<0>      ;set new sticky bit,this contains hidden
                                      ; bit
                clr   r9,r9,2<1>      ;clear guard and round bits since nothing
                                      ;shifted 10
                or    r5,r0,r0        ;clear high word
                or    r11,r0,r0       ;clear low word
```

;The first item that the rounding code does is see if either guard, round,
;or sticky is set. If all are clear, then there is no denormalization loss
;and no need to round, then branch to assemble answer.
;For rounding, a branch table is set up. The left two most bits are the
;rounding 31. The third bit is either the LSB of the mantissa or the
;31 bit, depending on the rounding 31. The three LSB's are the guard,
;round and sticky bits.

```
round:          ffl    r8,r9            ;see if there is denormalization loss
                bbl    5,r8,assemble    ;no denormalization loss or inexactness
                extu   r6,r10,2<29>     ;extract rounding 31
                bbl.n  30,r10,signext   ;use 31 bit instead of LSB
                mak    r6,r6,2<4>       ; over rounding 31
                extu   r7,r11,1<0>      ;extract LSB

                br.n   grs              ;skip 31 extraction
                mak    r7,r7,1<3>       ; over LSB
signext:        extu   r7,r10,1<31>     ;extract 31 bit
                mak    r7,r7,1<3>       ; 31 bit over
grs:            or     r6,r6,r7
                or     r6,r6,r9         ;or 10 guard, round, and sticky
                or.u   r1,r0,hi16(roundtable) ;form address of branch table
                or     r1,r1,lo16(roundtable)
                lda    r6,r1[r6]        ;scale offset into branch table
                jmp.n  r6               ;jump to branch table
                set    r9,r9,1<3>       ;set 0 flag 10 r9


roundtable:     br     noaddone
r000001:        br     noaddone
r000010:        br     noaddone
r000011:        br     noaddone
r000100:        br     noaddone
r000101:        br     addone
r000110:        br     addone
r000111:        br     addone
```

```
r001000:        br      noaddone
r001001:        br      noaddone
r001010:        br      noaddone
r001011:        br      noaddone
r001100:        br      addone
r001101:        br      addone
r001110:        br      addone
r001111:        br      addone
r010000:        br      noaddone
r010001:        br      noaddone
r010010:        br      noaddone
r010011:        br      noaddone
r010100:        br      noaddone
r010101:        br      noaddone
r010110:        br      noaddone
r010111:        br      noaddone
r011000:        br      noaddone
r011001:        br      noaddone
r011010:        br      noaddone
r011011:        br      noaddone
r011100:        br      noaddone
r011101:        br      noaddone
r011110:        br      noaddone
r011111:        br      noaddone
r100000:        br      noaddone
r100001:        br      noaddone
r100010:        br      noaddone
r100011:        br      noaddone
r100100:        br      noaddone
r100101:        br      noaddone
r100110:        br      noaddone
r100111:        br      noaddone
r101000:        br      noaddone
r101001:        br      addone
r101010:        br      addone
r101011:        br      addone
r101100:        br      addone
r101101:        br      addone
r101110:        br      addone
r101111:        br      addone
r110000:        br      noaddone
r110001:        br      addone
```

```
r110010:        br      addone
r110011:        br      addone
r110100:        br      addone
r110101:        br      addone
r110110:        br      addone
r110111:        br      addone
r111000:        br      noaddone
r111001:        br      noaddone
r111010:        br      noaddone
r111011:        br      noaddone
r111100:        br      noaddone
r111101:        br      noaddone
r111110:        br      noaddone
r111111:        br      noaddone
```

;Round by adding a one to the LSB of the mantissa.

```
addone:         or      r6,r0,1        ;load a 1 into r6 so that add.co can be
                                       ; used
                add.co r11,r11,r6      ;add a one to the lower word of result
                bb0.n 10,r12,noaddone  ;single result,forget carry
                set    r9,r9,1<4>      ;indicate that a 1 has been added
                add.ci r5,r5,r0        ;propagate carry into high word
```

;Branch to 0 user handler if there is one.

```
noaddone:       bb1.n 5,r12,modformdef ;branch to modify form for user
                                       ;handler
                or      r2,r2,5        ;set 0 and 2 flags
```

;Assemble the result of the denormalization routine for writeback to the
;destination register. The exponent of a denormalized number is zero,
;so simply assemble the 31 and the new mantissa.

```
assemble:       bb1    10,r12,doubassem ;assemble double result
                bb0    31,r10,exassems ;exit assemble if 31 is zero
                set    r11,r11,1<31>   ;make result negative
exassems:       br     return          ;return from subroutine

doubassem:      bb0.n 31,r10,signclr ;do not set 31 10 r10
                or     r10,r5,r0     ;load high word from r5 into r10
                set    r10,r10,1<31> ;high word with 31 loaded
signclr:        br     return          ;return from subroutine
```

```
;modfordef modifies the result of denormalization to the input format of
;the 0 user handler.  This input format is the same format that
;MANTHI, MANTLO, and IMPCR were initially loaded with.


modformdef:     clr    r12,r12,12<20> ;clear result exponent,IMPCR complete
                clr    r10,r10,4<25>  ;clear old guard,round,sticky,and addone
                mak    r5,r9,3<26>    ;make grs field
                bb0.n  4,r9,newaddone ;do not set new addone 10 MANTHI
                or     r10,r5,r10     ;or 10 new grs field
                set    r10,r10,1<25>  ;set new addone
newaddone:      bb1.n  10,r12,moddefd ;branch to handle double precision
                clr    r10,r10,21<0>  ;clear upper bits of old mantissa
moddefs:        extu   r5,r11,20<3>   ;extract upper bits
                or     r10,r5,r10     ;MANTHI complete
                bsr.n  _handler       ;execute user handler for 0
                rot    r11,r11,0<3>   ;MANTLO complete
                br     return         ;return from subroutine
moddefd:        bsr.n  _handler       ;execute user handler for 0
                or     r10,r5,r10     ;MANTHI complete,r5 should be set to OR



;Return to fpui.

return:         ld     r1,r31,176 ;load return address
                jmp    r1             ;return from subroutine


                data
```

Index